Unleashing the
Positive Power
of Differences

*For Brian, my favorite teacher and perfect
partner for our lifelong dance of opposites*

Unleashing the Positive Power of Differences

Polarity Thinking in Our Schools

Jane A. G. Kise

A Joint Publication With

CORWIN
A SAGE Company

FOR INFORMATION:

Corwin
A SAGE Company
2455 Teller Road
Thousand Oaks, California 91320
(800) 233-9936
www.corwin.com

SAGE Publications Ltd.
1 Oliver's Yard
55 City Road
London EC1Y 1SP
United Kingdom

SAGE Publications India Pvt. Ltd.
B 1/I 1 Mohan Cooperative Industrial Area
Mathura Road, New Delhi 110 044
India

SAGE Publications Asia-Pacific Pte. Ltd.
3 Church Street
#10-04 Samsung Hub
Singapore 049483

Printed in the United States of America

Library of Congress Cataloging-in-Publication Data

A catalog record of this book is available from the Library of Congress.

ISBN: 978-1-4522-5771-6

This book is printed on acid-free paper.

Acquisitions Editor: Dan Alpert
Associate Editor: Kimberly Greenberg
Editorial Assistant: Cesar Reyes
Production Editor: Melanie Birdsall
Copy Editor: Linda Gray
Typesetter: C&M Digitals (P) Ltd.
Proofreader: Caryne Brown
Indexer: David Luljak
Cover Designer: Rose Storey

SFI   Certified Sourcing
www.sfiprogram.org
SFI-00453

13 14 15 16 17 10 9 8 7 6 5 4 3 2 1

Contents

List of Professional Development Activities   vii

Acknowledgments   viii

About the Author   x

PART I. UNDERSTANDING POLARITY THINKING

Chapter 1. Introduction: Let's Put Our Differences to Work for Us   2

Chapter 2. Getting Unstuck in Education   7

PART II. THE BIG PICTURE OF POLARITY
THINKING IN EDUCATION REFORM

Chapter 3. Leveraging Education Goals:
Academic Success AND Whole Child Success   32

Chapter 4. Ensuring Effective Teachers: Evaluation as a
Measure of Effectiveness AND a Guide for Professional Growth   53

Chapter 5. A Math Wars Truce: Mastery of Knowledge
AND Mastery of Problem Solving   78

Chapter 6. Making Diplomas Meaningful: Standardization
AND Customization   105

PART III. PUTTING THE SMALL POLARITY
THINKING TOOLS TO WORK

Chapter 7. Introducing Polarity Thinking to Your Team   130

Chapter 8. Guiding Your Team Through Polarity Thinking   140

Chapter 9. Using Polarity Tools to Explore Initiatives and
Opposing Experts   156

Chapter 10. Working With Common Polarities in Education   172

Chapter 11. Students and Polarities: A Tool for Critical Thinking   190

PART IV. A CLOSER LOOK AT WHY
WE BELIEVE WHAT WE BELIEVE

Chapter 12. Carl Jung, Neuroscience, and the
Truth That We're Wired to Develop Different Viewpoints   212

Conclusion: Moving Beyond Polarization in Education   243

Appendix A. A PACT Process Case Study   246

Appendix B. Chapter 9 Reading:
How Do We Help Students Succeed?   252

References   256

Suggestions for Further Reading   265

Index   266

List of Professional Development Activities

Activity 2.1: Using Polarity Thinking to Analyze
a Failed Initiative   52

Activity 5.1: Mastering Calculations and
Mastering Mathematical Thinking   99

Activity 7.1: A Forty-Five-Minute Introduction
to Leveraging Differences   131

Activity 8.1: Mapping by Moving Through a Polarity   142

Activity 9.1: Reading With the Lens of Polarities   159

Activity 9.2: Mapping Any Article   161

Activity 9.3: Incorporating Polarity Mapping
in a Book Discussion   163

Activity 10.1: Demonstrating Respect   179

Activity 10.2: Point of View Debate   182

Activity 11.1: Student Discipline   195

Activity 11.2: On-Your-Feet Arguments   199

Activity 12.1: Reflecting on Biases   239

Acknowledgments

Not a word of this book could have been written without Barry Johnson, founder of Polarity Partnerships, who not only gave me permission to use his theories and tools in the arena of education but also invited me to training sessions, brainstormed ideas, cofacilitated with me, critiqued early chapter drafts, and in so many ways gave generously of his time and intellect. His passion for polarity thinking as a framework for helping people leverage the dilemmas of life is contagious! Thank you, Barry!

Barry also connected me with many of his colleagues in the world of polarity thinking. Yarrow Durbin was instrumental in helping me frame some of the book's ideas and navigate between theory and practicality. Todd Johnson shared his wisdom, exercises, and practical advice gained from years of working with educators on polarity thinking. Rebekah Marler provided stories and shared her experiences in using polarities in schools. Ann Deaton and Cliff Kayser also critiqued chapters, and Cliff helped me develop PACT assessments to use with schools. Leslie DePol of Polarity Partnerships provided guidance on how we might best make the tools available to schools.

Thank you, also, to my many education colleagues who willingly worked with me on early mapping of the issues in Part II of this book. Joellen Killion not only expanded my thinking on teacher evaluation but brought together a group of educators for a daylong workshop that was invaluable for tailoring the book to educators. Lois Easton provided key writing advice and feedback on early chapters. Robert Marzano, Marilyn Burns, and Lucy West listened to my early ideas and gave key suggestions. Bryan Goodwyn, Charles Kyte, Wendy Behrens, Lynnell Mickelsen, and Kari Ross all contributed to helping me present balanced views on the issues. Susan Powell, Erin Boltik, and Mary Rynchek allowed me to guide their teams in applying polarity thinking to real issues in their organizations as a way to develop the slides and scripts included in this book. And as always, Sue Blair, my psychological type colleague, helped me make these concepts practical and clear.

The advice of the peer reviewers was also invaluable, including Dr. David Petrovay.

PUBLISHER'S ACKNOWLEDGMENTS

Corwin gratefully acknowledges the contributions of the following reviewers:

Scott Bailey
Assistant Professor, Stephen F. Austin State University
Longview, TX

Janice Bradley
Assistant Professor, New Mexico State University
Las Cruces, NM

Lois Brown Easton
Educational Consultant and Author
LBE Learning and Learning Forward Senior Consultant
Tucson, AZ

Ron Fielder
Clinical Professor of Education Psychology and Leadership Studies
University of Iowa
Iowa City, IA

Ruth A. Rich
Mentor Coordinator/Teacher (Retired)
Matteson, IL

Dana Salles Trevethan
Interim Assistant Superintendent Educational Services
Turlock Unified School District
Turlock, CA

Rosemarie Young
Principal, Jefferson County Public Schools
Louisville, KY

About the Author

 **Jane A. G. Kise,** EdD, is an educational consultant specializing in team building, coaching, and professional development. She is also the author or coauthor of over twenty books, including *Differentiated Coaching: A Framework for Helping Teachers Change; Differentiated School Leadership: Effective Collaboration, Communication and Change Through Personality Type; Intentional Leadership;* and *LifeKeys: Discover Who You Are.* She holds an MBA in finance from the Carlson School of Management and a doctorate in educational leadership from the University of St. Thomas, both in Minnesota.

Kise has worked with diverse organizations across the United States and in Saudi Arabia, Europe, Australia, and New Zealand. Her clients include Minneapolis Public Schools and various public and private schools, the Bush Foundation, NASA, Twin Cities Public Television, and numerous other institutions. She is a frequent workshop speaker and has presented at Learning Forward, Association for Supervision and Curriculum Development (ASCD), National Council of Teachers of Mathematics (NCTM), National Council of Supervisors of Mathematics (NCSM), World Futures, and Association for Psychological Type International (APTi) conferences, including keynoting in Paris, Berlin, Sydney, and Auckland.

Kise's research on coaching teachers for change has received several awards. Her research on patterns in Jungian type and how students approach mathematics became a TEDx talk. She is a faculty member of the Center for Applications of Psychological Type and a past president of APTi.

Part I

Understanding Polarity Thinking

1 Introduction

Let's Put Our Differences to Work for Us

"**W**hat's this book about?" my colleagues asked as I was writing.

"Have you ever put a ton of effort into implementing a new education initiative, only to have the pendulum swing back to the way things were after just a few years—or a few months?" I'd reply. "Or witnessed educators gridlocked over an issue, unable to move forward?"

"Only all the time!" was everyone's response.

Unleashing the Positive Power of Differences provides tools and processes for avoiding those pendulum swings by listening to the wisdom of multiple points of view—and then strategizing to move forward. We'll explore *polarity thinking* to clarify the goals, values, and fears of each side in language that compels everyone to collaborate rather than compete.

What is polarity thinking? Here's a quick illustration. Take a deep breath. Inhale slowly. Now exhale.

Which is better, inhaling or exhaling?

It's a silly question, isn't it? Our bodies require both. You can "map" this energy system that is reality for the breathing cycle (see Figure 1.1).

Inhaling brings needed oxygen, but breathing in for too long causes a problem: too much carbon dioxide. Exhaling releases that carbon dioxide, but eventually a new problem will arise: too little oxygen. We can't choose either inhaling or exhaling. We need both. It's a polarity. Each pole accurately describes something we need, yet neither side is complete without the other. They're interdependent. In fact, you can't exhale unless you've inhaled, nor inhale unless you've exhaled.

Polarities are thus part of our lives literally from our first breath. However, learning to handle them *well* can take years. Take the polarity of

Figure 1.1 The Breathing Cycle

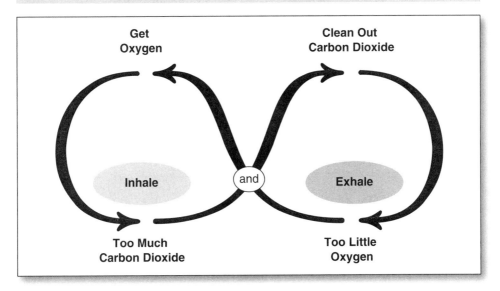

Individual AND Family, for example. My dad insisted we see other points of view with his oft-repeated phrase, "Your rights stop where your brothers' rights start." With five children sharing two bedrooms, Dad's maxim had practical origins. He and Mom wanted peace in the house, good relationships among siblings, and children who solved their own problems.

"If you can't be civil, take it outside!" We heard that whenever our attempts to sort out whose rights were impinging on whom got too boisterous.

We lived in Minnesota.

It's cold outside half the year.

We learned to respect each other's rights AND look out for our own.

Once-and-for-all solutions were rare, though. Yes, we all agreed on *Get Smart* for Sunday night television, but the week The Beatles premiered on *Ed Sullivan*, my eldest brother's right to fit in with his high school buddies triumphed over Maxwell Smart.

Our ongoing negotiations illustrate the push/pull between Individual AND Family, one of the many variations of the Individual AND Community polarity. If parents concentrate too much on the left, we raise selfish brats who dislike their siblings. If we concentrate too much on the right, we raise children who never quite find their own unique interests and potential. Astute parents help children learn to negotiate using both fairness and empathy and to examine circumstances, such as The Beatles, whose friends are coming over, or who got to watch a favorite show the night before.

Individual AND Community encompasses a multitude of issues: classroom behavior, cell phone etiquette, road rage, peanut allergies, taking (or not taking) a sick day, placing luggage in airplane overhead bins, and more. How well we work with this one polarity often affects whether others see us as kind, rude, effective, delinquent, and so on.

Life is full of universal polarities:

Continuity AND Change

Individual AND Team

Top-Down AND Participatory Leadership

You could easily add a dozen to this list, right? And you could quickly think of an example for each where one side "won" and jettisoned just about everything the other side valued. Problem solved!—until the downside of their own position surfaced, for which the solution was the other side. Thus, the pendulum swings back and forth because each solution is incomplete—just as inhaling, great as it is, is incomplete without exhaling. Things spiral down. No one wins.

The question isn't, "Have you dealt with polarities?" They permeate our lives. The question is, *"How well are you leveraging the value of each pole?"*

On many fronts in education right now, the answer is, "Not so well."

Think about the contentious debates, policy conundrums, and reversals in educational practices, whether you're looking at a school, a district, a state, or the nation. Reformers announce, "This is the problem. We have the solution." The solution gets implemented. And we end up with a *different* set of problems.

Education "reform" parallels the results my parents would have gotten if they'd solved squabbles with, "Stay away from your siblings." Maybe we'd have spent less time negotiating our differences, but we'd have missed the upsides of learning to work things out and building the relationships we still have today.

F. Scott Fitzgerald wrote, "The test of a first-rate intelligence is the ability to hold two opposed ideas in the mind at the same time, and still retain the ability to function" (*Columbia World of Quotations*, 2013). Shouldn't adult educators be modeling this ability and then passing it on to students? We can, if we stop using right/wrong and either/or thinking and instead learn to listen to the reasoning of those with whom we disagree, validate their needs and fears, and vow to work together, no matter how difficult it is.

In short, this book is about reframing conversations about many educational issues as polarities. When we choose to see two points of view, we expand our own knowledge of an issue, we better understand how someone else can hold a different opinion, and we find far more common ground and ways to work together than we suspected were possible. We can even use these tools to help our students think at higher levels.

None of this is easy, but unless we learn to listen to the values and fears of those who disagree with us, we'll continue to come up with half-right, nonsustainable "solutions." My dad would say, "Half a job." Or "There's just no sense in it." Or both.

Either way, Dad would be right. We *need* new tools, or we'll continue to swing from one reform to another. Join me in exploring how thinking in terms of polarities can help us stop wasting energy on debates, find common ground, and together, move forward. After all, we *are* all on the same side, that of the children, aren't we?

HOW TO USE THIS BOOK

Part I of *Unleashing the Positive Power of Differences* introduces the process of mapping polarities through a dilemma just about all educators have faced: helping students become responsible *and* providing support to ensure students succeed.

Then, decide what you need most right now.

If you're interested in exploring how polarity thinking could influence some of the bigger issues facing education today, continue with **Part II.**

If, after reading Chapter 1, you want to start using polarity thinking tools right away, turn to **Part III.**

Part II explores four major education issues that are being approached as problems to solve when in fact polarities are involved.

Chapter 3 explores *why* we provide education, through the polarity of Academic Success AND Whole Child Success

Chapter 4 looks at *who* should teach, through the lens of teacher effectiveness through Evaluation AND Professional Development

Chapter 5 examines *how* we teach with an in-depth look at the "math wars" and the polarity of Mastery of Knowledge AND Mastery of Problem Solving

Chapter 6 focuses on *what* we teach and the polarity of Standardization AND Customization

Part III provides the practical tools you need to start embedding polarity thinking in your team or organization's short-term and long-term approach to many issues. While you can probe the depths of polarity thinking for years, you can also make use of the tools immediately.

Chapter 7 provides a script, slides, and examples for introducing polarity thinking to a team.

Chapter 8 provides activities to help your team apply the tools to a relevant dilemma, using the example of Homogeneous Grouping AND Heterogeneous Grouping.

Chapter 9 provides tools for introducing and gaining acceptance for initiatives and strategies that involve polarities, using the example of Teaching Reading Skills and Strategies AND Student Choice in Reading.

Chapter 10 presents common polarities in education and tools for determining the ones on which your team might focus.

Chapter 11 provides ideas for introducing polarity thinking to students, from discussing classroom norms to lesson ideas that align with the Common Core State Standards.

Finally, **Part IV** takes a hard look at our hardwiring to better understand why great educators can hold opposing points of view. Chapter 12 explores how the personality theory of Carl Jung and neuroscience can inform our understanding of how we teach and learn. You can use polarity thinking without using personality type theory. However, time and again, I've successfully used this rich framework to help educators understand how and why they developed their beliefs about education and why those beliefs may not serve all teachers or all students well.

However you choose to journey through these pages, may the tools of polarity thinking give you new ideas for bridging what can seem like insurmountable differences. As a participant in one of my workshops put it,

I wish I had this model when I was a school administrator and was dealing with changes across the system (teachers, students, counselors, other administrators). Life would have been so much easier for me.

May polarity thinking enhance your work to improve the education of our children.

2 Getting Unstuck in Education

Are you suffering from initiative fatigue? That frustration stemming from being handed yet another "program" or "reform" when you don't have enough time or resources to fully implement the ones already under way (Freedman, 1992)? Whenever I'm asked to work with a school, I ask what other initiatives they're undertaking so I can make connections with my work and estimate the potential level of initiative fatigue. "Doing more with less" only goes so far, doesn't it?

Symptoms of initiative fatigue include the following:

Abbreviating. For example, one school district insisted that professional learning communities limit weekly meetings to twenty minutes, which probably isn't enough time for deep conversations about student learning.

Assuming. Here, leadership might provide high-quality professional development but fail to evaluate whether the ideas are being implemented or where additional support is needed.

Animosity. Anger toward "initiators" saps energy that could go toward implementation.

Abandonment. Frequently, initiatives are barely under way before they are replaced by new ones.

Apathy. Teachers are thinking, "Tomorrow, it'll be something else. I'm ignoring this and doing what I know works."

Take a look at the following list of initiatives where each side was seen as a "solution" to the other side. Have you been involved in initiatives that swung the pendulum of practice from one side to the other? Have you seen it swing back again? And as you read, does one side or the other strike you as more "right"?

Project-based instruction	Standards-based instruction
Whole language instruction	Phonics instruction
Direct instruction	Inquiry-based instruction
Performance assessments	Standardized assessments
Student self-esteem	Student academic progress
Teacher autonomy	Teacher collaboration

If you've seen the pendulum swing back, chances are it's because one side was seen as a "problem to solve." The other side was proposed as a "solution." Initiative fatigue is often one result. Who can find energy when past efforts didn't bring results?

Think, though, how the conversation changes if the pairs in the list are seen as *interdependent* rather than independent. Each side holds a partial solution for improving education. They're paradoxes, or tensions, or both/and rather than either/or thinking. Barry Johnson (1992) coined the term *polarity* as he developed organizational tools for working with them.

> Polarities are interdependent pairs that can support each other in pursuit of a common purpose. They can also undermine each other if seen as an either/or problem to solve. Polarities at their essence are unavoidable, unsolvable, unstoppable and indestructible. Most importantly, they can be leveraged for a greater good. (Johnson, 2012, p. 4)

What does interdependent mean? Neither pole can be "the" solution. If you want to guarantee that a change effort will fail, build it solidly on the positive results one pole has to offer to the exclusion of the other.

This book is about changing conversations in education so that we

- discern when we are dealing with ongoing polarities rather than problems that can be solved once and for all and
- learn the art of leveraging polarities by responding to shifting tensions so that we benefit from what each pole has to offer.

Let's dive right in and look at a common polarity to explore how we'll reach these goals.

WHO IS RESPONSIBLE FOR STUDENT LEARNING?

At a high-poverty school I worked with, only about 70% of the students were completing longer assignments such as reports, science investigations, and essays. That's a problem to solve, isn't it?

One of the teaching teams implemented a set of "No more Fs" strategies:

- Students learned to break projects into steps. What specific tasks did they need to complete? By when?
- Students updated their planners each day with assignments, test dates, and the next steps on their projects.
- Any work not worthy of a C or better had to be redone.
- If students fell too far behind on a major project, the teacher could require them to do a structured alternative assignment such as a test. We dubbed this rule "The make them do something rather than allow them to do nothing principle."

Within just a few weeks, one teacher reported that the passing rate in her room had climbed to 98% for the current unit. "Some of these kids had *never* finished a unit project," she told the team. "Their smiles were so big that I took pictures as they showed me their work," she added as she passed around the snapshots.

Soon, two other teachers reported similar results. "No More Fs" seemed to have erased failure from the grade books!

Problem solved, right? Moving from a failure rate of nearly 30% to close to zero?

After a rather euphoric team meeting, one of the teachers—let's call him Pete—pulled me aside to voice some concern, summarized below:

Are we helping students succeed? Or are we enabling them to continue to be irresponsible? If they know they're always going to be reminded of what they need to do—what to take home, what is due the next day—where's the incentive to develop their own organizational system?

Pete was rightly pointing out that by solving one problem, we may have created another. He correctly identified a tension between supporting students and teaching responsibility. Too much emphasis on either one creates new problems.

Perhaps you've seen the extremes of teachers who take responsibility for student learning—they keep student work in bins from one day to the next so students can't lose it or provide a bottomless supply of pencils and paper or schedule endless after-school catch-up sessions so that students feel no urgent need to attend.

And you've probably seen the extremes of expecting students to be responsible—teachers who give zeroes for any work turned in late or who accuse students of laziness when in fact they lack organization skills or who assume that Fs are "natural consequences that will teach responsibility" even though students continue to fail.

If Pete's team takes on too much of the responsibility for student learning, Pete is right. The sixth graders could easily flounder the following year without identical teacher support. Or they might internalize, "It's the teacher's fault if I'm not motivated to do the work."

But the team already knows that teaching responsibility has its limits. As one of Pete's colleagues put it, "These students have mastered failure. We need to help them experience and then master success."

So how can this team take responsibility AND teach responsibility? I've seen teams paralyzed by this very issue, with "sides" accusing each other of either babysitting students *or* being not just tough but cruel. Recognizing the tension between two poles of a *polarity* is a first step toward tapping the wisdom each side holds.

Too often, though, we attack the core issues of these debates as problems to solve. If Pete's team interpreted the "No More Fs" results as problem solved, they'd eventually see students become too dependent on teachers. They would devise an initiative along the lines of "No More Apron Strings," insisting that students organize their own schoolwork. And students would start to fail again . . . and they'd resurrect "No More Fs" . . . and . . .

THE PROBLEM OF POLARIZATION IN EDUCATION

Are you making any connections with the education "reforms" of the past 150 years? Just think of the cost—in terms of curriculum, professional development, meetings, policy formulation, and more—of the "reading wars" alone as we swung from phonics instruction to "whole language" to the Reading First initiative to "balanced instruction" to "scripted" programs and so on. Linda Darling-Hammond (2010) points out how our inability to solve these problems once and for all has stymied true reform in the United States.

> U-turns in education policy and practice are not unusual in U.S. education. Local, state and, sometimes, federal policies frequently force schools to change course based on political considerations rather than strong research about effective practice. In the long run, the fact that these battles must be continually refought means that we make less headway on student learning than we could and

should—and the students most harmed are the most vulnerable students in urban and poor rural schools where the political currents are strongest and changes of course most frequent. (p. 15)

While there are problems to solve within the issues that we'll discuss, right now the issues are being "solved" without considering key underlying polarities. Naming these polarities allows us to be intentional about leveraging, not working to solve, these inherently unsolvable tensions. If we treat them as problems, we simply create more problems for ourselves and, more important, for the students.

First though, let's deepen our understanding of polarities. Then we'll see how polarity thinking can help us transform debates into productive strategies, returning to the dilemma Pete's team faces to learn the basics of mapping a polarity.

A DEEPER LOOK AT POLARITIES

Polarities are all around us. They aren't new. They've been written about in philosophy and religion for centuries. We all know that either/or thinking can lead to problems—we need both/and thinking as well. Consider the tensions that arise when we need to honor traditions AND implement needed changes or work independently AND collaborate or meet individual needs AND build community. In each case, both sides are right. A more appropriate phrasing might be that both sides are accurate, but each is also incomplete.

We briefly visited the breathing cycle in Chapter 1:

Figure 2.1 The Breathing Cycle Infinity Loop

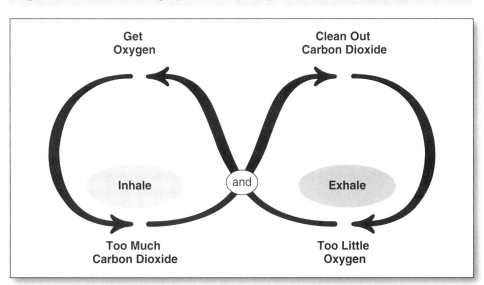

Breathing in and out is a *virtuous cycle* between two polarities. In the figure, note that the majority of the area inside the loop encompasses the space above the poles; this represents maximizing the positive sides of inhaling and exhaling. All too often, though, the two sides of a polarity fall into a *vicious cycle*, occupying the negative space below the poles.

Think for a moment about the tension between *Activity AND Rest* for someone whose goal is to finish a marathon. In Figure 2.2, the person has achieved balance—a virtuous cycle of intense training AND rest that allows muscles to both recover and increase in strength.

Figure 2.2 Marathon Virtuous Cycle

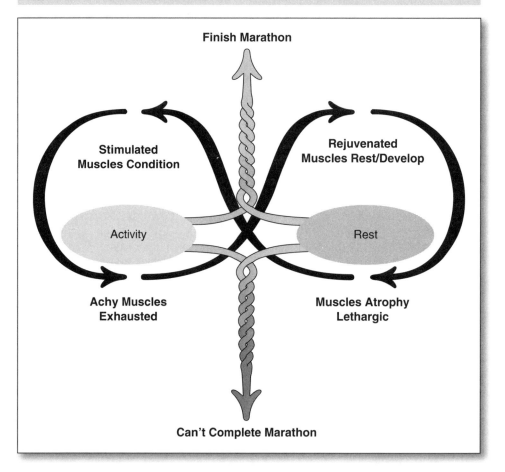

Note: The potential positive synergy between the two poles leading to a virtuous circle is depicted on a polarity map by upward spiraling arrows coming from the two poles. The potential negative synergy leading to a vicious circle is depicted by the downward spiraling arrows.

But the person shown in Figure 2.3 is training too hard. Too much training leads to achy muscles and exhaustion, and even perhaps injury, forcing rest. Too much rest stymies optimal training, and the person spirals down, caught in a vicious cycle, unable to complete the marathon. The infinity loop balloons into the lower half of the map. Every athlete leverages this polarity. The trick is to leverage it well enough to optimize performance.

Figure 2.3 Marathon Vicious Cycle

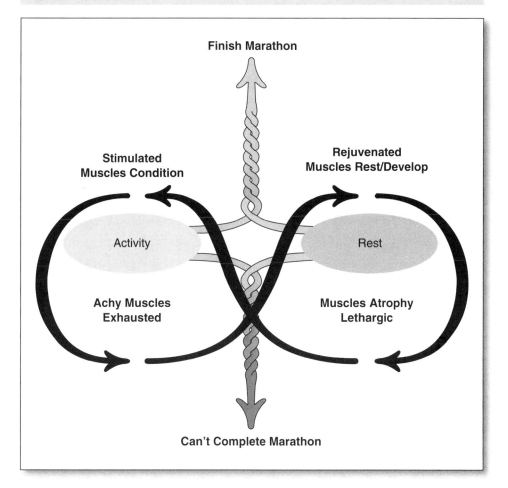

Likewise, we're already working within many polarities in education. However, just as working within the Activity AND Rest polarity doesn't automatically lead to effective marathon training, simply working within educational polarities doesn't automatically lead to highly effective education systems. Marathoners need to intentionally and systematically benefit from Activity AND Rest to ready themselves for a marathon; educators need to intentionally and systematically leverage key polarities to move toward an improved education system.

The energy wasted by animosity in debates, by swings in policies far more frequent than the three- to five-year implementation period required for deep change, and by lack of action caused by feuding shows that we're caught within polarization. Rather than leveraging the energy of various sides to move ahead, we're wasting energy on efforts that are inherently one-sided. Let's look at the steps that take us toward virtuous, not vicious, cycles.

THE CORE TOOLS FOR UNLEASHING THE POSITIVE POWER OF DIFFERENCES

We'll use the *Teacher Responsibility AND Student Responsibility* polarity that Pete's team faced to see how polarity thinking tools help reframe debates.

The Polarity Approach to Continuity and Transformation (PACT)

The example of Pete's team illustrates the value of recognizing a polarity and the values and fears of each pole for developing a wise path forward. The full PACT model involves five SMALL steps (as listed next), although for most of the book we'll be focusing on three core processes (the *see*, *map*, and *leveraging* steps described here).

See it (a polarity). We recognize when either/or thinking is perpetuating a vicious cycle and move to both/and thinking. We have a polarity to leverage, not a problem to solve. Four questions help us analyze this:

- Is it ongoing? Like breathing?
- Are the alternatives interdependent? Like inhaling and exhaling?
- Over time, are both poles or solutions needed?
- Finally, if we focus on only one upside, will we eventually undermine what we'll term our *greater purpose statement*, or GPS?

Map it. We take time to map the values and fears of each pole, identify a GPS, and acknowledge a *deeper fear* that has kept us rooted in our own position.

Assess it. Stakeholders can measure where an individual, team, or organization is on a particular polarity. Which pole is being honored more? Is the polarity in a virtuous or vicious cycle? In Part III, you'll be introduced to some quick ways to assess. Appendix B has a case study with a formal PACT assessment for the Teacher Responsibility AND Student Responsibility polarity.

Learning. In this step, we consider the assessment results, what they tell us about current and past actions, and how we might move forward. Common questions include the following: How well are we handling this polarity? How might we improve?

Leveraging. We channel the energy being wasted on either/or thinking into identifying early warning signs that a polarity is getting out of balance and action steps that can harness the essential truths of both sides.

The diagram that follows shows the two poles the team identified. At the start of our work together, the team operated within the Student Responsibility pole, resulting in a failure rate that was to them unacceptably high. The No More Fs initiative moved them to the Teacher Responsibility pole.

Figure 2.4 No More Fs Strategy

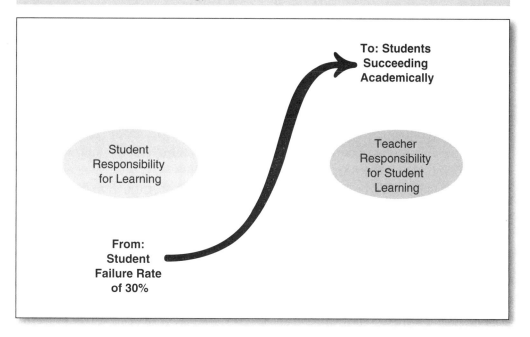

Remember, though, that Pete had some fears about the legitimacy and sustainability of that significant reduction in the student failure rate. All too often, those who raise opposition to change (especially when initial results are encouraging) are viewed as resisters or as lazy or uninformed or worse. When we map polarities, however, we recognize those fears as potential downsides of the pole toward which we're moving. Too much focus on the "No More Fs" strategies, if we fail to teach students responsibility, will have the unintended consequence of students who are too dependent on teachers.

Figure 2.5 Negative Results of Overfocus on Teacher Responsibility

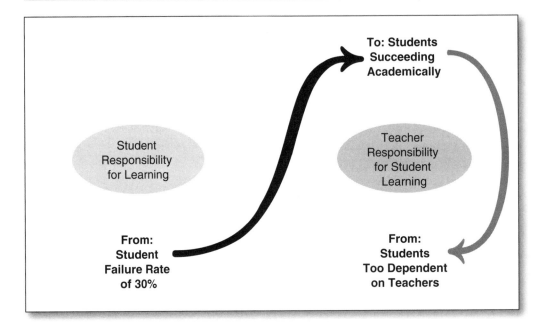

Pete's concerns reflect his equally important consideration of wanting students to take ownership of their schoolwork, which can be mapped as the upside of Student Responsibility (Figure 2.6).

However, Pete also knew that if they stopped *all* of the "No More Fs" strategies, they'd once again return to high failure rates, the downside of giving adolescents more responsibility than they can handle. Follow the arrows in the Figure 2.7 and you'll see the "vicious cycle," the infinity loop that will continue unless the team continues with the polarity thinking process to *transform* this into a virtuous cycle.

The team has completed Steps 1 and 2 of polarity thinking:

See it. They recognized Teacher Responsibility AND Student Responsibility for learning as a polarity.

Map it. They identified the upside and downside of each pole. Describing the values and fears in a polarity is the starting place for constructive dialogue. Each "side" can now step into the other's shoes and understand the differences in how each views the truth—two views of the truth that, over time, inform each other.

Figure 2.6 Positive Results of Focus on Student Responsibility

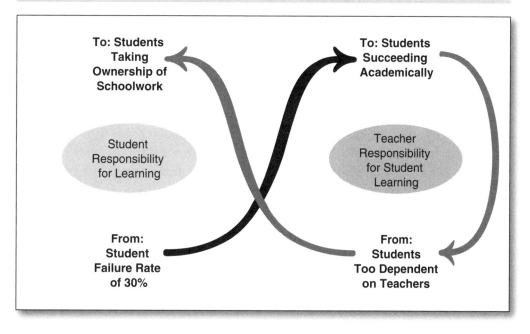

Figure 2.7 Vicious Cycle for Teacher Responsibility AND Student Responsibility

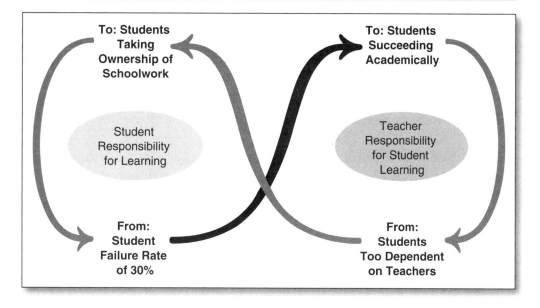

Now the team needs to *leverage* how they work with this polarity into something that accomplishes their real goal—that their students leave sixth grade with the confidence, knowledge, and habits they need to progress toward being lifelong learners.

TRANSFORMING AN UNSOLVABLE PROBLEM INTO A WELL-LEVERAGED POLARITY

This team had a common goal; we will call it a greater purpose statement, or GPS. The GPS provides motivation for learning to leverage a polarity. In this case, it answers the question, "Why should those who favor teaching responsibility and those who favor supporting students bother working together?"

The team also has a deeper fear, an awareness of what might happen if they fail to optimize this polarity. Note the additions of these in the polarity map shown in Figure 2.8, pages 20–21, as well as the more detailed lists of the values and fears of each pole. Note, too, that every map has the word *AND* in the middle as a constant reminder that to be effective over time, we need both poles.

Now the real work begins: *leveraging* the polarity to transform that vicious cycle into a virtuous cycle. In other words, we want to maximize the upside of each pole while minimizing the downsides.

The team's "No More Fs" strategies are *action steps* in the terminology we'll be using—concrete actions to be taken to maximize positive results from each pole. Some steps capture the energy of both sides—these are the most leverage-able.

To make the map useful, though, the team needs to be able to judge when they're overfocusing on one pole to the neglect of the other—either providing too much support while neglecting to help students take responsibility or focusing on responsibility without helping students develop necessary skills. *Early warnings* help us recognize when too much focus is being given to one pole. In Figure 2.9, pages 22–23, note the greater purpose statement, the specific positive and negative results each pole embodies, the deeper fear, action steps, and early warning signs.

See it. Map it. Leverage to transform it. These steps form the foundation of effectively working with polarities. The alternative is fighting the same battles over and over. Why? Because when polarities are treated as solvable problems, when one side "wins" and implements its solution, the "solution" isn't sustainable. Eventually, the overfocus on that pole to the neglect of the other will lead to its downside as well. The "win" will be seen as a mistake, to which the solution is the upside of the other pole. However, it wasn't a mistake; it just wasn't a solution. Remember, polarities are inherently unsolvable. It was a necessary self-correction in a system that over time includes its pole partner.

We don't have to look far to see the emerging downsides of "winners" in education policy. Again, remember the costs of implementing "whole language" to the neglect of phonics instruction and subsequent pendulum swings.

HOW SMART EDUCATORS CAN
HOLD OPPOSING VIEWS

That these battles continue—with the perennial losers being the students who have just one chance to be six, or eight, or fourteen years old—is, unfortunately, understandable, given human nature. The more scientists learn about neuroscience, psychology, and the decision-making process, the more humble we need to be about the stands we take and the positions we hold.

Recent research provides a very real clarion call for tools that get us beyond the paralysis of polarized sides. Jonathan Haidt (2012), a professor at New York University, shares his extensive research on the subject of how we form and defend beliefs in his book *The Righteous Mind: Why Good People Are Divided by Politics and Religion*. His conclusions also apply to why great educators find themselves on opposite sides of reform issues. Four conclusions from his research and that of others bolster the case for using polarity thinking as we work toward creating truly great educational policies and practices.

We have biases, which often come from our genetic makeup, cultural background, and experiences. Recent research confirms what realists have known for centuries. Our moral judgments usually happen before we engage in conscious processing. In other words, rather than being rational beings, we tend to react to things and then justify the positions we take (Damasio, 1994). Human beings are very good at this. Further, Perkins, Farady, and Bushey (1991) found that the higher the subjects' IQ, the more reasons they found to support their own side. Our ability to cement a one-sided argument seems to increase with intelligence!

We are all subject to "confirmation bias." Haidt (2012) documents what Wason (1960) defined as confirmation bias—a tendency to seek, note, and interpret only evidence that supports or confirms our prior conclusions. Exacerbating this, if we want to believe something, we look only for supporting evidence. We stop thinking when we've found it, even if it's somewhat flimsy. Note that because Internet search engines incorporate data from prior searches, online research is more likely to surface information that supports our current viewpoint. In contrast, if we don't want to believe something, it often only takes a single piece of evidence for us to convince ourselves that it isn't true (Gilovich, 1991).

We need input from others to overcome biases and *opinions.* We're frequently unaware that what is true in our culture may not be in another. Our initial

Figure 2.8 Elements of the Student Work Completion Polarity Map

Polarity Map for Student Work Completion

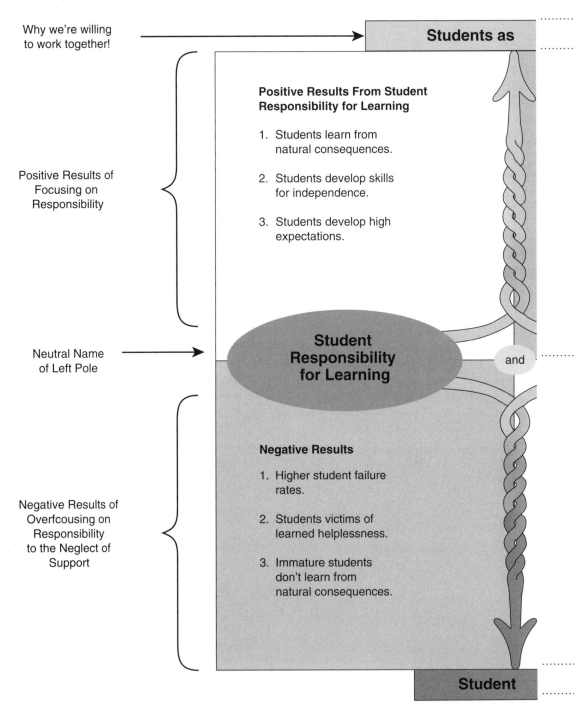

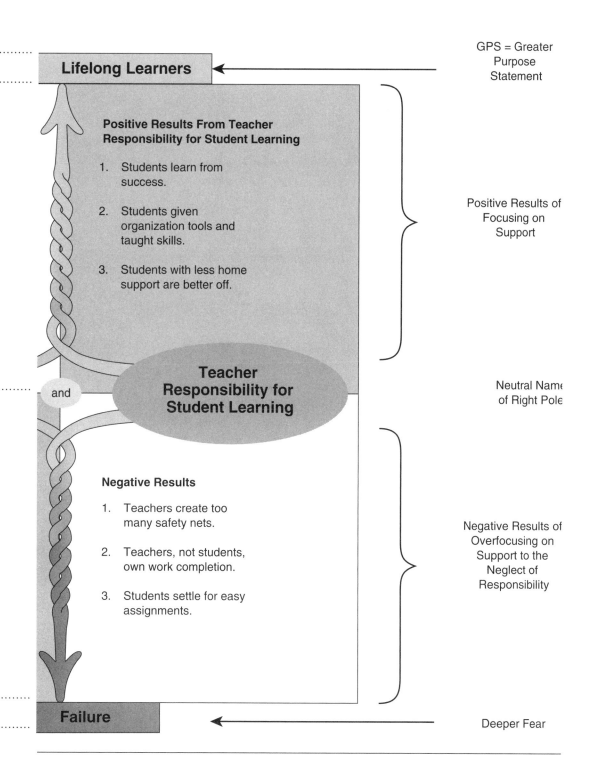

GPS = Greater Purpose Statement

Lifelong Learners

Positive Results From Teacher Responsibility for Student Learning

1. Students learn from success.

2. Students given organization tools and taught skills.

3. Students with less home support are better off.

Positive Results of Focusing on Support

Teacher Responsibility for Student Learning

and

Neutral Name of Right Pole

Negative Results

1. Teachers create too many safety nets.

2. Teachers, not students, own work completion.

3. Students settle for easy assignments.

Negative Results of Overfocusing on Support to the Neglect of Responsibility

Failure

Deeper Fear

Figure 2.9 Elements of the Student Work Completion Polarity Map

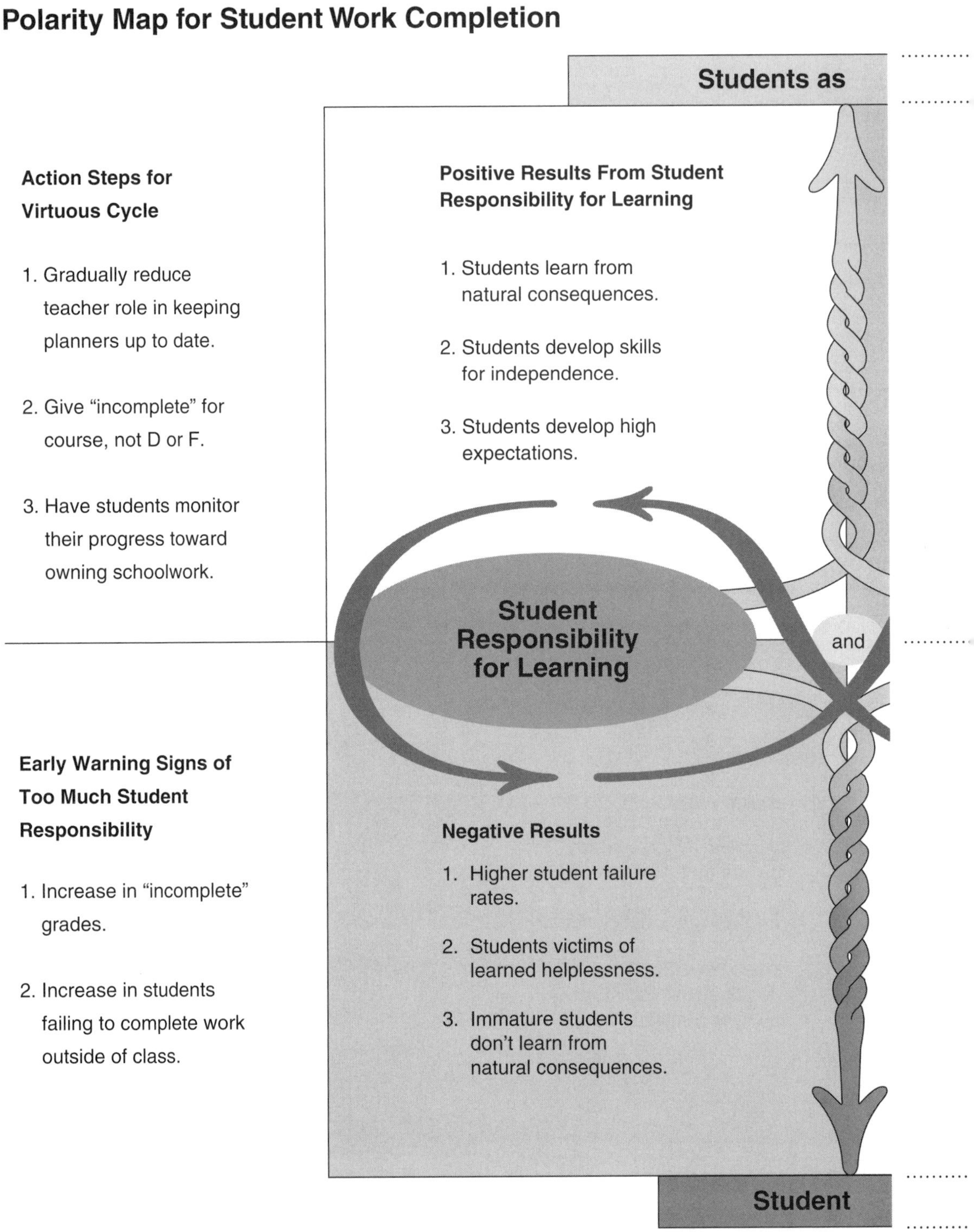

Polarity Map for Student Work Completion

Students as

Action Steps for Virtuous Cycle

1. Gradually reduce teacher role in keeping planners up to date.

2. Give "incomplete" for course, not D or F.

3. Have students monitor their progress toward owning schoolwork.

Positive Results From Student Responsibility for Learning

1. Students learn from natural consequences.

2. Students develop skills for independence.

3. Students develop high expectations.

Student Responsibility for Learning

and

Early Warning Signs of Too Much Student Responsibility

1. Increase in "incomplete" grades.

2. Increase in students failing to complete work outside of class.

Negative Results

1. Higher student failure rates.

2. Students victims of learned helplessness.

3. Immature students don't learn from natural consequences.

Student

Source: Map template copyright by Polarity Partnerships, LLC.

Lifelong Learners

Positive Results From Teacher Responsibility for Student Learning

1. Students learn from success.

2. Students given organization tools and taught skills.

3. Students with less home support are better off.

Action Steps for Virtuous Cycle

1. Teaching project planning.

2. Accept only C or better work.

3. Insist students complete project or alternatives.

Teacher Responsibility for Student Learning

and

Negative Results

1. Teachers create too many safety nets.

2. Teachers, not students, own work completion.

3. Students settle for easy assignments.

Early Warning Signs of Too Much Teacher Responsibility

1. Planner checks show students put in only teacher-required entries.

2. Increase in students doing only teacher-designed alternative tasks.

Failure

experiences with an idea or educational practice may have colored our opinion of it. And we often have no reason to question ourselves. We need others to point out the validity of data that support other positions—and we need tools that help us *listen* to such data, such as working with polarities. We're rewarded—by peers and by our physiology—for being one-sided. Whether or not we want to admit it, we care what the people in our work, social, and political circles think of us because, speaking in evolutionary terms, belonging to a group is necessary for our survival. Our brains fire dopamine, that pleasure-producing neurotransmitter, when we do something that improves our chances of survival, and that includes retaining an opinion that helps us fit in with our group (Westen, Blagov, Karenski, Hamann, & Kilts, 2006).

Great decisions come from reason and emotions. Damasio (1994) documented how people whose emotional centers of the brain are damaged are often unable to reach decisions. It also seems that psychopaths reason without emotion. Trying to stay too objective, such as by relying on only objective data for educational research, can weaken decisions.

Is it any wonder that educational issues are polarizing and that we need tools to unleash the positive power of our differences of opinion? I'd like to share a personal example of how wrong we can be if we don't seek out our own biases, dialogue with others, and use tools to examine the polarities involved in so many of the dilemmas educators face.

Recently at a bookstore, I spotted a book by Isaac Asimov that I hadn't read. Eagerly I pulled it off the shelf, only to see a phrase—"collection of short stories"—that fills me with disgust. Yes, disgust, thanks to my first formal learning experience with a short story, "The Lottery" by Shirley Jackson. (If you've never read this *New Yorker* classic, it's freely available online, and I'll try not to spoil it.)

Part of the reason Jackson's story disgusted me was my habit in adolescence of skimming assigned readings; I missed Jackson's textual clues that might have alerted me to the horror to come. In Chapter 12, we'll explore how we're sometimes hardwired to favor one pole or the other on many education issues, using research that supports Jungian type theory, popularized through the Myers-Briggs Type Indicator. For now, just note my tendency to grasp the big picture rather than details on a first read and that I am easily upset by cruelty. These factors—my habits, my wiring, "The Lottery's" cruel ending, and the ensuing class discussion—created a bias. They gave me a permanent aversion to short stories that has persisted for several decades now.

Because of "confirmation bias," these unconscious reactions are very difficult to overcome. As an English major, I certainly had plenty of exposure to excellent short stories taught by professors who loved the genre. I enjoyed Gogol's "The Nose."

Flannery O'Connor's "A Good Man Is Hard to Find" was so compelling that I bought a complete collection of her stories (but have only read a few). When my neighborhood book club chose Richard Russo's story collection *The Whore's Child*, I forced myself to read one—and liked it enough to read them all. Still, that Asimov book went right back on the bookstore shelf around the same time.

Then my daughter, assigned in seventh grade to read "The Most Dangerous Game" by Richard Connell (another gruesome classic available online), burst out, "How could a teacher make us read such a horrid tale? I hate short stories!" See how easy it is for biases to get reinforced?

I know why I have an aversion to short stories, but my reaction remains involuntary. For similar reasons, I seldom choose to read poetry. You may be wondering how I ever became an English major, right? Well, I love novels. Old, new, classic, modern, adventure, coming-of-age, science fiction, fantasy, historical—you name it. And here's where I could go wrong with my educational beliefs:

> Never in my thirteen years of public school was I required to read an all-class novel in an English or language arts class. I could easily conclude that being subjected to all-class novels would have caused me to hate those as much as I dislike poetry and short stories. That conclusion could drive a belief that assigning reading material is detrimental to student learning. I might thus advocate for student choice in reading, all day and every day.

> I've learned, though, that when educators I admire hold a different belief, I need to find out why. I dialogued with fans of all-class novels. I've observed great classroom discussions. I've seen a common text become a touchstone for future learning. I still believe that choosing assigned texts is a sacred task. I've developed a framework to assist teachers in making good choices—that is, less likely to result in what I call "The Lottery Effect," referencing that story I detested. Yet I also understand it's a polarity between Individual (choice in what we read) AND Community (connections in a classroom through shared experiences), a universal polarity we deal with continually when working with individuals within a community.

Although I'm having a bit of fun with the subject of assigned texts, it's a hotly debated topic in education. I've worked with schools and districts where teachers at each grade level are told exactly which books to assign to students. This allows for excellent collaboration around curriculum planning, but the lack of choice degrades teacher professionalism and autonomy, besides increasing incidences of my Lottery Effect. I've worked with other schools where the choices are left to the teachers. This ensures that teachers are introducing texts that they love, and can tailor choices to their particular students in any given year. However, students are sometimes required to read the same texts in multiple grades, and teachers lose the benefits of common points of reference.

I recognize that students benefit from reading choices AND assigned readings. It isn't either/or. It is both/and. We can see the polarity, map the upside and downside of each pole, and then transform the polarity into a system that engages students in reading.

CAN WE MOVE FORWARD?

We are failing, though, in the world of education, to have these conversations. Haidt (2012) suggests a path that seems a great fit with learning to use polarity-thinking tools.

> We should not expect individuals to produce good, open-minded, truth-seeking reasoning, particularly when self-interest or reputational concerns are in play. But if you put individuals together in the right way, such that some individuals can use their reasoning powers to disconfirm the claims of others, and all individuals feel some common bond or shared fate that allows them to interact civilly, you can create a group that ends up producing good reasoning as an emergent property of the social system. This is why it's so important to have intellectual and ideological diversity within any group or institution whose goal is to find truth (such as an intelligence agency or a community of scientists) or to produce good public policy (such as a legislature or advisory board). (p. 90)

As educators, we are both searching for the truth about how to help students succeed and for public policy that can bring that truth into reality, yet we so far seem to lack the tools to bring opposing "sides" together in productive dialogue. Let's now turn to how the tools of polarity thinking might help productively channel the energy in these debates. The next chapters map the dialogue on four current yet long-standing issues in education. Rather than solutions, we'll be looking at the upsides and downsides of each position and how we might transform each side's values and fears into key actions that capture as much as possible of the best of both poles.

The alternative is continuing to let the pendulum swing on major educational priorities. Again as Darling-Hammond (2010) put it,

> In the long run, the fact that these battles must be continually refought means that we make less headway on student learning than we could and should—and the students most harmed are the most vulnerable students in urban and poor rural schools where the political currents are strongest and changes of course most frequent. (p. 15)

REFLECTION

1. Before diving into the big issues in the next chapters, take a moment to think about your own education beliefs and possible sources. Below is a list of terms that probably involve polarities. Chances are, you think of at least a few of these as problems, based on real-life experiences with them. And chances are, you've seen related policies implemented, jettisoned under new leadership, and revived when leadership changes again. As you read through them, note your initial reaction as positive (+), negative (–), or neutral (. . .). And think about an educator you know who might give the same term the opposite rating

___ Gifted education

___ Phonics instruction

___ Academic rigor

___ Direct instruction

___ Individualized instruction

___ Standardized testing

___ Cooperative learning

___ Common Core State Standards

___ Inquiry-based learning

___ Performance assessments

___ Competency-based grades

___ Shared leadership

___ Middle school model

___ Constructivist learning

___ Project-based learning

___ Social/emotional learning

Now, choose one of the terms that provoked a strong reaction. Use the following questions to reflect on how you developed the viewpoint you hold. The questions revisit the dilemmas we face in understanding and influencing educational beliefs—both our own and those of others.

○ Reflect on the basis of your beliefs. Can you recall an experience, teacher, family rule, or other factor that might have fostered your belief about this topic in education? How has it contributed to your success as an educator?

○ Does anything about your own learning style or habits influence your belief?

○ Consider opportunities you've had (or made) to rethink that belief. Have you worked with people who hold an opposite belief, or have you read about their positions? Conversely, what factors might have reinforced your position?

○ Might your belief lead to any unintended consequences? List them.

○ Can you name how your belief might be part of a polarity? What are some of the downsides of your own pole? The upsides of the other?

2. Consider how you are leveraging the Student Responsibility AND Teacher Responsibility polarity. How would you position an arrow on the infinity loop in Figure 2.9 on pages 22–23? Moving toward the upside or downside of each pole?

○ How well are you leveraging this polarity? Is it a vicious or virtuous cycle?
○ Did specific policies, decisions, or beliefs move you to your current position on the infinity loop?
○ What action steps and early warning signs might increase student readiness for moving to the next grade level?

Chart 2.1 Summary of Polarity Realities

Reality 1. **Polarities are energy systems** within all interdependencies in life. Where there is interdependence, polarities are at play.

Reality 2. **Polarities are not new.** They have been a part of our personal lives since our childhood when we learned things like sharing. They've been written about in philosophy and religion for centuries and reaffirmed in research on leadership and organizational effectiveness over the last fifty years.

Reality 3. **Polarities are interdependent pairs** for which both/and thinking is required. They show up in literature as polarities, dilemmas, paradoxes, or tensions.

Reality 4. **Both/and thinking is an essential addition to either/or thinking.** It is not a replacement for either/or thinking. These two types of thinking are themselves an interdependent pair, a polarity.

Reality 5. **In an argument over a polarity, both sides are right.** A more appropriate phrasing might be that both sides are accurate but incomplete.

Reality 6. **Polarities are leverage-able.** We don't have to accept swinging from one pole to the other but can see, map, assess, learn, and leverage the energy system, putting to productive use the time and energy each side is expending in trying to "win," redirecting it toward a mutual greater purpose.

Reality 7. **Each pole has an upside and a downside.** When we acknowledge the downside of our own pole, we are acknowledging the legitimate fears of the other side, thus opening dialogue about the portion of truth each side holds.

Reality 8. **Polarities are unsolvable.** The downside of one pole is often seen as a "problem" with the upside of the other pole as a "solution."

Reality 9. **Seeing one upside as a solution leads to it being called a mistake later on.** There are natural self-corrections in the ongoing oscillation between the two poles, but both are needed over time.

Part II

The Big Picture of Polarity Thinking in Education Reform

3 Leveraging Education Goals

Academic Success AND
Whole Child Success

> What the best and wisest parent wants for his own child, that
> must the community want for all of its children. Any other ideal
> for our schools is narrow and unlovely; acted upon, it destroys
> our democracy.
>
> —John Dewey, 1902/1990, p. 7

"**W**hat does your ideal school look like?"

Wendy, a colleague, asked me that question as we were discussing
her recent visit to Finland. Comparing schools we've visited in countries
as diverse as China, Saudi Arabia, New Zealand, Poland, and now
Finland helps us unearth assumptions about education that we didn't
know we'd made.

I had recently read about Finland's dedication to equity in its schools
and had cited the Dewey quote above to express my understanding of
their philosophy. While Finland's great public school system is well worth
studying, a host of significant factors make comparison among countries
quite difficult. For example, Finland has no private schools, so parents,
government, businesses—in fact the country as a whole—are vested in
making public schools work. All education is free, even advanced university degrees. Teachers are highly regarded and well paid. Gaining entrance
to teacher education programs is competitive. Also, children do not begin

formal schooling until age seven; the Finns believe that academics shouldn't spill down into early childhood education too quickly. Still, delving into what they value provides great insights into the beliefs that drove their reform efforts, beginning in the 1970s.

Wendy thought about the Dewey quote for a moment and then replied, "As much as there was to admire about the Finnish schools I visited, there were some I wouldn't want to send my children to."

"I don't interpret Dewey to mean that there is one school ideal that we should uniformly seek," I clarified, "but rather that any school designed to meet the needs of a particular child would be as good as any other of a similar design, whether parents wanted a neighborhood school, an arts magnet school, or some other category."

Once we had an agreed-upon *greater purpose statement*, our GPS—good schools for all students—we were able to quickly articulate the values at play in the educational choices being made in each country.

SEEING THE POLARITY

The battle over what makes an ideal school goes back more than a century—actually several centuries. E. D. Hirsch, Jr. (2001b), in an indictment of what is often called progressive education, defines "classic" schools as those with a "rich and demanding curriculum, requir[ing] a lot of drill and practice, and expect[ing] every child to reach minimal goals in each subject during the year. As a result, disadvantaged children prosper academically (as do their advantaged peers)" (p. 16). He contrasts these with "progressive" schools, characterized by "multi-age groupings, where each child can go at his or her own pace; individualized assessments rather than objective tests; teachers as coaches rather than sages; projects instead of textbooks; and so on" (p. 15). He points to longitudinal studies of Catholic schools, international comparisons, and recent research on the most effective school reform efforts and concludes, "One could take each of the principles of effective-schools research (such as uniform and explicit learning goals), negate them, and you would usually have a description of progressivist principles" (p. 17). He concludes that progressive education is more of a religion than a theory or it would have been abandoned long ago in light of evidence that it doesn't work.

Those who favor the progressive view, though, claim that there was no "Golden Age" of classic education. In the past, a high school education, or even an eighth-grade education, wasn't necessary for most occupations. If we are now educating everyone, does it change our definition of school? Or is that an excuse? Or have we swung between classic and progressive education as problems to solve when in fact polarities are involved? Often, when debate over an issue has continued for decades, or for centuries, this is this case. Recognizing the polarity of *Classic AND Progressive* education allows us to apply tools to leverage the truths of both kinds of education. Then we can create a virtuous cycle from the vicious infinity loop in which we've been caught for far too long.

As a starting place, take a close look at the full title of the U.S. Elementary and Secondary Education Act, better known as "No Child Left Behind" (NCLB):

> To Close the Achievement Gap With Accountability, Flexibility, and Choice, So That No Child Is Left Behind (NCLB, 2002)

If you read further in NCLB, passages refer to coordinating community resources and other nonacademic elements, but its title focused implementation on the academic achievement gap.

Compare those words with the summary statement of the Association for Supervision and Curriculum Development (ASCD) Whole Child Initiative:

> Each child, in each school, in each of our communities deserves to be healthy, safe, engaged, supported, and challenged. That's what a whole child approach to learning, teaching, and community engagement really is. (ASCD, 2012b)

ASCD explains the purpose of its initiative in the era of NCLB: "Launched in 2007, ASCD's Whole Child Initiative is an effort to change the conversation about education from a focus on narrowly defined academic achievement to one that promotes the long term development and success of children" (ASCD, 2012b). While the poles could be named in many ways, we'll start by reflecting the character of these two very different emphases: *Academic Achievement AND Whole Child Achievement*.

A tremendous amount of energy is being expended within each pole. For example, fifteen major business groups, including the Business Roundtable and U.S. Chamber of Commerce, formed the Tapping America's Potential Coalition to improve an education system that they do not believe is currently producing enough math, science, and engineering graduates for the United States to stay globally competitive in research, defense, and innovation. *The Education for Innovation Initiative* (Tapping America's Potential, 2005) states their recommendations. Accountability, flexibility, and choice are the themes, just as named in NCLB.

ASCD's (2012a) *Making the Case for Educating the Whole Child* is perhaps the largest organized effort for whole child achievement. Foundations that support arts in the schools, the American Academy of Pediatricians, Rethinking Schools, and many other organizations are pulling together research that shows the positive impact on academic achievement of music, movement, health education, free play, a curriculum that lets children explore a wide range of subjects, and less emphasis on grades and testing. They also advocate programs that give schools ways to deal with the health and safety needs of students.

Seeing these as opposing viewpoints rather than as a polarity to leverage has resulted in swings in programs from one pole to the other, competition for funding, and different forms of inequity. What if we could capture the energy of both sides and move forward toward schools that encompass both? That's the goal of polarity thinking—clarifying the goals, values, and fears of each side in language that compels everyone to collaborate instead of compete. The map shown at the end of this chapter comes from a review of literature on "both sides" of this issue to document the values and fears each holds. We'll also name early warning signs that the polarity is moving toward a vicious rather than a virtuous infinity loop and action steps that can help schools tap the wisdom of both poles.

MAPPING THE POLARITY

Our first step is finding common ground, a GPS that answers the question of why people from the Academic and Whole Child poles should work together.

Advocates from both sides seek to define markers of well-educated public school graduates. Common phrases (although not used with equal frequency by those at each pole) include the following:

- Globally competitive
- Ready to participate in a democratic society
- Lifelong learners
- Equipped with 21st-century skills
- Proficient with at least a basic level of literacy
- Prepared for life
- College or career ready

Perhaps the phrase with the greatest potential for an effective GPS is the notion of lifelong learners, for two reasons. First, it reminds us that with the information explosion, schools can no longer provide students with a significant percentage of the knowledge they will need in life. Roland Barth (2005) estimated that whereas people graduating from high school forty years ago had probably learned about 75% or so of this knowledge, today's graduates master less than 3%—not because schools are failing but because knowledge is exploding. According to a study, the increase in available information each year now is approximately five exactabites, the equivalent of 37,000 libraries the size of the Library of Congress (Regents of the University of California, 2003).

Second, although there are not official estimates even before the recession, general consensus among career counselors was that people change careers between three and seven times. As the popular YouTube video *Did You Know* (Fisch, McCleod, & Xplane 2009) memorably put it, "We are currently preparing students for jobs that don't yet exist, using technologies that haven't been invented, in order to solve problems that we don't even know are problems yet." Thus, knowing how to learn on one's own is at least as important as mastering any prescribed set of knowledge or skills.

The *deeper fear* of both sides—the direction this polarity will take if we fail to capture the wisdom of *both* poles—can be summarized as student failure. Schools would fail to ready students for life. As always, it is in the long-term interest of both poles to seek the wisdom of the other pole. Overfocus on one's own pole eventually leads to its downside—and the downside of the other pole as well. You get what you are attempting to avoid!

POSITIVE RESULTS OF FOCUSING ON ACADEMIC ACHIEVEMENT

While the positive results from focusing on the Academic Achievement pole can and have filled books, here we will try to capture the most important points. The full map can be found at the end of the chapter on pages 50–51.

1. Academic achievement is the top priority, providing access to the American Dream.

Lengel (2012) points to a study by Sean Reardon of Stanford, who found that the achievement gap at the start of kindergarten between low-income and high-income children, regardless of race, has increased over the last fifty years and does not seem to lessen over years of schooling. The goal of ensuring that all high school graduates are college or career ready reflects the very sobering truth that lifelong wages are considerably lower for people lacking college degrees and even lower for those without a high school diploma. These facts have spurred more academic content in Head Start programs and kindergarten.

2. We show true caring by insisting that all students meet high standards.

Setting high expectations that all students can achieve, and then seeking research-based strategies that work to bring this about, is foundational to this pole. Because the United States is perceived as losing the race in producing scientists, STEM (science, technology, engineering, and mathematics) courses are emphasized at this pole. For example, introducing algebra in earlier grades is often championed since it is a predictor of college success.

3. Extra class time and hard work help students who are below grade level.

Since the implementation of NCLB, most schools (71% according to the Center on Education Policy; McMurrer, 2008) have increased time spent on literacy and mathematics to give children extra time to master these crucial, tested subjects. Lavon (2009) reported that students at the KIPP charter schools, often held up as an example of institutions that are closing the achievement gap, spend 60% more hours at school than students in regular public schools. Time and sufficient support are considered the key ingredients for ensuring that students achieve at high levels.

In the last few years, the possibilities provided by technology for personalizing learning are also being championed. Project RED (Redesigning Education; 2012) conducted research with nearly 1,000 schools and, besides identifying nine key components of effective technology implementation, found that well-implemented use of technology in interventions was more predictive of improved high-stakes test scores, dropout rate reduction, course completion, and improved discipline than any other factor they studied.

4. Leaders provide vision, establish a culture of achievement and accountability, and recruit and retain effective teachers.

While nearly all school reform advocates recognize the importance of leadership, supporters of this pole often advocate and invest in transferring effective business practices to school management.

A report from the Wallace Foundation (Leithwood, Louis, Anderson, & Wahlstrom, 2004) summarized findings compiled by the Universities of Minnesota and Toronto. It describes how successful school leaders bring about reform by setting a clear direction with high expectations and then using data to measure progress, by providing adults with the support and training they need, and by working to ensure that the system conditions and incentives support both teaching and learning. They and other foundations have invested heavily in school leadership development programs that concentrate on these factors. The Broad Foundation, for example, reports that thirty alumni of its Superintendents Academy, launched in 2002, are running big-city school districts in the United States (Jehlen, 2012).

5. Accountability, measurement of academic progress, and school choice result in academic success for all.

NCLB (2001) specifically lists accountability, flexibility, and choice as strategies for closing the learning gap. Reliance on standardized tests, teacher accountability initiatives, and support for vouchers and charter schools are three common themes that tie into these strategies.

NEGATIVE RESULTS OF OVERFOCUSING ON ACADEMIC ACHIEVEMENT TO THE NEGLECT OF WHOLE CHILD ACHIEVEMENT

If academic achievement accurately captures part of a polarity, then too much focus on its values will eventually lead to its downside. Below are possible outcomes from failing to consider the values of educating the whole child.

1. Rating schools and providing school choice means that some students have access to a better education than others.

Opponents of school choice claim that if we're ranking schools, we're failing to strive for excellence in all schools. They point out that while choice would seem to empower everyone, it often disadvantages those with the fewest resources. Many parents prefer having their children in neighborhood schools, especially low-income families who rely on public transportation and might struggle to participate in schools farther away from home. Also, parents with more resources, in terms of time, money, and knowledge of the system and how to research other opportunities, are more likely to opt out of the default public school to which their child is assigned. This concentrates students with the biggest academic and other struggles in certain buildings.

Charter schools are often championed by advocates of choice. A major unintended consequence of charter schools and other choice programs, though, is the resegregation of public school in the United States. The most highly segregated public schools at the start of the 21st century were in New York, Michigan, Illinois, and California. In Chicago, where increasing the number of charter schools is a policy priority, less than 10% of children in public schools were white in 2000; in Washington, DC, less than 5%; in Detroit, the percentage is slightly lower still. And we know that these urban schools are not "separate but equal" any more now than at the time of *Brown vs. Board of Education.* Inequity seems to be increasing, not decreasing, in public schools.

However, an even bigger inequity seems to be surfacing. Children not making adequate yearly progress can be seen as problematic in struggling schools. Further, the lower the socioeconomic status of the school, the more likely that there will be a police presence in the school. Certain factors known to increase a student's chances of dropping out are on the rise:

- Students' in-school arrests have increased, with a high percentage of arrests being for offenses that result in suspensions, not criminal records, for students in schools without police presence.
- In states with high school exit examinations as a requirement for graduation, graduation rates are lower. In 2006, twenty-three states had such requirements, but 74% of the nation's minority populations attended school in these states, meaning they had a lower chance of graduating than if they lived in other states.

Organizations such as Rethinking Schools and Dignity in Schools are calling attention to this "school-to-prison pipeline" for our most disadvantaged students. Both organizations see a link between pushing for academic success and removing students who struggle academically.

2. School curriculum narrows to tested areas for students who struggle.

Because student enjoyment of school is often tied to subjects in which they can excel, narrowing the curriculum can decrease their chances of becoming lifelong learners. For secondary school students, days are often split into six or seven periods. With one period for each core subject (math, science, language arts, and social studies) plus an extra period of math and/or reading for struggling students, little time is left for anything else.

According to the Center on Educational Policy, nearly two-thirds of school districts have increased the amount of instructional time for reading and math by an average of 32%. This increase came at the expense of time for social studies, science, the arts, physical education, and recess

(McMurrer, 2008). Approximately 28% of schools serving low-income populations have no recess at all (Ramstetter, Murray, & Garner, 2010). There have also been complaints about decreased opportunities and curriculum for multicultural education. In contrast, high-achieving and wealthier students still take arts, humanities, and other elective courses and thus have more opportunities to discover their talents.

3. Students receive a standardized, sometimes scripted, curriculum.

The Gallup Student Poll (Lopez, 2011) reports that about 23% of students don't find schoolwork engaging and another 14% are actively disengaged and "likely to undermine the teaching and learning process for themselves and others" (p. 72). Further, whereas about 80% of elementary students are engaged at school, that percentage drops to 40% by high school. Brandon Bust (2013), the executive director, summarizes as follows:

> The drop in student engagement for each year students are in school is our monumental, collective national failure. There are several things that might help to explain why this is happening— ranging from our overzealous focus on standardized testing and curricula to our lack of experiential and project-based learning pathways for students—not to mention the lack of pathways for students who will not and do not want to go on to college.

The High School Survey of Student Engagement (Yazzie-Mintz, 2010) reports that of the 98% of students reporting being bored at school, 81% stated that the material they were studying wasn't interesting. While the facts are somewhat contradictory on whether graduation rates have increased or decreased under NCLB (there are at least four ways to measure this rate), dropouts themselves report disengagement as a major reason. And the lower student test scores are, the bigger the chance the school will be using more standardized or scripted curricula while at the same time cutting untested content areas.

4. Fears from top-down pressures of high-stakes testing drive out innovations by teachers and students, who stop taking risks to ensure higher grades or test scores.

If academic achievement is being emphasized, especially in STEM courses, then are creativity and uniqueness at risk? Kim (2011) found that measures of student creative thinking have decreased significantly since 1990 even as IQ and SAT scores have climbed.

Teachers have been concerned about the amount of time going to test prep, assessing for learning, and other activities that crowd out time for student research projects, group activities, and project-based learning.

5. Wisdom based on teacher experience is ignored in favor of what can be tested or measured.

I asked an experienced teacher, who had just tallied the results of the reading unit tests her students had spent three hours taking, what she had learned from the results. "Nothing," she said. "I already knew which students had mastered which skills by watching, listening, and asking questions, but the district insists that we collect all this data."

While some may argue that not all teachers have this knowledge, denying them the ability to use their experience is akin to insisting that experienced airline pilots fly by the book when their plane is malfunctioning. Like pilots, teachers gain the ability to "know" what to do through experience and reflective practice, especially in collaboration with other professionals. *Assessments AND Teacher Wisdom* is a polarity for how student growth is measured.

POSITIVE RESULTS OF FOCUSING ON WHOLE CHILD ACHIEVEMENT

When too much focus is directed toward one pole, the cycle moves toward seeking the upside of the other pole. Again, this is a summary of the values and positive results described in the literature by advocates of the Whole Child Achievement pole.

1. Schools need to ensure that students are healthy, safe, engaged, supported, and challenged (ASCD, 2012b).

Imagine trying to learn algebra when you are hungry or if you or friends you care about were threatened at the bus stop or if the schoolwork is too easy or too difficult for you or if no adults seem invested in your success. Advocates at this pole stress that academic readiness is only one of a host of factors for student learning. Noncognitive skills are as important as cognition to success in life, including learning to cooperate, self-motivation, perseverance, and so on. Teaching social skills, for example, has a significant positive impact on academic achievement (Durlak, Weissberg, Dymnicki, Taylor, & Schellinger, 2011).

Further, we've known for a long time that people with the highest IQs aren't necessarily destined for greater success than the rest of us. In his book *How Children Succeed*, Paul Tough (2012) documents how character is created by encountering and overcoming failure. Often, high-income children don't encounter enough failure, and low-income students don't have the support necessary to learn to overcome it. Advocates of a whole child approach believe schools can help students develop what Tough calls "grit."

2. Equity gives every child an equal opportunity to learn regardless of family background, income, or geographic location.

Advocates suggest that rather than giving parents and students access to excellent schools through choice, our democracy would be better served by bringing all schools up to excellence. Note that this echoes the priorities of the Finnish school system, as summarized by Pasi Sahlberg, the Director of the Finnish Ministry of Education's Center for International Mobility:

> Since the 1980s, the main driver of Finnish education policy has been the idea that every child should have exactly the same opportunity to learn, regardless of family background, income, or geographic location. Education has been seen first and foremost not as a way to produce star performers, but as an instrument to even out social inequality.
>
> In the Finnish view, as Sahlberg describes it, this means that schools should be healthy, safe environments for children. This starts with the basics. Finland offers all pupils free school meals, easy access to health care, psychological counseling, and individualized student guidance. (Partanen, 2011, pp. 4–5)

3. Play, movement, and opportunities for creativity all promote intellectual development.

Study after study shows that free play, imaginative play, and chances to learn to cooperate in play with other children are valuable learning tools. A report from the American Association of Pediatrics documents that play

- contributes to healthy brain development,
- increases a child's ability to remember new information,
- enhances learning readiness and problem-solving skills, and
- develops creative, imaginative, and leadership abilities. (Milteer, Ginsburg, & Council on Communications and Media, Committee on Psychosocial Aspects of Child and Family Health, 2012)

In other words, play is a natural way to develop many of the so-called 21st-century skills. A too-narrow focus on academics often displaces the forms of play that improve cognitive abilities—and that would make the school day more developmentally appropriate for children.

4. Meeting needs of the whole child requires collaboration among the student, school staff, parents, and sometimes, outside professionals and community services.

We wouldn't expect school personnel to diagnose appendicitis and then operate. Similarly, we shouldn't expect schools by themselves to meet the significant mental health or family counseling or learning disability needs of some children. Initiatives such as the Harlem Children's Zone are able to provide preventive care to students with conditions such as asthma and emphasize coordination of community services to ensure that children are safe, healthy, and ready to learn. The Centers for Disease Control (Akinbami & Liu, 2011) estimated that students with asthma missed 10.5 million school days in 2008, and the disease is more prevalent among low-income students, who often also lack access to adequate health care.

5. Intrinsic motivation is essential to becoming a lifelong learner. Engagement flows from caring adults and time every day doing what one does best.

The Gallup Student Poll found that 79% of students who agreed with the statement, "My school is committed to building the strengths of each student" are fully engaged at school, compared with only 11% who disagreed with that statement (Lopez, 2011). In this regard, it's interesting to compare the purpose statements of the Singapore Ministry of Education and the U.S. Department of Education:

> The Ministry of Education aims to help our students to discover their own talents, to make the best of these talents and realize their full potential, and to develop a passion for learning that lasts through life. (Ministry of Education, 2006, p. 2)

> The mission of the Department of Education is to promote student achievement and preparation for global competitiveness by fostering educational excellence and ensuring equal access. (U.S. Department of Education, 2012)

The first is distinctly individual centered, characterized by the factors necessary to create lifelong learners, while the second is more community centered, emphasizing our national need for excellence and competitiveness. *Individual AND Community* is a universal polarity. Within the context of education, are we creating schools that honor individuals *and* meet our society's needs?

NEGATIVE RESULTS OF OVERFOCUSING ON WHOLE CHILD ACHIEVEMENT TO THE NEGLECT OF ACADEMIC ACHIEVEMENT

However, if we overfocus on whole child achievement to the neglect of academics, we will get the downside of both poles as the cycle spirals toward our deeper fears of student failure. Key negative results might include the following.

1. Inequality continues when struggling students fall further behind due to lack of academic emphasis.

I frequently hear from teachers that for all that they dislike about the high-stakes testing environment created by NCLB, they recognize that prior to its enactment, the poor performance of some student groups was somewhat taken for granted. Yes, schools created caring environments, but less attention was paid to accelerating academic achievement.

2. Too many accommodations are made for student learning differences, resulting in low academic expectations.

While allowing students to learn in different ways is essential to honoring their diverse needs, the substitutions don't always demand enough. Making shoebox dioramas, posters, or other projects, without specific rubrics that emphasize learning goals or the literacy skills to be employed, is not the equivalent of writing essays.

Sometimes, the "dumbing down" is obvious, as when some students read college prep materials such as *The Iliad* while classmates learn about the plot and characters from a comic book or movie version. If the goal is simply factual knowledge of *The Iliad*, then these substitutions may be fine. However, the graphic novel version probably won't prepare students for encountering complex texts in college freshman classes, and they may need remediation courses.

Excess concern over children's self-esteem can also lead to dilution of grades. Examples of this include grading on effort rather than results, where children who fail to master material still pass a course because they did their best.

3. When benchmarks for academic progress are unclear or underemphasized, students, teachers, and parents are unaware of progress rate.

As more and more students received high school diplomas yet were unprepared for college course work, critics pointed out that academic standards were simply too low. Frequently, teachers did not set clear learning targets and therefore had no way of assessing whether students had met them. The emphasis in NCLB on making adequate yearly progress stemmed from this dilemma. Marzano (2003) found that a guaranteed and viable curriculum is, of those studied, the variable most related to student achievement. "Guaranteed" means that teachers deliver that curriculum as a minimum to all students. "Viable" means that enough time and resources are available for students to master it.

4. Academics get squeezed out by curriculum for bullying, self-esteem, cooperation, values instruction, and so on.

Every whole child initiative takes time away from core academics. As proponents speak of educating students for life, more and more topics are suggested for the school day, from nutrition to personal finance to career and college planning in elementary classrooms. Others raise concerns that providing a multicultural learning environment or allowing for dual-language instruction also takes away from precious academic time. While all of these experiences can have a positive impact on students, learning time is finite.

5. In an effort to engage students, schools de-emphasize academic content.

Critics can give very real examples of lessons or assessments that appear to have little rigor but that students enjoy. I've heard complaints about assignments involving creating board games or a daylong simulation of a Roman marketplace, that weren't structured with learning objectives in mind. Some teachers accept student complaints that memorizing math facts is boring and lower their expectations. Others substitute a movie version of a classic novel, assuming that there is no way to make the real thing compelling to students or that an equivalent text that is more engaging can't be found. Mintz (2012) describes how these instructional decisions involve a misunderstanding of the progressive education value for education to be exciting and pleasurable. She points out that Rousseau, whose writings are often cited as the basis for progressive education, gave examples of how we learn best from our mistakes and that those mistakes are sometimes necessarily painful. We also learn from perseverance. Modern educators should thus design experiences that allow some pain without developing fearful attitudes or discouragement.

TRANSFORMING THE POLARITY

Given that this debate has raged for centuries, albeit without the current emphasis of trying to close the achievement gap, using the tools of polarity thinking to transform the energy into useful dialogue might forge new partnerships. The next step is assessing where we currently are in the infinity loop this polarity encompasses. Which of these early warning signs are evident in your organization?

Early Warnings for the Downside of Academic Achievement

    A. Decrease in school time for arts, physical education, recess, and other non-core subjects. Not all students have daily chances to engage in areas where they excel.

    B. Increase in incentive systems to motivate students on tests, to take more AP classes, or to read more books.

    C. Decrease in measures of overall student health: obesity, bullying, untreated mental health issues, burned-out college freshmen.

    D. Increase in use of technology to "personalize" learning; students lose time with caring adults.

    E. Surveys show decrease in student engagement, increase in boredom.

Early Warnings for the Downside of Whole Child Achievement

    A. Decrease in students making acceptable academic gains.

    B. Increase in educators attributing student failure to poverty and other factors outside their control.

    C. Increase in school segregation as motivated students/families choose charter or private schools that emphasize academic success.

    D. Increase in students who state plans to attend college but whose college entrance test scores may not qualify them.

    E. Increase in students who avoid taking intellectual risks or challenging themselves because of being overly protected from tasks at which they might fail.

STEPS TOWARD MANAGING THIS POLARITY WELL

Here is one way to describe the ideal outcome of leveraging Academic Achievement AND Whole Child Achievement:

> Parents no longer need to worry about finding a great school because every school works to ensure that students have the instruction and support they need to become lifelong learners.

Below are action steps that might get us there. Note that all of these are "high leverage," supporting not one but both poles. Frequently, though, action steps also include ones specific to each pole.

A. Focus on equity instead of choice so that all schools are ones to which you might send your own child.

This is the route that countries such as Finland have taken. It doesn't mean that all schools would be exactly the same, but when looking for a particular kind of school, whether a neighborhood school or a STEM school or an arts school or a K–8 building or a language immersion program or any other type of school, parents would know with confidence that any school would be as good as another one of its kind.

While the lack of private schools in Finland means that resources are more easily focused on achieving such a goal than in the United States, accepting this goal rather than accountability and choice would shift resources toward ensuring that at least in public schools, students would all be educated in buildings that are healthy, suited to learning, and equipped with modern science, technology, physical education, and media facilities.

B. Ensure that all students are exposed to a wide variety of disciplines to engage students in multiple ways and maximize talent diversity among students.

In his book *Catching Up or Leading the Way,* Yong Zhao (2009) lays out that U.S. schools have long nurtured individual differences and unique talents among children, leading to greater creativity and our historical excellence in science and related fields. However, while the United States is embarking on increasing high-stakes testing, countries with a history of reliance on high-stakes testing are working to decrease the importance of tests in order to nurture creativity. In other words, current reforms may be squelching the very conditions that have traditionally nurtured our finest minds. Zhao claims that the current emphasis on a narrow definition of school success will hurt, not help, students in reaching their full academic potential.

Further, we're learning more and more about how the arts and hands-on problem solving prepare students for excellence in science and other "hard" disciplines. Einstein credited his scientific reasoning to violin playing, observation skills learned through drawing, and his job at a patent office tearing apart new devices to see how they worked—to music, arts, and shop class, one might say (Root-Bernstein & Root-Bernstein, 2013).

C. Develop collaborative partnerships to ensure that students' academic, physical, social, emotional, and safety needs are met.

This action step acknowledges that students need more than academic support to succeed and that schools often need help in meeting the tremendous mental, physical, and social needs of some of their students. Returning to the consequences of asthma illustrates the issues. Approximately one in three urban children of poverty suffer from asthma, which results in poorer sleep and missed school days. School-based asthma care results in fewer emergency room trips, better symptom management, and fewer missed days of school.

Many initiatives are working to make such services available for a wide range of needs. The Harlem Children's Zone, where medical, dental, and social services are coordinated through the neighborhood schools, is one example of concerted effort to bring this about. In Minneapolis, the Washburn Center for Children has at least eighteen school-based offices where they provide mental health services to children whose families would struggle to transport them to traditional clinics.

D. Emphasize intrinsic motivation methods, including involving students in setting learning targets and goals, while decreasing reward/punishment incentives for learning.

In *Drive*, Daniel Pink (2009) gathers the research to show how carrots and sticks—monetary incentives, pizza parties, or bad grades and lost free time—fail to motivate human beings. Instead we crave the following:

- *Autonomy.* Adults and children alike need some say in what they do and how they do it. When students have some say in how or when or what they learn, they become more motivated from within.
- *Mastery.* Children need chances every day to do something they are good at, as stated above.
- *Purpose.* The payback from knowing why they are learning something is huge.

E. Ensure that the data informing instruction have information on student engagement and motivation as well as academic test results.

Again, if students need to become lifelong learners, then we need to be tracking their attitudes toward schooling. Yes, we need data that track whether students are growing academically, but we also need data such as the Gallup Student Poll's information on students' attitudes toward reading for pleasure, information on engagement in extracurricular activities, and student self-assessments of their own study habits and organizational skills.

Going further, schools might consider ways of including student voices to understand what is and isn't working. A few years ago I had the wonderful opportunity to meet with a half dozen students whose teachers considered them at risk for underachieving. All qualified for free and reduced lunch. All of them told me they valued education but didn't always feel supported by their teachers. *All* of them leaned forward into the discussions, made meaningful contributions, stayed seated and focused, and seemed to bask in the fact that they were being heard. Here are some of their comments:

> The smart kids get to learn new things. We're stuck with the same stuff over and over.

> Teachers need to be fair and give compliments to everyone. Compliments are something you'll work hard for.

> Teachers need to work with you until you get it. I can't get help at home. The worst is when you don't get it and they say, "Didn't you listen?"

> No teacher should be telling me I can't do something. If I want to try a harder task or read a harder book, let me do it!

> Teachers and students look at me like I'm retarded. Once in a while, tell me I'm doing a good job.

> The smart kids have all been a teacher's pet at some time.

> I learn when teachers listen and ask questions, trying to understand what I'm saying.

They're asking to succeed academically. And they're asking to be treated as a whole child. Listening to the students may just help us leverage this polarity.

REFLECTION

1. Consider your own organization or team's current position by examining the map at the end of the chapter on pages 50–51. Which of the positive results of each pole have you experienced? Which

Polarity Thinking Map for Leveraging Academic Goals

Students as

Action Steps

A. Focus on equity instead of choice so that all schools are ones to which you might send your own child.

B. Ensure that all students are exposed to a wide variety of disciplines to engage students in multiple ways and maximize talent diversity among students.

C. Develop collaborative partnerships to ensure that students' academic, physical, social, emotional, and safety needs are met.

D. Emphasize intrinsic motivation methods, including involving students in setting learning targets and goals, while decreasing reward/punishment incentives for learning.

E. Ensure that the data informing instruction have information on student engagement and motivation as well as academic test results.

Values = positive results from focusing on the left pole

1. Academic achievement is the top priority, providing access to the American Dream.

2. We show true caring by insisting that all students meet high standards.

3. Extra class time and hard work help students who are below grade level.

4. Leaders provide vision, establish a culture of achievement and accountability, and recruit and retain effective teachers.

5. Accountability, measurement of academic progress, and school choice result in academic success for all.

Academic Achievement

and

Early Warnings

A. Decrease in school time for arts, physical education, recess, and other non-core subjects. Not all students have daily chances to engage in areas where they excel.

B. Increase in incentive systems to motivate students on tests, to take more AP classes, or to read more books.

C. Decrease in measures of overall student health: obesity, bullying, untreated mental health issues, burned-out college freshmen.

D. Increase in use of technology to "personalize" learning; students lose time with caring adults.

E. Surveys show decrease in student engagement, increase in boredom.

1. Rating schools and providing school choice mean that some students have access to a better education than others.

2. School curriculum narrows to tested areas for students who struggle.

3. Students receive a standardized, sometimes scripted, curriculum.

4. Fears from top-down pressures of high-stakes testing drive out innovations by teachers and students, who stop taking risks to ensure higher grades or test scores.

5. Wisdom based on teacher experience is ignored in favor of what can be tested or measured.

Fears = negative results from overfocusing on the left pole to the neglect of the right pole

Student

Lifelong Learners

*Values = positive results from
focusing on the right pole*

1. Schools need to ensure that students are healthy, safe, engaged, supported, and challenged (ASCD, 2012b).

2. Equity gives every child an equal opportunity to learn regardless of family background, income, or geographic location.

3. Play, movement, and opportunities for creativity all promote intellectual development.

4. Meeting needs of the whole child requires collaboration among the student, school staff, parents, and sometimes, outside professionals and community services.

5. Intrinsic motivation is essential to becoming a lifelong learner. Engagement flows from caring adults and time every day doing what one does best.

and

Whole Child Achievement

1. Inequality continues when suggling students fall further behind due to lack of academic emphasis.

2. Too many accommodations are made for student learning differences, resulting in low academic expectations.

3. When benchmarks for academic progress are unclear or underemphasized, students, teachers, and parents are unaware of progress rate.

4. Academics get squeezed out by curriculum for bullying, self-esteem, cooperation, values instruction, etc.

5. In an effort to engage students, schools de-emphasize academic content.

*Fears = negative results from overfocusing
on the right pole to the neglect of the left pole*

Failure

Action Steps

A. Focus on equity instead of choice so that all schools are ones to which you might send your own child.

B. Ensure that all students are exposed to a wide variety of disciplines to engage students in multiple ways and maximize talent diversity among students.

C. Develop collaborative partnerships to ensure that students' academic, physical, social, emotional, and safety needs are met.

D. Emphasize intrinsic motivation methods, including involving students in setting learning targets and goals, while decreasing reward/punishment incentives for learning.

E. Ensure that the data informing instruction have information on student engagement and motivation as well as academic test results.

Early Warnings

A. Decrease in students making acceptable academic gains.

B. Increase in educators attributing student failure to poverty and other factors outside their control.

C. Increase in school segregation as motivated students/families choose charter or private schools that emphasize academic success.

D. Increase in students who state plans to attend college but whose college entrance test scores may not qualify them.

E. Increase in students who avoid taking intellectual risks or challenging themselves because of being overly protected from tasks at which they might fail.

negative results? Toward which pole is the energy in your system moving? Is it a virtuous or vicious cycle right now, moving toward the GPS or deeper fear? Consider the following:

○ How is our current handling of this polarity working for our students?
○ What initiatives have focused on each pole?
○ Which action steps might accelerate us toward the GPS?

ACTIVITY 2.1: USING POLARITY THINKING TO ANALYZE A FAILED INITIATIVE

2. Think of a failed initiative you experienced that could be categorized as "whole child" (such as character education or arts experiences) or "academic" (such as providing math tutors or implementing new instructional strategies). What was valued—that is, what was the upside of the initiative? What was ignored? Make a miniature polarity map, filling in the boxes that follow *in the order of the numbers, starting in the lower left quadrant* to mimic the system's natural energy flow.

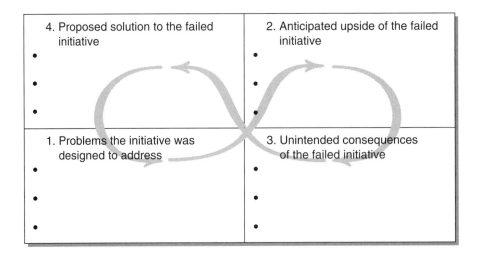

What action steps during the initiative might have included the values of the other "pole" and perhaps led to more success?

4 Ensuring Effective Teachers

Evaluation as a Measure of Effectiveness AND a Guide for Professional Growth

As I began working on this chapter, Chicago Public Schools teachers were on strike. While disagreement over class size, salaries, school closings, and more led to the strike, the proposed teacher evaluation system was the Chicago Teachers Union's main concern.

Objecting to the heavy reliance on student standardized test scores, the union declared

> There is no way to measure the effectiveness of an educator. Further, there are too many factors beyond our control which impact how well some students perform on standardized tests, such as poverty, exposure to violence, homelessness, hunger and other social issues beyond our control. (Omar, 2012, p. 1)

And thus the issues became so polarizing in Chicago that a strike resulted and students missed seven days of school. Note that when disagreements over goals and values are so severe that neither side can see any common ground, circumstances often degenerate into a "vicious cycle" in which both poles—and the entire system—lose.

SEEING THE POLARITY

When conflict moves to the streets, stopping to search for polarities might be helpful! Teachers everywhere have long mistrusted evaluation systems, and unions have worked to protect their rights. After all, observations can be biased, the one year a student spends in a teacher's classroom isn't always enough to overcome learned helplessness, and parents and administrators have both been known to seek dismissal of effective teachers who disagreed with them on a philosophical point.

However, unions weren't listening to the rationale of those calling for new evaluations: Teachers are hired to help students learn. Shouldn't they be evaluated on how well they succeed at this primary task? This resistance to *any* changes in evaluation systems opened the way for a revolutionary change in how teachers are evaluated.

The Obama Administration's Race to the Top initiative required states to implement a measure of teacher accountability based on student performance. In its wake, more and more states (thirty-four as of this writing) passed laws requiring teacher evaluation systems to include a measure of student achievement, usually in the form of standardized test scores.

Yet the "teacher accountability" movement is creating new problems. Quick implementation of some systems has resulted in crazy events such as the following:

- Unreliable systems can have statistical error rates of 35% when using one year's worth of data and 25% when using three years of data (Schochet & Chiang, 2010).
- One of the best eighth-grade mathematics teachers in New York City, whose students all passed the tenth-grade Regents examination, was ranked in the New York Post as the lowest-performing teacher, based on performance on the eighth-grade standardized test (Pallas, 2012).
- There is heavy reliance on standardized test scores in the evaluation systems, even though studies show their unsuitability for this purpose. For example, one study from five school districts showed that of the teachers who scored in the bottom 20% one year, between 25% and 45% moved to the top half of the distribution the next year while most who scored in the top 20% moved to lower parts the next year (Newton, Darling-Hammond, Haertel, & Thomas, 2010).
- How teachers rank varies widely, depending on which test is used (Bill & Melinda Gates Foundation, 2010).

With the current overfocus on using test scores to rank teachers, we're quickly seeing the downside of this polarity. Still, the other pole can't be

No Evaluation; nearly all teachers want feedback that helps them improve their craft. The American Federation of Teachers (n.d.) advocates that educators to play an active role in developing a better approach:

> Teachers need to take responsibility for their profession, define what it means to be a good teacher, and play a role in deciding who should enter and remain in the profession. Teachers can do this by leading the effort to overhaul teacher evaluation rather than reacting to others' evaluation plans. . . . Good teachers are not born; rather, they are carefully and systematically cultivated through rigorous recruitment, preparation, induction and continuous professional development. Yes, comprehensive teacher evaluation, when done right, can weed out those who should not remain in the profession. But more important, it can take good teachers and make them great. Teaching is a profession built on the hard work, reflection, care, persistence and intellect of great teachers.

This statement acknowledges the reasoning of those seeking more accountability while emphasizing educator leadership in developing evaluation systems. After all, teachers are public servants; the public school system needs to listen to and work with critics if it is to hold on to public trust. There is an interdependency between schools and their communities.

MAPPING THE POLARITY

When I first began discussing this polarity with educators, the general reaction was laughter. "Rank and Fire" was how they first named the pole favored by those who call for accountability. They'd seen too much rhetoric in the press and in the political arena targeting "bad teachers" and "inflexible unions" as the primary causes of student failure. Because educators know full well that many other factors affect student learning, the force of these attacks simply increased their resistance to the call for accountability. *In fact, when polarities are misdiagnosed as problems to solve, the resulting "solutions" often increase resistance, thus decreasing the speed at which change can take place.* Further, sustainability decreases since the system will experience not just the upside but also the downside of the pole that is receiving too much focus. Eventually, the values of the other pole will be seen as the "solution" and the system will once again overcorrect. A vicious cycle.

Yet once we stopped laughing about ranking and firing, we quickly found common ground. For this issue, the *greater purpose statement*, or GPS, is straightforward: *Everyone* wants an effective teacher in every classroom.

- Students know that effective teachers mean more engagement, safety, and success.
- Parents know that effective teachers mean fewer homework battles and better preparation for postsecondary education.
- Businesspeople and politicians know that effective teachers mean a better-prepared, more competitive workforce.
- And teachers know the benefits of being able to draw on best practices as well as the positive, building-wide effects of working with competent colleagues.

Similarly, the *deeper fear* of failing to help students succeed motivates people at both poles.

Having effective teachers requires identifying those who *are* effective and those who need to improve; hence the push for accountability systems. However, educators know that they need more than a score or a ranking to become more effective. They need timely, personalized, helpful feedback and related professional development to show continuous improvement. Mielke and Frontier (2012) point out that high-stakes teacher evaluations have the same problems as high-stakes student examinations.

> Like high-stakes student assessment, high-stakes teacher evaluation threatens to be an occasional event that is disconnected from day-to-day teaching and learning, producing results that do not help teachers improve their performance and placing teachers in a passive role as recipients of external judgment. (p. 10)

Before agreeing on exactly how to assess teachers, there needs to be agreement on how such a system might be used. Some proponents wish to see "ineffective" teachers dismissed. There are four main problems with this approach:

- Replacing teachers is expensive. While exact figures vary based on the quality of teacher induction programs as well as the effort needed to recruit teachers for high-demand subjects or difficult working environments, estimates run from $10,000 to $20,000 per teacher replacement. In Chicago, for example, with a cost per replacement of nearly $18,000 and 4,844 teachers leaving in one year, the cost totals over $87 million dollars. Researchers estimated that for Chicago's highest-turnover schools "implementing a comprehensive induction program in these schools would only cost the district $750,000 more than it is currently spending on teacher turnover due to the increase in teacher retention" (Barnes, Crowe, & Schaefer, 2007, p. 88). Further, turnover is most common and has the highest negative impact on student learning at high-poverty schools. Retaining and training teachers may truly be in the best interest of students at these schools.

- Replacing teachers only slowly improves teacher quality, as Dylan William (2011) points out. If one dismisses the bottom 10% of teachers each year (assuming one finds a method for accurately identifying them) and replaces them with more effective teachers (which is difficult, given that first-year teachers are not as effective as those with more experience), it will take years to improve the overall average quality of teachers.

- There aren't enough higher-quality replacements waiting to take jobs. In countries such as the United States where teaching has not been valued as a profession, teacher education programs seldom receive students from the top percentiles of their high school classes. William (2011) determined that even if programs became more selective, with only about 3% of the teaching force coming from those more highly qualified candidates in any given year, it would take 30 years for the full effect to be felt. He estimates that about one extra student would pass an accountability test every three years as a result of more selective recruitment.

In other words, we need a different strategy to reach our GPS of effective teachers in every classroom.

Stepping back from the drama of teacher strikes, legislated deadlines for new evaluations systems, and teacher rankings being published in newspapers, each "side" truly holds part of the truth:

- The "accountability" champions are right to insist on a way to measure and sort teachers so that the best can be identified, recognized, used as resources for other teachers, and retained in classrooms.

- Those opposed to using evaluations to rank and rate teachers call attention to the need for continuous growth in all professions; they ask for evaluation processes that provide feedback they can use to make improvements.

Acknowledging both the problems created by decades of teacher evaluation that failed to measure effectiveness and the need for continuous professional growth, we will name the poles *Teacher Evaluation as a Measure of Effectiveness AND As Guide for Professional Growth.*

THE POSITIVE RESULTS OF TEACHER EVALUATION AS A MEASURE OF EFFECTIVENESS

Following is a summary of the main arguments being made for new teacher accountability systems. The full map is at the end of the chapter on pages 76–77.

1. We have a way to measure the impact of teacher practices on student learning.

Most proponents recognize how meaningless using a single test score would be in evaluating teacher effectiveness. Considerable resources are being poured into value-added measures (VAM), which are systems that analyze changes in student test scores to isolate the impact of a teacher on student learning. These usually involve more than one year's worth of data to improve validity. Compared to No Child Left Behind, which measured students with regard to a set benchmark no matter their level of knowledge when they entered a teacher's classroom, the VAM method of looking at student gains seems much more fair.

The Measures of Effective Teaching (MET) project, supported by $45 million from the Bill & Melinda Gates Foundation, includes universities such as Harvard and Stanford, nonprofit organizations such as the Educational Testing Service, and for-profit groups such as Cambridge Education. The American Federation of Teachers and Teach for America have also been involved. Their summary report *Working With Teachers to Develop Fair and Reliable Measures of Effective Teaching* (Bill & Melinda Gates Foundation, 2010) states, "The MET project is based on two simple premises: First, a teacher's evaluation should depend to a significant extent on his/her students' achievement gains; second, any additional components of the evaluation [e.g., classroom observation] should be valid predictors of student achievement gains" (pp. 4–5).

In other words, this extensive project flows from evaluating other measures of teacher effectiveness against student growth on VAM. Their final report (Bill & Melinda Gates Foundation, 2013) found that combining three measures is an effective predictor of student achievement on standardized tests: test scores received by a teacher's prior students, observation ratings, and student survey ratings. They summarize: "Through this large-scale study involving random assignment of teachers to students, we are confident that we can identify groups of teachers who are comparatively more effective than their peers in helping students learn. Great teaching does make a difference" (p. 9).

Supporters point out that other professions such as law and medicine have developed clear standards of professionalism and police their members, but education hasn't. VAM is frequently held up as a way to easily accomplish this.

2. Teachers, like other professionals, can be rewarded based on excellence.

In the past, teacher salary increases were based on years of service and completion of additional degrees or training. Because neither of these factors adequately predicts teacher effectiveness, as measured by student achievement on standardized tests, businesspeople and politicians have advocated merit pay.

3. Ineffective teachers can be more easily identified and removed.

Many of the criticisms of teacher evaluations and union contracts center on how seldom teachers who receive poor performance ratings are removed from classrooms. While the primary purpose of tenure for teachers is to ensure access to fair processes and shelter them from politics, tenure is often perceived as a barrier to dismissing ineffective teachers. A survey of ten school districts, including Chicago, Denver, and Cincinnati, found that only fourteen teachers in total were subject to formal dismissal during a four-year period. Further, two-thirds of the teachers surveyed believed that administrators failed to take action against tenured teachers who were poor performers (Weisberg et al., 2009).

A community organization, Put Kids First Minneapolis (2011), lists several statistics on its website to support its demands for teacher contracts that allow schools to hire the best available teachers.

According to The New Teacher Project's study, *only one percent* of tenured MPS teachers are referred to the Peer Assessment Review process (PAR), which under our current contract rules is the prescribed method for dealing with under-performing teachers and can take up to 18–24 months. *Out of this one percent less than half* are dismissed, resign, or retire. That means under the current PAR criteria 99.5 percent of our tenured teachers are considered effective. *This isn't credible for any profession.* The PAR process either needs to be scrapped or drastically changed.

4. Fair, just, and equitable evaluation systems are able to stand up to legal and ethical considerations.

One of the reasons this pole favors using objective data such as test scores is the perceived consistency. While observation ratings can reflect the bias of observers and can therefore be disputed as inaccurate, "hard" data such as test scores seem less open to dispute.

5. Site teams have control over hiring the personnel best suited to their buildings.

One of the catch phrases from *Good to Great* (Collins, 2001) that resonates in the business world is "Get the right people on the bus." The executives who ignited the transformations from good to great did not first figure out where to drive the bus and then get people to take it there. No, they *first* got the right people on the bus (and the wrong people off the bus) and *then* figured out where to drive it. They said, in essence,

> Look, I don't really know where we should take this bus. But I know this much: If we get the right people on the bus, the right people in the right seats, and the wrong people off the bus, then we'll figure out how to take it someplace great. (p. 41)

Businesspeople are wondering why, if Collins (2001) is right and this is a hallmark of effective organizations, schools aren't following this notion and getting the right teachers into classrooms. Besides the perceived difficulties with removing ineffective teachers, many district teacher contracts require principals to hire from designated pools of teachers, decreasing flexibility for hiring the best person for a given position. If the needs of students to have the highest-quality teachers available, not the needs of adults, come first, then these contract clauses are obsolete.

NEGATIVE RESULTS OF OVERFOCUSING ON THE MEASUREMENT MODEL FOR TEACHER EVALUATION

Now that we've explored five of the key reasons proponents are advocating teacher accountability, from a polarity perspective, we can predict that an overfocus on this pole to the neglect of professional growth will have some negative results, as discussed below. The full map can be found at the end of the chapter on pages 76–77.

1. Professional judgment and creativity are threatened by a perceived need to focus on elements of teaching that are being evaluated.

In every field, distortion is likely to follow decisions about what is measured and evaluated. Citing examples from business, medicine, and many other fields, Donald Campbell coined his namesake law in 1975: "The more any quantitative social indicator is used for social decision-making, the more subject it will be to corruption pressures and the more apt it will be to distort and corrupt the social processes it is intended to monitor" (p. 35).

Teachers are already reporting that evaluation criteria are changing how they teach. For example, measuring student engagement is often done by counting the number of students working on an assignment, the number who speak in class discussions, or the number who are looking directly at the teacher. None of these criteria actually measure whether students are actively engaged in learning the content or whether the work requires them to think, which is a higher standard than mere engagement. With such criteria, though, worksheets and simple rules such as "eyes on me" quickly become the norm rather than more risky activities.

If the criteria are valid indicators of teacher effectiveness, then measuring them is in the best interest of students. However, most of the evaluation systems being suggested are untested; while the criteria may be based on research, the suggested measures themselves have yet to be validated.

2. Resources are concentrated on evaluation systems at the expense of supporting teacher development.

Good evaluation systems require an investment of both time and money. For example, a review of the Teacher Evaluation Work Group site for the Minnesota Department of Education shows that about fifty people, including educators and department employees, are devoting time to developing an effective system. With limited resources in education, such an emphasis will take time away from other priorities.

As I was completing the final version of this chapter, Bill Gates (2013), in a *Washington Post* editorial, acknowledged the danger of focusing on teacher accountability to the exclusion of supporting professional growth:

> Even in subjects where the assessments have been validated, such as literacy and math, test scores don't show a teacher areas in which they need to improve. If we aren't careful to build a system that provides feedback and that teachers trust, this opportunity to dramatically improve the US education system will be wasted. (p. 1)

3. Teachers are demoralized by the lack of ability to meet individual student needs, which was their motivation for entering the profession.

The MetLife Survey of the American Teacher (Marklow & Pieters, 2012) showed that the percentage of teachers satisfied with their jobs dropped from 59% in 2009 to 44% in 2011. Further, the percentage of teachers planning to leave the profession increased from 17% to 29%. Of those likely to leave, only about 45% are optimistic that student achievement levels will improve over the next five years. Doris Santoro, a professor at Bowdoin College, points to overall demoralization within the profession.

> Demoralization occurs when the job changes to such a degree that what teachers previously found "good" about their work is no longer available.
>
> Moral rewards are what bring many of us to teaching: finding ways to connect meaningfully with students, designing lessons that address students' needs, using our talents to improve the lives of others. It is a sense that the moral dimension of the work is taken away by policy mandates that affect their teaching directly. (Rosales, 2012)

Note: Nested within this polarity is the more universal polarity of conditional AND unconditional respect. Teaching as a profession needs to be respected regardless of specific issues or controversies, yet it is also true that teachers are to earn respect by carrying out their profession to the best of their abilities. Low morale and feelings of helplessness are often the result of an overfocus on conditional respect to the neglect of unconditional respect; thus, it could be affecting teacher morale.

4. Processes for removing teachers rather than processes for improvement are emphasized.

This fear is based on how such systems have been implemented in Texas; Washington, DC; and other districts and states. While in some places, teachers who are rated as ineffective are provided with tailored support to make improvements, other evaluation systems provide little feedback that is useful for seeking appropriate professional development.

Darling-Hammond (2012) reports that teachers in Houston are already learning to avoid high-need students by, for example, not teaching fourth grade, where the inclusion of English language learners in regular classrooms usually results in a drop in test scores. She relates this story.

In Houston, where teachers are dismissed or rewarded based substantially on value-added scores, teachers can find little relationship between what they do and how they rate each year. As one put it, "I teach the same way every year. [My] first year got me pats on the back. [My] second year got me kicked in the backside. And for year three, my scores were off the charts. I got a huge bonus. What did I do differently? I have no clue."

Paige (2012) points out that court challenges are inevitable once VAM are used as the basis for firing tenured teachers. He advocates using extreme caution. He also points out that case law for dismissing teachers is built on observations, so continuing to build a high-quality observation system for evaluation will remain essential.

5. **Relationships among administration, district, union, and teachers suffer.**

The strike in Chicago, the testing scandal in Atlanta, the nationwide drop in teacher morale, and the long contract negotiations in Los Angeles and Boston are just a few of the events precipitated by the proposed implementation of new teacher evaluation models. Trust, a crucial foundation for any change effort, has been damaged.

THE POSITIVE RESULTS OF TEACHER EVALUATION AS A GUIDE FOR PROFESSIONAL GROWTH

Given the list of legitimate concerns with an overfocus on a measurement model to the neglect of a growth model, it is easy to understand educator interest in moving toward the positive results of focusing on a growth model. From a polarity perspective, this is a natural and necessary self-correction. As we look at the positive results listed below, try to frame them as helpful self-corrections rather than "solutions" to a problem.

1. **Embed evaluation within an apprenticeship model that acknowledges the four to six years of classroom experience it takes to become an expert teacher.**

It's a fact: The average new teacher is not as effective as the average experienced teacher. While people may be born with a love of children, becoming a great teacher takes practice, just like any other profession.

Ericsson, Prietula, and Cokely (2007), in a synthesis of over 100 studies on developing expertise, point to deliberate practice of specific skills as the key and that it takes time and mentoring. Mielke and Frontier (2012) add,

> Why, then, are we reluctant to acknowledge that a teacher may take dozens of hours to learn a new instructional strategy? As a profession, we need to transcend the idea that only teachers who are struggling need an improvement plan. If the school views the need for improvement as a liability, why would teachers ever acknowledge their need for deliberate practice? (p. 12)

Proponents of this view recommend evaluation systems with different standards for new versus experienced teachers, along with benchmarks for expected movement toward expertise. Marzano (2011) suggests language that emphasizes development rather than judgment, proposing a rubric based on "not using, beginning, developing, applying, and innovating" (p. 12).

2. Use evaluation systems to provide timely, effective feedback and meaningful, individualized professional development for improvement.

Traditionally, teachers have received little feedback that helped them improve practice. With principal observations, the most common form of evaluation, teachers received a scored rubric that often didn't contain recommendations. Weisberg et al. (2009) found that 73% of the 15,000 teachers they surveyed had no identified areas for improvement in their most recent performance appraisal. Of those who were given such feedback, only 45% received useful support to make improvements.

The Montgomery County, Maryland, Professional Growth System is often held up as a model by those who favor the Evaluation for Professional Growth pole. Since 1997, the district's personnel and union representatives have worked together to design and improve the system. At its heart are consulting teachers, recommended by their peers, who work full-time with new or struggling teachers. With caseloads of about eighteen teachers, the consulting teachers have the time to provide the intensive support needed to help teachers develop expertise.

3. Competition for bonuses is carefully implemented to ensure continued teacher collaboration.

For decades, teachers in the United States were isolated in their own classrooms. Only very recently have deep collaborative practices, such as working in professional learning communities, grown in popularity. Advocates for collaboration point out that creating school environments where teachers willingly share practices and coach each other helps everyone improve. Competitive systems—where teachers are ranked publicly or paid based on test scores or otherwise incentivized to perform well as individuals—have the potential to detract from collaboration.

In districts such as Washington, DC, where student test scores are not only used to determine 50% of a teacher's rating score but are also used to distribute pay, collaboration is no longer in one's own best interest. Darling-Hammond (2012) points out that no other country in the world is using test scores to evaluate teachers.

> Singapore's minister of education explained at last year's International Teaching Summit that his country would never rank teachers by student test scores because doing so would create the wrong incentives and undermine collaboration, which is emphasized in Singapore's schools and teacher evaluation system.

4. Evaluation systems are based on sound research and educator input.

While people from outside the education profession often assume that good teaching can be quantified through a checklist of characteristics supported by research, such a tool by itself will not capture the complexities of teaching. Margolis (2010) points out that

> "good teaching" involves not a "knowing that" but a "knowing when" a particular approach to teaching is appropriate. This, to a large extent, will change based on location, time, circumstance, and basic human variation . . . while still being based in research and analysis. (p. 2)

Intense training of observers is needed to help them understand, for example, quality instruction in Grade 1 and Grade 5 mathematics classrooms or student engagement in culturally diverse classrooms.

5. "Tenure" provides access to fair processes that appropriately shield teachers from politics and censorship.

Jeff Mirel, a professor with the University of Michigan School of Education, differentiates between the lifetime guarantee of employment that tenure guarantees university professors and the right to due process it provides public school teachers if someone wants to dismiss them. The public school tenure clauses exist to keep public schools from becoming embroiled in politics and are *not* lifetime employment guarantees. He points out,

> It is impossible to imagine a time when tenure protection is more vital than now. The country is so divided that on any given school day teachers can be denounced, "tried," and fired over an amazingly wide range of issues (e.g., discussing the age of the earth, accuracy of the theory of evolution, the appropriateness of reading *Huck Finn*, what the Founders meant by the separation of church and state, the effectiveness of the New Deal, or what Shakespeare meant when he wrote in "Romeo and Juliet:" " . . . the bawdy hand of the dial is now on the prick of noon") (Act II, Scene 4). (quoted in Ravitch, 2012)

A correct understanding of tenure is key, since a misunderstanding of it as guaranteed job security has been used in states such as Wisconsin to attack teacher unions and the rights of teachers to pursue collective bargaining.

NEGATIVE RESULTS OF OVERFOCUSING ON TEACHER EVALUATION FOR PROFESSIONAL GROWTH

It is clear from the previous section that there is a lot to be said for a professional growth focus. At the same time, a polarity lens reminds us that no matter how essential these upsides are, they are unsustainable without also including the positive results from the measurement model. If in a power struggle, the professional development model advocates "win," the school system will predictably find itself with the following negative results from an overfocus on the growth model.

1. Educators lack clear standards for effectiveness and expected progress.

Traditionally, teachers worked alone in the confines of their classrooms— or, further back in time, in one-room schoolhouses. This led to cultural norms such as these:

Teaching is an art form rather than a set of teachable skills.

Teachers are born, not made.

What works for one teacher won't work for another.

There is some truth in each of these statements, yet the lack of effort in the past to define common characteristics, or to construct a typical time line for becoming an effective teacher, have exacerbated the problem of identifying and supporting ineffective teachers. Although several research-based standards of practice models exist (e.g., Danielson, 2007; Marzano, 2011), as of now, what constitutes "excellence" varies from school to school, district to district, and state to state.

2. Teachers have little ability or incentive to seek or plan for professional development that has a direct impact on student learning outcomes.

Without a system of feedback on effective teaching practices, teachers have no outside information to assist them in determining the most helpful professional development goals.

While teachers need to pursue continuing education credits for license renewal, usually a wide array of options meet the requirements, whether or not they relate to specific developmental needs or to improving student achievement. Teachers are free to select options based on convenience and interest. Further, many in-school professional development activities, usually one-size-fits-all in design to further school goals, count toward these "clock hours." They may or may not mesh with the professional development needs of struggling teachers.

3. Tenured teachers have no incentives to improve practice.

Weisberg et al. (2009) found that over 80% of tenured teachers rated themselves an 8, 9, or 10 on a scale of 1 to 10 regarding instructional performance. The researchers commented that this is a natural response in an environment that reinforces a norm that everyone is above average. Why in such an environment would teachers actively seek improvement?

Most teachers work extremely hard, putting in more hours than their contracts require. Many have less than an hour a day to prepare lessons, grade papers, contact parents, collaborate with colleagues, and more. Yet without targeted feedback, much of their effort can go to work that isn't effective in helping students learn. A better system of evaluation and professional development might result in more efficient efforts by teachers and better outcomes for students.

4. Too many teachers are rated highly effective, even when a large percentage of students lack proficiency.

A study from The New Teacher Project called "The Widget Effect" (Weisberg et al., 2009) showed that in systems where teachers were rated as either satisfactory or unsatisfactory, 99% were rated as satisfactory. In systems with more rating categories, 94% of tenured teachers are placed in the top or second rating category. With so much media attention given to test score rankings among schools, and among students in different countries, such statistics provide plenty of opportunities for critique.

5. It is too difficult to remove ineffective teachers.

Weisberg et al. (2009) found that 86% of the administrators surveyed had not taken action to dismiss teachers they knew were ineffective. While tenure does not guarantee lifetime employment, the due process procedures require documentation. Because the inadequate teacher evaluation systems do not provide it, documenting means more work for already overburdened administrators. The very low rates of teacher removal have become rallying cries for dismissal of tenure rules in Wisconsin, New Jersey, and other states.

TRANSFORMING THE POLARITY

The next step in creating a virtuous cycle is selecting *early warnings*, those measurable indicators that let you know when the system is overfocusing on one pole to the neglect of the other. Again, even most educators agree now that we focused too long on the upside of a growth model for teacher evaluation.

Let's look at some early warning signs of an overfocus on measurement as the "solution" and some signs that might have led to an earlier self-correction by educators themselves if they hadn't been so worried about the downside of a more objective evaluation system.

Early Warnings for the Downside of a Measurement Model for Teacher Evaluation

A. Increase in teachers planning to leave the profession because of lack of support or unfair evaluation practices.

B. Increase in educator-driven cheating on standardized tests and other ways to undermine what teachers perceive as unfair evaluation.

C. Narrowing of professional development options to generic or online programs rather than the investment of individualized coaching or specially designed workshops.

D. Increase in funds spent on evaluation systems to the neglect of teacher development.

E. Decrease in teacher autonomy concerning curriculum, pacing, testing, schedules, and so on.

Early Warnings for the Downside of
a Growth Model for Teacher Evaluation

A. Increase in complaints claiming that a teacher is ineffective and should be removed, as well as trends in how teachers who are rated as ineffective are handled.

B. Increase in level of parent activism over "bad teachers" and teacher tenure—websites, public forums, blogs, letters, and so on.

C. Time and resources invested in professional development to the neglect of training evaluators.

D. Increase in year-to-year fluctuations in teacher ratings.

E. Decrease in teachers with lower ratings or who are removed.

STEPS TO MOVING BEYOND POLARIZATION

To flesh out the GPS, everyone wants the following:

Motivated, effective teachers who love their profession and foster success for all of their students

Remember the data from William (2011) mentioned earlier—that if we focus only on firing ineffective teachers and hiring better ones, we are decades away from school improvement? We need to work together to assist every teacher we have in becoming highly effective, providing individualized support for those who are struggling while encouraging those who already are highly effective to develop further expertise.

While in the last chapter all the proposed *action steps* supported both poles, here, some are "high-leverage" and support both, whereas others access the upside of one pole or the other. This is a more typical pattern for action steps.

HIGH-LEVERAGE ACTION STEPS THAT ACCESS THE UPSIDE OF BOTH POLES

A. Professionalize the teaching profession, as has been done in Finland, Singapore, and other high-achieving countries.

In Finland, education programs recruit candidates from the top 15% of graduates. In America and many other countries, candidates from the top 15% are attracted to medicine, law, and many other professions rather than education. Emily Moore, a magna cum laude Princeton graduate, was so tired of the question, "But you have such a good degree. Why waste it teaching?" that she developed a ready response: "Who would you rather have teaching your children?" (Moore, 2000).

Increasing the professionalism of teaching starts with increasing respect for the profession. Higher pay, yes, but other notable differences in systems such as Finland's include the following:

- Less accountability testing. It is assumed that teachers are doing their best to help students learn. All students are tested once, in high school, although schools follow their own programs for progress assessment.
- More teacher education. At the government's expense, all teachers acquire masters' degrees before entering the classroom.
- A balance between national and local control. Through a generalized rather than specific national curriculum and other factors, teachers are free to collaborate and determine what will work best for their students and schools.
- Teachers, not politicians or business leaders, are determining what will work best for children, based on experience and research.

B. Make use of research on motivation in teacher evaluation, incentive, and development systems.

Recall Pink's (2009) summary of what really motivates people and consider how it applies here.

- *Autonomy.* Care needs to be taken with tools such as scripted curriculum, pacing calendars, reading lists, professional development choices, and other decisions to ensure that teachers are not stripped of the motivating power of taking responsibility for some of these choices.
- *Mastery.* All of us strive to work toward excellence. Too many reform efforts, changing agendas, and unclear goals can place restraints on a teacher's ability to master promising practices.
- *Purpose.* We know that teachers are motivated by helping students. They do not choose the profession for prestige or financial rewards! Yet policies and mandates can undermine their efficacy. Jonathan Kozol, speaking of his book *Letters to a Young Teacher*, suggests that to stay focused, teachers need to sometimes be subversive:

Yes, children have to be prepared for the economic world—but the invasion of the public schools by mercantile values has deeply demoralized teachers. I've been in classrooms where the teacher has to write a so-called mission statement that says, "The mission of this school is to sharpen the competitive edge of America in the global marketplace."

[A teacher] once said to me, "I'm damned if I'm going to"—I don't think she said "damned," because she's too polite; maybe "darned"—"treat these little babies as commodities or products. Why should they care about global markets? They care about bellybuttons, and wobbly teeth, and beautiful books about cater-pillars." I think we have to protect those qualities [in teachers]. (quoted in Fishbane, 2007, p. 4)

C. Monitor money, time, and effort spent on evaluation models AND on improving professional development.

Developing and implementing effective teacher evaluation models will take time and money. Most will require extensive training of observ-ers, collaboration to ensure that ratings are consistent across observers, record systems, and more, once the initial criteria and measurement tools are developed. Further, because many systems require more observations, additional personnel will be needed to conduct observations.

However, budgets for these expenditures might be compared to com-mitment of resources for professional development to ensure that measur-ing teacher effectiveness isn't occurring at the expense of developing effective teachers. For example, are instructional coaches being cut to fund observers? What is the ideal balance?

ACTION STEPS THAT SUPPORT THE UPSIDE OF A MEASUREMENT MODEL FOR TEACHER EVALUATION

D. Develop a consistent evaluation model, based in research, that includes multiple measures and sound research, with input from educators and other qualified contributors.

As I was writing this chapter, the current editions of the *Phi Delta Kappan* and *Educational Leadership,* the magazines of two well-respected education organizations, were dedicated to the issue of evaluating teacher effectiveness. Across the nation, states and school districts are working on models for teacher evaluation. While there is hope for the emergence of an excellent model, there is also great duplication of effort, a lack of research, and a rush to implement. Pointing to a long string of reforms that were rushed to implementation without careful evaluation and implementation planning, Schmoker (2012) warns,

> Our silver bullet du jour is teacher evaluation (a good thing) on steroids (a bad thing). It is being driven by popular, time-gobbling, anxiety-inducing evaluation "frameworks." Don't misunderstand me: I have always been a fan of simple, effective teacher observation and evaluation. . . . My complaint is with the frameworks themselves—their sheer bulk and their sloppy, agenda-driven language. (p. 70)

Schmoker goes on to point to solid research showing that performance improves when training and evaluation are centered on a few key criteria and goals. However, some of the new systems have as many as 116 criteria (the current version of Tennessee's system) on which teachers are to be evaluated.

Yet the model also needs to incorporate some way of evaluating whether teachers are helping students learn. If the systems currently being implemented continue to produce unfair results (and unintended consequences such as Texas teachers avoiding fourth-grade classrooms), then we need to go back to the drawing board rather than work with all-too-convenient standardized test scores. After all, we know that increased standardized test scores can occur while scores *decrease* on creativity and innovation.

E. Clearly demonstrate how an evaluation model adjusts for teachers with higher percentages of students in various categories.

Fairness is also central to any effective evaluation system. With the push to link teacher evaluation to student achievement test scores, little is being said of the very real fact that such scores are available for only 20% of teachers and for almost no teachers in Grades 9 through 12. There are no standardized tests for art, special education, physical education, languages, and many other subjects—and students do not need more days spent on tests rather than on learning. If, as is often proposed, these teachers are measured by criteria upon which they and their administrators agree, fairness is quickly lost; they will have far more control over their evaluations than teachers in tested subject areas.

Several other factors will quickly lead to the perception that evaluations are unfair:

- Lack of randomness in class configurations. Often, to balance gender, special needs, and many other factors, students aren't randomly assigned to classrooms. Most VAM assume that they are.
- Public humiliation. With the wide swings in how teachers are rated, especially if different tests are used, publishing teacher rankings in public newspapers is at the very least misguided. There is evidence that rankings are measuring factors that are simply not under teacher control and have contributed to the suicide of a teacher.
- Continued poor results with systems that are already implemented. The fallout from publishing teacher names, the wide swings in places like Texas as to how teachers are ranked, and teachers being driven by fear to avoid teaching our neediest students are just a few examples.

Bill Gates (Downey, 2012), in a speech to the Education Commission of the States, emphasized the danger of rushing to implement untested solutions.

Let me start with one overarching point: a strong teacher evaluation and improvement system costs money. We have estimated that it will cost between 1.5 and 2 percent of the overall budget for teacher compensation and benefits to implement an evaluation system based on multiple measures of teaching performance. This price tag might cause people to try to do this cheaply—to skimp on paying teachers to do classroom observations, to cut corners on training the evaluators, to get stingy on providing the feedback that will help teachers improve. But saving money on those measures would be like saving money on a car by leaving out the engine.

ACTION STEPS THAT SUPPORT A GROWTH MODEL FOR PROFESSIONAL DEVELOPMENT

D. Establish clear, manageable markers for professional growth as well as a general time line for expected progress.

Killion and Kennedy (2012) describe what is needed in such a system:

These standards, frequently crafted through years of collaborative work among professionals, are often overlooked as the core content for professional learning. For teachers, this means that their professional learning may fail to support them to achieve expertise in the sophisticated knowledge, skills, and dispositions required of masterful, professional teachers. These areas include content knowledge; pedagogical content knowledge; respecting and addressing individual backgrounds, language, and academic abilities; differentiating learning to meet the needs of all learners; and general instructional pedagogy. The standards also include effective professional communication; collaborative teamwork; creating a collaborative culture; and garnering parental involvement. Professional learning that uses these standards as the content focus elevates practice by developing educators' capacity to demonstrate the essential attributes of effectiveness. (pp. 13–14)

E. Develop a "response to intervention" model for teachers to provide support in developing expertise.

"Response to intervention" models for students work on the principle of devoting the most resources to students who need the most help. Similarly, models for increasing teacher effectiveness need to encourage continuous improvement for everyone while dedicating resources to new and struggling teachers. While there is still good reason for schoolwide professional development sessions, these usually support initiatives or school goals, not the specific needs of struggling teachers.

With the rush to meet the requirements of Race to the Top grants, some states purchased online course services with "personalized learning paths" on topics such as learning assessment and classroom management. The courses, though, require passing only multiple-choice quizzes. Other than for procedural or fact-based knowledge, generic online modules are not the equivalent of targeted instructional coaching.

In contrast, where systems focus on instructional coaching, such as Montgomery County, Maryland, teachers learn to trust the evaluation system. Although more teachers have been dismissed since their Peer Assistance and Review system was implemented, the teachers know that they will be given the support to change and a fair hearing if it seems they are not making adequate progress.

Wisely, some school districts such as Boston compromised on the implementation of new teacher evaluation systems with the promise of beginning with a pilot program. Instead of immediately switching every building to the new system, they will be testing it in pilot sites, receiving feedback, and making adjustments and improvements. This measured, collaborative approach may save resources, avoid trust-busting mistakes, and smooth the transition to a new way of looking at what it means to be an effective teacher.

REFLECTION

1. Many evaluation systems use one of two basic sets of descriptive terms to rate teachers, which in themselves form a polarity. What are the upsides and negative results of using each set?

   ○ Highly effective, effective, marginally effective, not effective
   ○ Innovating (with this strategy or characteristic), applying, developing, beginning, not using (Marzano, 2011)

2. If you are (or were) a classroom teacher, how long did it take you to master lesson planning? Classroom management? Building relationships with students? Collaborating with other teachers? Writing good assessment items? How would you factor this learning curve into teacher evaluations?

Polarity Thinking Map for Teacher Effectiveness

Effective Teachers

Action Steps

A. Professionalize the teaching profession, as has been done in Finland, Singapore, and other high-achieving countries.

B. Make use of research on motivation in teacher evaluation, incentive, and development systems.

C. Monitor money, time, and effort spent on evaluation models AND on improving professional development.

D. Develop a consistent evaluation model, based in research, that includes multiple measures and sound research, with input from educators and other qualified contributors.

E. Clearly demonstrate how an evaluation model adjusts for teachers with higher percentages of students in various categories.

Values = positive results from focusing on the left pole

1. We have a way to measure the impact of teacher practices on student learning.

2. Teachers, like other professionals, can be rewarded based on excellence.

3. Ineffective teachers can be more easily identified and removed.

4. Fair, just, and equitable evaluation systems are able to stand up to legal and ethical considerations.

5. Site teams have control over hiring the personnel best suited for their buildings.

Measurement Model for Teacher Evaluation and

Early Warnings

A. Increase in teachers planning to leave the profession because of lack of support or unfair evaluation practices.

B. Increase in educator-driven cheating on standardized tests and other ways to undermine what teachers perceive as unfair evaluation.

C. Narrowing of professional development options to generic or online programs rather than the investment of individualized coaching or specially designed workshops.

D. Increase in funds spent on evaluation systems to the neglect of teacher development.

E. Decrease in teacher autonomy concerning curriculum, pacing, testing, schedules, etc.

1. Professional judgment and creativity are threatened by a perceived need to focus on elements of teaching that are being evaluated.

2. Resources are concentrated on evaluation systems at the expense of supporting teacher development.

3. Teachers are demoralized by the lack of ability to meet individual student needs, which was their motivation for entering the profession.

4. Processes for removing teachers rather than processes for improvement are emphasized.

5. Relationships among administration, district, union, and teachers suffer.

Fears = negative results from overfocusing on the left pole to the neglect of the right pole

Student

Source: Map template copyright by Polarity Partnerships, LLC.

in Every Classroom

Values = positive results from focusing on the right pole

1. Embed evaluation within an apprenticeship model that acknowledges the four to six years of classroom experience it takes to become an expert teacher.

2. Use evaluation systems to provide timely, effective feedback and meaningful, individualized professional development for improvement.

3. Competition for bonuses is carefully implemented to ensure continued teacher collaboration.

4. Evaluation systems are based on sound research, and educator input.

5. "Tenure" provides access to fair processes that appropriately shield teachers from politics and censorship.

Growth Model for Teacher Evaluation

and

1. Educators lack clear standards for effectiveness and expected progress.

2. Teachers have little ability or incentive to seek or plan for professional development that has a direct impact on student learning outcomes.

3. Tenured teachers have no incentives to improve practice.

4. Too many teachers are rated highly effective, even when a large percentage of students lack proficiency.

5. It is too difficult to remove ineffective teachers.

Fears = negative results from overfocusing on the right pole to the neglect of the left pole

Failure

Action Steps

A. Professionalize the teaching profession, as has been done in Finland, Singapore, and other high-achieving countries.

B. Make use of research on motivation in teacher evaluation, incentive, and development systems.

C. Monitor money, time, and effort spent on evaluation models AND on improving professional development.

D. Establish clear, manageable markers for professional growth as well as a general time line for expected progress.

E. Develop a "response to intervention" model for teachers to provide support in developing expertise.

Early Warnings

A. Increase in complaints claiming that a teacher is ineffective and should be removed, as well as trends in how teachers who are rated as ineffective are handled.

B. Increase in level of parent activism over "bad teachers" and teacher tenure—websites, public forums, blogs, letters, etc.

C. Time and resources invested in professional development to the neglect of training evaluators.

D. Increase in year-to-year fluctuations in teacher ratings.

E. Decrease in teachers with lower ratings or who are removed.

5 A Math Wars Truce

*Mastery of Knowledge AND
Mastery of Problem Solving*

Note: While this chapter discusses issues in approaches to teaching mathematics, similar disagreements exist in all curricular areas. For example, the "reading wars" juxtaposed phonics instruction with "whole language" instruction. Teachers of history grapple with how much content (names, events, dates, and known motivations or reasoning) students need to master and the historian's work of understanding contexts, interwoven causes and forces, and other aspects of the study of history. While chapter reflection exercises apply polarity thinking to all content areas, I chose to concentrate on mathematics because of how "math anxiety" increases polarization on this issue. Math anxiety is just about unknown in countries such as Hong Kong and Korea, where students in general do well in math. They believe everyone can learn math with effort and concentration. In contrast, math anxiety is high in many countries like the United States, where most people believe you either are or aren't good at math.

Carly and Tim had seen a lot of fads come and go in their 20 years of teaching middle school mathematics. Still, they'd taken time to thoroughly review the new "reform" curriculum their district had chosen. Before the workshop on implementation, they narrowed down their list of questions to just two carefully chosen ones. First, they didn't understand the initial sequencing of topics. They'd never seen a group of seventh graders who were ready for variables without first working with positive and negative integers, yet this curriculum reversed the order. Second, how would students master forms of linear equations with this curriculum? They liked the hands-on problems that introduced the topic, but they didn't think there was enough practice for mastery.

The workshop presenters hadn't allowed time for questions, though. Carly and Tim's polite yet detailed e-mail to the math leaders in the district went unanswered. Both teachers decided to continue using their old curriculum, stating, "Wouldn't they point us to good answers if they existed? We know how to get the most out of what we're using, and we won't experiment on our students!"

Note that both Carly and Tim prefer a "let me master it" learning style, explained in more detail on page 234. As students, they learned best through clear assignments, developed proficiency through practice, and wanted questions answered up front so they didn't waste time. With this new curriculum, no one met their needs for a clear understanding of why it was an improvement or presented data on its effectiveness. Further, because the texts arrived the week before school started, they didn't have time for the detailed preparation that gave them confidence in the classroom. They both closed their classroom doors and continued using the old curriculum, teaching via lecture, demonstration, practice problems, and gradual release of responsibility to students.

Just down the hall, Wes worked hard to implement the new curriculum. He agreed with the general idea that by connecting mathematics ideas to the real world, students could ground new learning in familiar situations. His students, though, didn't seem to be catching on to concepts when he turned them loose on the investigative activities. They never quite finished, and Wes ended up summarizing what they might have learned if they'd had time to complete the activities. He found himself demonstrating the concepts with review problems from some supplemental materials.

Wes has a "let me think" learning style (see page 234), thriving on chances to develop his own insights and figure things out for himself. The new curriculum met his need for something new and interesting; he'd always thought the old curriculum was too full of "drill and kill." But none of the training had covered how to successfully launch, facilitate, and summarize the new style of tasks. Because Wes didn't realize the importance of activating prior knowledge, anticipating student responses, and asking for justification, he was setting his students up for failure.

Roslyn, the school's principal, knew that not everyone was using the required curriculum, but several reviews of common assessments showed that students in Carly's, Tim's, and Wes's classrooms were doing equally well. She'd observed each of their classrooms and had noted how each of them seemed to be making the most of their own strengths as teachers. She hadn't seen any reason to require Carly and Tim to switch to the new books, especially after Wes had voluntarily talked with her about the difficulties he was having with the new curriculum.

> Roslyn has a "let me brainstorm!" learning style (see page 234) and naturally takes a big-picture approach to implementation issues, preferring to provide options and make room for experimentation. It's easy for her to live with seeming contradictions such as allowing curriculum choice. She was well aware that the district hadn't addressed teacher concerns, and she believed in giving her staff flexibility to implement changes at their own pace, as long as students were learning.

Brad, the district curriculum coordinator, was furious when he learned that some teachers weren't using the new curriculum. He and a committee of teachers and instructional coaches had thoroughly reviewed several curricula. They'd chosen the best with regard to high-level cognitive demands, alignment with standards, and supplemental resources such as assessments and online texts and practice problems. He asked the superintendent if the criteria for evaluating math teachers in the district could include whether they used the designated curriculum.

> Brad's decisive, logical style is shared by about 80% of leaders worldwide (Myers, McCaulley, Quenk, & Hammer, 1998). He believes that he and his committee both accurately diagnosed the needs of the district's students for learning mathematics and chose the best curriculum. What further justification could anyone want? He tends to see teacher resistance as rooted in laziness or an inability to learn new ways.

AN ALL-OUT BATTLE

This tale of the "math wars" is fictionalized from the patterns and events I've seen in many districts to show how a single polarity can affect every level of a system. Compared with discourse elsewhere, though, the "war" is still pretty calm in the composite district described here; a couple of my colleagues were reluctant to discuss this polarity with me because of how they'd been lambasted in the media over this issue.

In 2012, Dr. Jo Boaler, a Stanford professor, researcher, and advocate for mathematics education that actively involves students, revealed the details of how colleagues have attacked her professionalism, questioning her data and accusing her of harming students with "reform" mathematics

(Boaler, 2012). Either/or thinking is being applied in a way that is destructive to research and collaboration. And this battle is being fought at many levels—among professors, between parents and teachers, between teachers and administrators, at PTO meetings, and on YouTube (watch *Math Education: An Inconvenient Truth* for an example). Let's take a look at one of the core polarities involved.

SEEING THE POLARITY

Schoenfeld's (2004) historical overview of the math wars (a thorough background resource) summarizes the issues this way:

> During the 1990s, the teaching of mathematics became the subject of heated controversies known as the math wars. The immediate origins of the conflicts can be traced to the "reforms" stimulated by the National Council of Teachers of Mathematics' *Curriculum and Evaluation Standards for School Mathematics*. Traditionalists fear that reform-oriented, "standards-based" curricula are superficial and undermine classical mathematical values; reformers claim that such curricula reflect a deeper, richer view of mathematics than the traditional curriculum. An historical perspective reveals that the underlying issues being contested—Is mathematics for the elite or for the masses? Are there tensions between "excellence" and "equity"? Should mathematics be seen as a democratizing force or as a vehicle for maintaining the status quo?—are more than a century old. (p. 253)

Yes, we've been arguing about the hows and whys of teaching math for over a century.

Mathematically Correct, a website created by parents as well as professionals in the sciences, states its position as follows:

> Mathematics achievement in America is far below what we would like it to be. Recent "*reform*" efforts only aggravate the problem. As a result, our children have less and less exposure to rigorous, content-rich mathematics.
>
> The advocates of the new, fuzzy math have practiced their rhetoric well. They speak of higher-order thinking, conceptual understanding and solving problems, but they neglect the systematic mastery of the fundamental building blocks necessary for success in any of these areas. Their focus is on things like calculators, blocks, guesswork, and group activities and they shun things like

algorithms and repeated practice. The new programs are shy on fundamentals and they also lack the mathematical depth and rigor that promotes greater achievement.

Concerned parents are in a state of dismay and have begun efforts to restore content, rigor, and genuinely high expectations to mathematics education. (http://wheresthemath.com)

We will talk about this as the Mathematics Education for Mastering Knowledge pole to capture the emphasis on achievement test scores and comparisons with the performance of students in other countries.

The "reform" position is a bit harder to state, but we'll use the label Mathematics Education for Mastering Problem Solving. In the 1980s, the National Council of Teachers of Mathematics (NCTM), recognizing that students would need more, not fewer, mathematical skills in the rapidly evolving digital age, published *An Agenda for Action* (NCTM, 1980), which provided general recommendations for improving math instruction. These included increased emphasis on solving problems, allowing students to use calculators and computers so that they could concentrate on mathematics rather than calculations, and increasing class time spent on cooperative activities and discussion instead of practice. They also suggested less focus on long division, memorizing algorithms, and rote practice.

New textbooks based on these reforms launched the math wars, beginning in California, for a host of reasons that will become evident as we map this polarity.

MAPPING THE POLARITY

For the math wars, it may seem obvious that the *greater purpose statement* (GPS) is "every student a mathematician"—teaching math in such a way that all students can work efficiently, understand concepts, and apply them in the real world. However, with our national math phobia, what it means to "understand math" has different connotations to different people. If I were working with a group in person to map this polarity, I would have each side provide its own definitions as the discussion evolved.

Adding to the polarization on the issues are the clear differences that I and others have documented on how people with different learning styles, like the teachers in the opening story, approach mathematical tasks. These underlying bases for our beliefs will be pointed out as well.

The *deeper fear* in the math wars is that students will graduate without proficiency in the math skills they will need in the workforce, in college course work, and for daily living.

POSITIVE RESULTS OF MATHEMATICS EDUCATION FOR MASTERY OF KNOWLEDGE

Again, entire books and websites address this polarity. What follows is a synthesis of the various positions being expressed. The full map can be found at the end of this chapter on pages 102–103.

1. Students master the body of established mathematics knowledge.

Two plus two really does equal four is one way to summarize what is valued here. Over the past few thousand years, mathematicians have discovered, developed, and sequenced a body of knowledge. Through good instruction, students can master the core content of the discipline of mathematics.

In this view, students move linearly through a well-documented pathway of mastering arithmetic operations with whole numbers, followed by fractions. Algebra comes before geometry and so on.

2. Teacher-led, algorithm-centered instruction efficiently conveys best practices for speed and accuracy.

Schoenfeld (2004) summarizes this pole's emphasis on mastering knowledge.

> From the (very) traditionalists' point of view, the role of schooling should be to provide authoritative knowledge. Certain things are right or wrong; it is the responsibility of the teacher to say what is right and make sure the students learn it. What the students feel is irrelevant and inappropriate for discussion in school; what counts is what the students are taught and what they should know. (p. 271)

Note that one of the key values here is efficiency. If over time a mathematical method has proved efficient in multiple applications, why wouldn't we teach students how to use it?

3. Children develop conceptual understanding through expert instruction and practice.

Teacher lecture and demonstration are usually seen as a preferred instructional method by this pole rather than small-group or hands-on tasks where students might hear or develop misunderstandings.

One model of instruction favored by this pole involves *gradual release of responsibility*, a term developed by New Zealand educator Margaret Mooney (1988). The teacher explains a concept or algorithm and demonstrates a problem. Then he or she leads the class through another problem or more. Often, students then work in pairs before at last working on their own. This works well for helping students master procedures and calculation rules.

4. Children need basic skills and efficient algorithms before they can apply them to complex problems.

People who value this pole emphasize a more concrete, or "let me master it" learning style (see page 234), such as that favored by Carly and Tim in the opening story. They see developing math knowledge as a linear process, with facts and known processes as the first steps.

In *Tackling the Mathematics Problem*, the London Mathematical Society (1995), pointed out that

> to gain a genuine understanding of any process it is necessary first to achieve a robust technical fluency with the relevant content. Progress in mastering mathematics depends on reducing familiar laborious processes to automatic mental routines, which no longer require conscious thought; this then creates mental space to allow the learner to concentrate on new, unfamiliar ideas (as one sees, for example, in the progression from arithmetic, through fractions and algebra, to calculus). (pp. 9–10)

5. Children are motivated by success in accuracy, efficiency, and speed, which prepares them to tackle increasingly rigorous tasks.

Automaticity—being able to perform calculations or procedures quickly and without conscious thought—is a clear goal for mathematics instruction at this pole. Usually, practice brings about greater automaticity. Many parents report having their children work with tutors or purchasing extra workbooks to give their children more practice and thus increase the speed with which they perform calculations.

Parents, teachers, and students can all easily measure progress on tasks, such as the number of addition or multiplication problems they can complete correctly within a given time frame. Being able to quantify such learning allows for easy analysis of student progress toward stated standards or benchmarks.

NEGATIVE RESULTS OF OVERFOCUSING ON MATHEMATICS EDUCATION AS MASTERING KNOWLEDGE TO THE NEGLECT OF PROBLEM SOLVING

As with any system that involves a polarity, overfocus on the upside of one pole without adequate attention to its pole partner leads to negative results. Here are some of the negative outcomes of overfocus on mastering the knowledge of the discipline to the neglect of understanding and applying that knowledge in problem solving.

1. Memorization of rules and procedures produces math anxiety and students who hate math and lack understanding.

In an AP–AOL poll conducted in 2005, four in ten adult Americans reported hating mathematics classes, more than twice the percentage of any other course (Lester, 2005). Nearly all these adults would have been taught through "traditional" methods. Stigler and Hiebert (1997) found, for example, that 96% of seatwork for students in U.S. eighth-grade mathematics classrooms was devoted to practicing procedures a teacher had demonstrated. And for nearly 80% of all mathematics topics, teachers demonstrated processes or ideas. They were not explained or developed.

In response to those who felt that traditional methods were more successful than reform curriculum, Hiebert (1999) summarized studies showing that students learned simple calculation procedures, terms, and definitions, but not how they might adapt what they know to solve new types of problems or how to engage in other mathematical process. And if they memorized procedures, they struggled more to understand why they worked than if they understood concepts before learning the procedures. He concludes, "The long-running experiment we have been conducting with traditional methods shows serious deficiencies, and we should attend carefully to the research findings that are accumulating regarding alternative programs" (p. 13).

2. Teacher-led instruction means teachers are working and learning more than students are.

Jackson (2009) describes the problem with teacher lecture/student practice this way:

> We underestimate our students' abilities and overestimate the value of our own contributions. When students are faced with a problem, our first impulse is to quickly solve the problem and

move on. But doing so transfers the work of learning from the student to us. Instead, we should pose questions that help them think through the problem, model problem-solving strategies, and point them to the resources they need. Rather than solve the problem for them, we show them how to solve the problem for themselves. (p. 174)

Somehow, the additional polarity of *Teacher-Centered Instruction AND Student-Centered Instruction* has become embedded within this polarity, with most "mastering knowledge" classrooms being teacher-centered and a majority of "mastering problem solving" classrooms being more student centered. "Nested" polarities such as these are best mapped separately for clarity on each issue.

3. Students get bored with repetition.

Students differ on the amount of practice needed to master a procedure or concept. Further, our reaction to practice problems has a lot to do with our learning style preferences. I've found these general patterns, more fully explained in Chapter 12, especially Chart 12.12 (page 242):

People who prefer a "let me master it" style tend to prefer reinforcing learning through practice. The more they practice, the more secure they feel that their knowledge becomes. Incidentally, a preponderance of secondary school mathematics teachers are in this category.

"Let me do something" learners also appreciate practicing until they feel that a concept has been cemented. However, as students, they need more breaks in repetitive tasks—they need to move, talk, sharpen a pencil, or even shoot a few hoops to regain focus.

"Let me think" learners—my people—may practice to please a parent or teacher or to ensure mastery of a skill. However, the inner worlds of their brains are often far more interesting than a worksheet. They will thus either daydream and take forever or rush through repetitive tasks and get several wrong (my typical math behavior until ninth grade, when the problems became intrinsically interesting).

"Let me brainstorm" learners may also practice to please others or develop competence but often refuse to continue if they know they have mastered something. One boy, for example, did the first 10 of 30 multiplication problems, turned them in and said, "These are right. I'm not doing any more."

Big point: What works for some in mathematics education may truly not be best for everyone; what is experienced as the upside of a pole for some may be experienced as a downside for others. Practice is one of those areas (Kise, 2007).

4. Students won't be ready for the high-tech workplace where flexible thinking, problem formulation, and collaboration are key.

To help parents and educators understand the mathematics needed for careers in the sciences, Boaler (2008) describes how engineers are required to go beyond standard algorithms and models to use math effectively.

> Typically the engineers needed to interpret the problems they were asked to solve (such as the design of a parking lot or the support of a wall) and form a simplified model to which they could apply mathematical methods. They would then select and adapt methods that could be applied to their models, run calculations (using various representations—graphs, words, equations, pictures, and tables—as they worked), and justify and communicate their methods and results. Thus the engineers engaged in flexible problem solving, adapting and using mathematics. (p. 8)

She ends her description with a quote from a study by Gainsburg (2003), "The traditional K–12 mathematics curriculum, with its focus on performing computational manipulations, is unlikely to prepare students for the problem-solving demands of the high-tech workplace" (cited in Boaler, 2008, p. 8).

5. The emphasis on skills proficiency prevents students from seeing math as a creative process that is worthwhile and enjoyable.

While many, many adults read for pleasure, few pursue mathematics recreationally beyond Sudoku puzzles. As the scientist Richard Dawkins (1996) pointed out, "It has become almost a cliché to remark that nobody boasts of ignorance of literature, but it is socially acceptable to boast ignorance of science and proudly claim incompetence in mathematics."

In *A Mathematician's Lament,* Paul Lockhart (2009) opens with a hilarious parable of what music and arts education would look like if they followed the current mathematics model, with children working on music theory worksheets before being allowed to hear or play music and memorizing brush bristle types before they can touch paint to a canvas. He concludes,

> Sadly, our present system of mathematics education is precisely this kind of nightmare. In fact, if I had to design a mechanism for the express purpose of *destroying* a child's natural curiosity and love of pattern-making, I couldn't possibly do as good a job as is currently being done—I simply wouldn't have the imagination to come up with the kind of senseless, soul-crushing ideas that constitute contemporary mathematics education. (p. 20)

Those who love mathematics claim that if people fail to love math in the same way they love their favorite books, then they experienced poor teaching. The mathematician Peter Hilton (1998) summarized the problem with instruction this way:

> Just as any sensitive human being can be brought to appreciate beauty in art, music or literature, so that person can be educated to recognize the beauty in a piece of mathematics. The rarity of that recognition is not due to the "fact" that most people are not mathematically gifted but to the crassly utilitarian manner of teaching mathematics and of deciding syllabi and curricula, in which tedious, routine calculations, learned as a skill, are emphasized at the expense of genuinely mathematical ideas, and in which students spend almost all their time answering someone else's questions rather than asking their own. (pp. 482–483)

POSITIVE RESULTS OF MATHEMATICS EDUCATION AS MASTERING PROBLEM SOLVING

After experiencing the downside of one pole, most systems begin to perceive the upside of the other pole as the "solution." Below are some of the key values of those who favor the Mastering Problem Solving pole.

1. Mathematics is conveyed as making meaning of the world through numbers and patterns, problem formulation/solving.

People who love math want other people to love math. Check out these quotes:

> Mathematics is the only instructional material that can be presented in an entirely undogmatic way. (Max Dehn, cited in Mathematics, 2005)

Computation involves going from a question to an answer. Mathematics involves going from an answer to a question. (Peter Hilton quotes, 2013)

The true spirit of delight, the exaltation, the sense of being more than Man, which is the touchstone of the highest excellence, is to be found in mathematics as surely as poetry. (Bertrand Russell, cited in Mathematics, 2005)

Thus, the drive for math as exploration rather than as demonstrations and practice problems is an effort to introduce students to math as an enjoyable pastime.

2. Mathematics as problem solving engages all students, not just those already college bound. This is a social justice issue.

Understanding this point requires remembering that there never was a "golden age" in mathematics instruction in the West, when all students mastered computation and concepts. Up until World War II, only about half of the population graduated from high school. Less than 30% of students took algebra. Even in the 1980s, students could take a college-bound math track or a regular math track; from ninth grade on, the attrition rate from advanced math courses was 50% per year (Madison & Hart, 1990).

In its *Principles and Standards for School Mathematics*, the NCTM (2000) makes clear that all students need access to math to be successful in life:

The vision of equity in mathematics education challenges a pervasive societal belief in North America that only some students are capable of learning mathematics. This belief, in contrast to the equally pervasive view that all students can and should learn to read and write in English, leads to low expectations for too many students. Low expectations are especially problematic because students who live in poverty, students who are not native speakers of English, students with disabilities, females, and many non-white students have traditionally been far more likely than their counterparts in other demographic groups to be the victims of low expectations. (pp. 12–13)

Alfie Kohn (1998), a constant voice for equity in reform, wondered if, besides the dichotomy of teaching basic skills or teaching for understanding, the "math wars" reflected a dichotomy of best practices for learning math or best practices for elite university admission. He questioned whether parents were so focused on the goal of top SAT or ACT scores, which might be improved by practice problem sets, that they had blinded themselves to the more important goal for higher college mathematics of grasping the underlying concepts.

3. Children develop conceptual understanding through real-world connections, discussion, collaboration, and practice.

The belief that students learn more when they are actively engaged in discussions, activities, and open-ended tasks than when listening to lectures drives this pole's emphasis on these instructional strategies. Further, when students are well-grounded in the concepts, they find it easier to access the knowledge in new situations (Bransford, Brown, & Cocking, 1999).

Often, this approach is called "constructivist learning," or "inquiry-based learning." A misunderstanding is that these techniques involve turning students loose to invent their own strategies and discover concepts on their own. "Structured (or guided) inquiry," as Marzano (2011) calls the more appropriate practice, would be a better term; teachers need to carefully craft the environment and tools students will use, preplan how to guide their discoveries and mistakes, and be ready to summarize and reinforce the main concepts. It is not unfettered exploration.

Developing understanding through guided inquiry may take more time. For example, a sixth-grade teaching team investigated how its first group of incoming students who had been taught with an elementary mathematics reform curriculum might be different from prior students. While the reform students scored lower on computational accuracy, in questioning them, teachers found they understood why the methods they were using worked. Their mistakes were simple calculation errors. The students said they didn't like using methods they didn't understand. They preferred learning "why" before "how" (Keiser, 2010). Their accuracy improved as the year went on.

4. Children can use tools to access math knowledge they haven't mastered to solve rich problems that build conceptual understanding.

While accurate calculation skills were essential until just a few decades ago (are you old enough to recognize a slide rule?), calculators, computers, and cellular phones perform many arduous tasks. I don't have a "smartphone," yet my basic model has sine, cosine, tangent, square root, and exponent functions in the calculator application, as well as a separate tip calculator.

Providing students with calculators is valued as a way to let them work on rich problems without having to perform time-consuming calculations. This frees up time to concentrate on how to best model problems and the underlying concepts. Calculators are not meant to be a substitute, however, for understanding how to perform the calculations.

5. **Children are motivated by engagement and achievement with meaningful work. Effort creates ability.**

A key value for people at this pole is helping students grasp that effort, not innate intelligence, creates ability. Students who believe that their intelligence is fixed give up far more quickly when given novel problems to solve than those who believe that working hard helps you get smart (Dweck & Legget, 1988; Resnick, 1999).

Given the number of adults who groan at the mention of "Two trains leave different stations, traveling in opposite directions . . ." one would think that the need for engaging curriculum would be obvious. Simply making things "relevant" or "real world" is not the answer here. As Lockhart (2009) points out,

> It may be true that you have to be able to read in order to fill out forms at the DMV, but that's not why we teach children to read. We teach them to read for the higher purpose of allowing them access to beautiful and meaningful ideas. Not only would it be cruel to teach reading in such a way—to force third-graders to fill out purchase orders and tax forms—it wouldn't work! We learn things because they interest us now, not because they might be useful later. But this is exactly what we are asking children to do with math. (pp. 47–48)

NEGATIVE RESULTS OF OVERFOCUSING ON MATHEMATICS EDUCATION FOR MASTERY OF PROBLEM SOLVING TO THE NEGLECT OF MASTERY OF KNOWLEDGE

Because problem solving is only one pole in this system, too much emphasis on it to the neglect of basic skills and efficiency will bring a downside, as shown below.

1. Students who lack proficiency with traditional math skills aren't prepared for advanced math or college admissions tests.

The NCTM (2000) included three aspects of mathematical proficiency: factual knowledge, procedural proficiency, and conceptual understanding. However, many reform efforts took an either/or approach, saying that inquiry methods should be used to the exclusion of teaching any procedures or "drill and kill" with math facts. Further, parents unfamiliar with techniques such as lattice multiplication or short division struggle to help their students with homework. Many feel compelled to hire tutors to ensure that their children master procedures.

One student whose school used a constructivist curriculum placed credit for his score of 5 on the Advanced Placement calculus exam on his parents and tutors, not the curriculum, stating,

> My whole experience in math the last few years has been a struggle against the program. Whatever I've achieved, I've achieved in spite of it. Kids do not do better learning math themselves. There's a reason we go to school, which is that there's someone smarter than us with something to teach us. (Freedman, 2005)

2. In seeking proficiency for all students, math gets watered down. Many constructivist problems lack rigor.

One of the problems with inquiry-based problems is that it is difficult to implement them well; Stein Smith, Henningsen, and Silver (2009) found that only about 30% of rigorous tasks were implemented in a way that maintained that rigor. Too often, teachers unintentionally overstructured the problems in ways that decreased rigor, they didn't prompt prior knowledge or making connections, they didn't require reasoning and justification, or they spent too much or too little time on concept exploration.[1] Wes in our opening story is a perfect example.

3. "Fuzzy math" leads to calculator dependency, inefficient methods, and lack of accuracy.

It isn't difficult to page through some of the reform curricula and find examples of questionable tasks that lack mathematical content: writing essays about a favorite number or performing time-consuming operations such as drawing pictures to represent 7 × 12 are two examples. Parents also

---

1. See page 235 for information on how teacher learning styles, as described by Jungian psychological type, correlate with their difficulties in implementing these tasks at a high level.

saw their children perform repeated addition to multiply 3 × 32 instead of using the standard algorithm and complained about how inefficient their children's techniques were. They were also concerned about the amount of instructional time spent on estimation, seeing it as a substitute for accuracy. Or their children punch in 4 × 3 on a calculator rather than recall a multiplication fact.

Another complaint centers on the use of manipulatives. Critics of the "new math" painted pictures of students forever dependent on buckets of blocks to solve problems. Many teachers choose manipulatives that poorly illustrate concepts or fail to adequately make connections between the representation and the concept being explored. Further, children need different amounts of hands-on activities to grasp a concept. My son once said, "Why do I have to move around slices of pizza when I can see them in my head?"[2]

4. Children are confused by multiple algorithms and lack of clarity about acceptable answers.

One of the strategies of teaching math for understanding is providing students with multiple methods of solving problems and helping them develop skills to recognize the best methods to use in different situations. However, multiple methods may be taught in a disjointed manner, without discussion of when and why each might be used. Further, students may make more mistakes in early grades than if they are taught more than one method, causing parental concerns about lack of skills mastery.

5. Writing, collaboration, inquiry, and use of estimation detract from efficiency in mathematics.

Proponents of this view see class time and homework time as precious; there is no doubt that teacher-directed instruction is a more efficient way of passing on facts and procedures than collaborative activities.

One film that I often use in professional development sessions shows a boy constructing a shape that is one-quarter red and three-quarters yellow. It takes him three tries as he looks at his work, rereads the instructions, and adjusts according to a new understanding, but he succeeds in solving the problem without any help. Most teachers say, "I'd have wanted to help him after his second mistake, but now I realize he just needed time

---

2. There is another type link here, further explained in Chapter 12. My research on how students with different type preferences approach math tasks showed that when given the option, Sensing types (see page 94) often used the manipulatives to solve a problem. Intuitive students were more likely to use numbers to solve a problem (Kise, 2011).

to figure it out." Other teachers point out, "But we don't have enough time for students to try every problem three times!"[3]

LEVERAGING THE POLARITY

As teachers make changes in mathematics instruction, below are some early warning signs that might indicate that the system is overfocusing on one pole to the neglect of the other.

Early Warnings of Overfocusing on Mathematics Education as Mastering Knowledge

   A. Students passing proficiency tests but failing tasks requiring flexible math thinking or struggling to apply learning in new contexts.

   B. Increase in student requests for teachers to show them what to do.

   C. Increase in top math students who do not plan to take college mathematics courses; fewer math majors.

   D. Decrease in student collaborative tasks.

   E. Increase in times when teachers ask questions with a "correct answer" in mind.

Early Warnings of Overfocusing on Mathematics Education as Mastery of Problem Solving

   A. Increase in parents hiring tutors for basic skills, buying workbooks.

   B. Increase in teachers covertly using old textbooks or worksheets for skills practice.

   C. Increase in students who use calculators automatically, even when there are obvious mental math strategies.

   D. Sound bites such as "fuzzy math" or "calculator dependency" being used by parents.

   E. Students confused by inefficient methods and unclear on progress toward standards mastery.

STEPS TO MOVING BEYOND POLARIZATION

To flesh out the GPS, everyone wants our graduates to be able to understand and apply mathematics. The differences arise over the best ways to

---

3. Again, personality type plays a role here (see Chapter 12, page 232). While none of us wish to waste time, there is a definite Sensing/Judging value around efficiency. Adults and students with these preferences are more insistent than other types about getting clear directions. They say, "If you know there's a better, faster way to do it, why would I want to waste my time figuring it out on my own?"

get to that goal. The following are some of the best practices that honor and leverage the values of both sides.

1. Provide teacher training in trajectories of math knowledge, rich tasks, structuring collaboration/discourse, best practices in basic skills.

What knowledge do mathematics teachers need? Studies show that teachers with mathematics degrees do not show better student results than other teachers at the elementary level and only minimally at the secondary level (National Mathematics Advisory Panel, 2008). While teachers of course need content knowledge, it isn't sufficient. In fact, once someone has mastered elementary mathematics and can easily apply processes to multiple problems, it is more difficult to ascertain why and how a seven-year-old might struggle with something as basic as place value. Hill and Ball (2009) found that teachers need special knowledge and skills, including the ability to do the following:

- Interpret and analyze student work. If, for example, students are going to approach tasks in multiple ways, a teacher's understanding of the concept needs to be far deeper than knowing the common algorithm.
- Determine the source of student errors.
- Choose examples, representations, and manipulatives that fit best with a given problem or idea.

Hill and Ball summarize:

> As we made progress in identifying and describing these teaching tasks, we began to appreciate the mathematical demands of ordinary teaching. We saw the mathematical understanding involved in posing questions, interpreting students' answers, providing explanations, and using representations. We saw it in teachers' talk and in the language they taught students to use. We realized that the capacity to see the content from another's perspective and to understand what another person is doing entails mathematical reasoning and skill that are not needed for research mathematics or for bench science. (p. 69)

Hill et al. (2008) developed an assessment to measure teachers' specific knowledge for teaching mathematics, such as the preceding list, and found that it was strongly related to improved student outcomes. It matters more than the curriculum chosen or the time spent on mathematics instruction or the socioeconomic status of the students. Hill et al. also found that students from a lower socioeconomic status are likely to be taught by teachers with lower scores on their assessment.

2. Implement a balanced curriculum (practice and rich tasks) that develops number sense, computation skills, reasoning, making connections.

In a response to critics, the NCTM (Matthews, 2005) stated the following:

> NCTM has never advocated abandoning the use of standard algorithms. The notion that NCTM omits long division is nonsense. NCTM believes strongly that all students must become proficient with computation (adding, subtracting, multiplying, and dividing), using efficient and accurate methods.
>
> Regardless of the particular method used, students must be able to explain their method, understand that other methods may exist, and see the usefulness of algorithms that are efficient and accurate. This is a foundational skill for algebra and higher math.

As an outside consultant, I need to work with whatever curriculum a school has adopted—and they vary greatly in how they balance these strands of mathematical proficiency. None of them do it perfectly, nor do students respond in the same ways to equal levels of practice, rich tasks, and reasoning and justification. In other words, "balanced" can change from classroom to classroom. Teachers need deep knowledge *and* autonomy to balance correctly for the students they are teaching.

3. Provide teachers with collaborative time for lesson study and refinement, task and rubric development.

The wisdom gained in one classroom isn't easily passed to another; you can't simply hand over a lesson plan and assume teachers can implement it in the same way. One needs to know why certain instructional decisions were made and then adjust the plan to one's own students—and to student reactions in the moment. Few successful one-size-fits-all lesson plans exist, in spite of all the scripted curriculum that is out there. More and more teachers are part of professional learning communities, where they might engage in activities such as studying teaching practices, student work, assessments, and data. However, teaching duties, especially the long hours of student contact, still result in a considerable amount of solo practice in many countries.

Contrast the one period of preparation time most teachers in the United States have with Chinese teachers, who teach about three hours a day and then spend the rest of their time reviewing work and preparing lessons in offices shared with colleagues (Ma, 1999). Besides an hour a week of formal collaborative time in what the Chinese call teaching research groups (Paine & Ma, 1993), sharing office space leads to considerable informal collaboration.

I frequently work with professional learning communities to engage them in Japanese lesson study. This practice involves planning a specific lesson together by identifying clear learning targets and how they will be assessed, optimal ways to capture student work, questioning strategies, how to activate prior knowledge, and so on. Then one teacher teaches the lesson while the others observe. They meet again to review student work, process observations, and improve the lesson. They often repeat this process more than once.

All the groups I work with have reported, "It is amazing how much we've learned about instruction and assessment from just one lesson. Why aren't we collaborating this way more often?" Teachers report that while time-consuming, lesson study gives them vital information about how to improve their teaching skills (Nakamura, Takahashi, & Kurosawa, 1989).

Making time in a teacher's day for this kind of collaboration would require agreement that more time is needed to prepare to teach children. University professors have better ratios of teaching time to preparation time. Yet why do we think it takes more preparation to teach university students, who have chosen to be in a classroom, than it does elementary students, who come with a wide variety of interests and skills? Thought of that way, teaching reading or arithmetic takes at least as much prep as calculus, doesn't it? *This is really another embedded polarity, where in general teachers are required to overfocus on Doing the Work to the neglect of Preparing to Do the Work.*

4. Have clear agreement on developmentally appropriate proficiency skills students need to master.

Many of the "big ideas" in mathematics are crucial for success in higher-level study, yet these concepts are often not taught to a mastery level. For example, in a study that compares U.S. and Chinese teacher knowledge of key concepts (Ma, 1999), teachers were asked what they would do if several students were struggling to multiply three-digit numbers such as 123×645. About 70% of the U.S. teachers said that students were struggling with "lining up" the answers. They proposed solutions such as having students work on graph paper so that it would be easier to keep the numbers in straight columns or putting flowers where the zeroes would go since the zeros are "artificial" (p. 33). They spoke of place value as the placement of the numbers and not, for example that the 2 in 123 represents 20.

In contrast, the Chinese teacher solutions showed a correct understanding of place value. Further, they pointed out that their students didn't make such mistakes because "it should have been solved in the stage of learning multiplication by two-digit numbers" (Ma, 1999, p. 45); it is a crucial stage of learning. There is no point moving on to bigger numbers until students have mastered the concepts and procedures in two-digit multiplication.

These crucial stages, or "big ideas." are often not specifically identified in benchmarks, learning goals, and standards, yet they need to be key targets of assessment and intervention. At one school, the teachers were exploring with me the big ideas students needed to master in Grades 1 and 2. We generated many ideas for reinforcing these concepts, such as the combinations of numbers that equal 5 and the difference between reciting numbers and counting objects. I repeated, "Work with these big ideas during interventions!" more than once.

At a meeting a month later, one of the special education teachers reported, "I did what you said. I worked with combinations of 5 and 10 with a struggling second grader for weeks. And suddenly he got it. I could see the change in his excitement. That day, he was sitting at a table with fifth graders. 'What are they doing?' he asked. 'Can I try it?' He not only tried it, but succeeded. Mastering that one big idea increased his confidence and his ability to explore."

5. Have clear agreement on power standards that are enduring, leverage-able, and essential.

The Common Core State Standards are a new step in this direction, yet there are still far more standards to teach than hours in which to teach them. Agreement on what every child really needs to learn and *can* learn during a school year is a proven strategy for student success (Marzano, 2012). Many countries have mathematics standards that are "a mile wide and an inch deep." Rather than decide whether statistics or calculus or geometric proofs are essential knowledge, they tend to include everything; they aren't leveraging the *Breadth AND Depth* polarity.

"Power standards" help teachers agree on what is most essential and are described by Reeves (2005) as being of enduring importance, associated with success with other standards, and essential for the next level of instruction. Without such common agreement, teachers feel compelled to "cover" every topic rather than teach for mastery. Emphasizing our GPS of students who understand and use math might help with difficult choices among topics. Collaborating to awaken mathematical wonder in children might help even more.

Can we get to where adults have as much fun comparing the math ideas we tackled over the weekend as the books or magazine articles we read? That GPS may seem impossible, but I've seen students crave more math when given the skills they need AND tasks that light up their inner motivation to put those skills to use.

REFLECTION

1. While this chapter explored the "math wars," nearly every content area involves similar polarities, with possible names such as these:

   Content Knowledge AND Process Knowledge

   Basic Skills AND Applications

   Factual Information AND Using the Information

   Core Discipline Knowledge AND Doing the Work of the Discipline

   o In language arts, the "reading wars" represent the most contentious polarity, where mastering skills such as phonics and fluency AND reading texts were seen as solutions rather than part of a system. Consider working alone or with a group to map Teaching for Reading Proficiency AND Teaching Reading for Enjoyment. The polarity mapping process, and team activities for working through it, is fully explained in Chapter 8.

   o In history and geography, the tension is between memorizing events, dates, and places AND studying trends, motivations, patterns, and the big ideas of civilization. What is emphasized in your team, building, or district? How are students assessed and graded?

   o In science, students need foundational knowledge, but learning to formulate and test hypotheses is the core work of the discipline. How much time do students spend mastering knowledge? How much time do they devote to formulating and investigating their own questions?

2. Reflect on your own school experiences. For different disciplines, consider how factual knowledge and basic skills were emphasized. How was the actual work of the discipline emphasized? In what ways did you act as historians, scientists, or mathematicians? How did it change at different grade levels? What experiences stand out as most valuable for your own learning?

ACTIVITY 5.1: MASTERING CALCULATIONS AND MASTERING MATHEMATICAL THINKING

3. Often, resistance to new ideas comes from a perceived overemphasis on one pole to the neglect of the other. Following is a professional development activity I use with mathematics professional learning communities when an action step involves helping students master efficient calculation methods that also support mathematical

Polarity Thinking Map for Mathematics Calculation Proficiency

Students Are

Action Steps

A. Agree on specific methods that will be taught to mastery and what mastery means.

B. Develop assessments to ensure students understand why as well as how an algorithm works.

Values = positive results from focusing on the left pole

1. Students have a universally reliable method.

2. Students have a common tool that allows easy communication.

Standard Algorithms

and

Early Warnings

A. Students use the standard algorithm when mental math should suffice, for example with 25 x 10.

B. Students cannot answer simple questions such as, "If 20 x 21 is 420, what is 21 x 21?" without writing out the standard algorithm.

1. Students have only one tool, and it can be cumbersome rather than efficient.

2. Students can use the algorithm without understanding why it works.

Fears = negative results from overfocusing on the left pole to the neglect of the right pole

Students Apply Procedures

Accurate and Efficient

Values = positive results from focusing on the right pole

1. Students are able to apply mathematics concepts to find efficient solutions.
2. Students understand how to calculate and why methods work.

Multiple Methods

and

1. Students become inefficient if they apply methods without reasoning which one is best.
2. Students need significant time and support to learn when and how to use multiple methods.

Fears = negative results from overfocusing on the right pole to the neglect of the left pole

Without Understanding

Action Steps

A. Collaborate on a plan for teaching multiple methods, including scaffolding students with lower levels of mathematics understanding.

B. Seek professional development on facilitating student discussions of the methods they used.

Early Warnings

A. Students are too slow at computation.

B. Students cannot articulate why they are choosing a method.

"Math Wars" Polarity Thinking Map

Every Student

Action Steps

A. Provide teacher training in trajectories of math knowledge, rich tasks, structuring collaboration/discourse, best practices in basic skills.

B. Implement a balanced curriculum (practice and rich tasks) that develops number sense, computation skills, reasoning, making connections.

C. Provide teachers with collaborative time for lesson study and refinement, task and rubric development.

D. Have clear agreement on developmentally appropriate proficiency skills students need to master.

E. Have clear agreement on power standards that are enduring, leverage-able, and essential.

Values = positive results from focusing on the left pole

1. Students master the body of established mathematics knowledge.

2. Teacher-led, algorithm-centered instruction efficiently conveys best practices for speed and accuracy.

3. Children develop conceptual understanding through expert instruction and practice.

4. Children need basic skills and efficient algorithms before they can apply them to complex problems.

5. Children are motivated by success in accuracy, efficiency, and speed, which prepares them to tackle increasingly rigorous tasks.

Mastering Math Knowledge

and

Early Warnings

A. Students passing proficiency tests but failing tasks requiring flexible math thinking or struggling to apply learning in new contexts.

B. Increase in student requests for teachers to show them what to do.

C. Increase in top math students who do not plan to take college mathematics courses; fewer math majors.

D. Decrease in student collaborative tasks.

E. Increase in times when teachers ask questions with a "correct answer" in mind.

1. Memorization of rules and procedures produces math anxiety and students who hate math and lack understanding.

2. Teacher-led instruction means teachers are working and learning more than students are.

3. Students get bored with repetition.

4. Students won't be ready for the high-tech workplace where flexible thinking, problem formulation, and collaboration are key.

5. The emphasis on skills proficiency prevents students from seeing math as a creative process that is worthwhile and enjoyable.

Fears = negative results from overfocusing on the left pole <u>to the neglect</u> of the right pole

Students Not

Source: Map template copyright by Polarity Partnerships, LLC.

a Mathematician

Values = positive results from focusing on the right pole

1. Mathematics is conveyed as making meaning of the world through numbers and patterns, problem formulation/solving.

2. Mathematics as problem solving engages all students, not just those already college bound. This is a social justice issue.

3. Children develop conceptual understanding through real-world connections, discussion, collaboration, and practice.

4. Children can use tools to access math knowledge they haven't mastered to solve rich problems that build conceptual understanding.

5. Children are motivated by engagement and achievement with meaningful work. Effort creates ability.

and

Mastering Problem Solving

1. Students who lack proficiency with traditional math skills aren't prepared for advanced math or college admissions tests.

2. In seeking proficiency for all students, math gets watered down. Many constructivist problems lack rigor.

3. "Fuzzy math" leads to calculator dependency, inefficient methods, and lack of accuracy.

4. Children are confused by multiple algorithms and lack of clarity about acceptable answers.

5. Writing, collaboration, inquiry, and use of estimation detract from efficiency in mathematics.

Fears = negative results from overfocusing on the right pole <u>to the neglect</u> of the left pole

Proficient in Mathematics

Action Steps

A. Provide teacher training in trajectories of math knowledge, rich tasks, structuring collaboration/discourse, best practices in basic skills.

B. Implement a balanced curriculum practice and rich tasks. that develops number sense, computation skills, reasoning, making connections.

C. Provide teachers with collaborative time for lesson study and refinement, task and rubric development.

D. Have clear agreement on developmentally appropriate proficiency skills students need to master.

E. Have clear agreement on power standards that are enduring, leverage-able, and essential.

Early Warnings

A. Increase in parents hiring tutors for basic skills, buying workbooks.

B. Increase in teachers covertly using old textbooks or worksheets for skills practice.

C. Increase in students who use calculators automatically, even when there are obvious mental math strategies.

D. Sound bites such as "fuzzy math" or "calculator dependency" being used by parents.

E. Students confused by inefficient methods and unclear on progress toward standards mastery.

thinking. As you study it, identify and outline a similar activity that you might develop for another discipline.

○ Provide copy paper or individual whiteboards to each participant. Ask them to solve the equation 19 × 24 and show their work. When they are finished, ask people to explain the methods they use. If no one suggests (20 × 24) − 24, write it on a piece of paper as it is probably the most efficient method. Note, when I work with a group of classroom teachers, the vast majority use the standard algorithm. I see a variety of methods if I work with mathematics coaches or at schools that use certain curricula such as Investigations.

○ Ask for the pros and cons of teaching students multiple methods for multiplication. Note that this lets them express fears associated with the Math for Mastery of Problem Solving pole. Typical concerns are that the methods don't always work, that they confuse the "low" students, and that students have more difficulty collaborating or helping each other if they use different methods. Point out that mathematicians generally look for the simplest method and would not use the standard algorithm for 19 × 24.

○ Ask the group to solve the problem 16 × 35, again showing their work on paper or the whiteboard. The easiest method is 8 × 70, worked by factoring 16 so that the problem becomes 8 × (2 × 35). Have the group discuss the mathematical concepts involved in this solution (the distributive and commutative properties, factoring, etc.). Ask what students might learn from looking for efficient ways to do such problems. Note that you are asking for the upside of the Math for Mastering Problem Solving pole.

○ Emphasize that the standard algorithm is still important. It is often more efficient and can be universally applied. Ask for the downsides of teaching only that method.

○ Post three or four other problems and ask the group to look for the most efficient way to solve them.

○ Share the Polarity Thinking Map for Mathematics Calculation Proficiency on pages 100–101 with the group and ask what they might add. What action steps might the team take to leverage the upside of both poles?

6 Making Diplomas Meaningful

Standardization AND Customization

Standards are nothing new; for centuries people have debated what students should learn. In the opening lines of Charles Dickens's *Hard Times,* Superintendent Gradgrind delivers a rousing message about *his* standards to a teacher and his class.

> NOW, what I want is, Facts. Teach these boys and girls nothing but Facts. Facts alone are wanted in life. Plant nothing else, and root out everything else. You can only form the minds of reasoning animals upon Facts: nothing else will ever be of any service to them.

In Gradgrind's mind, students *either* learned facts *or* what he terms "fancy"—fiction, poetry, the arts, and even "What if" reasoning. Students need to be taught, for example, that carpeting designs can't include flowers because you'd never walk on a bed of flowers, would you! The book then charts how Gradgrind's own son, guided by facts without critical thinking skills, ruins his life. The moral? Facts AND Fancy are valuable.

Over 150 years later, echoes of Gradgrind's speech still reverberate. Headlines such as "History Literacy Failing Among American Students" (2012, in *Huffington Post Education*) or "Failing Grades on Civics Exam Called a 'Crisis'" (Dillon, 2011, in the *New York Times*) cause public outcries. Only a handful of fourth graders can correctly identify Abraham Lincoln from a photo and give two reasons why he was important? Only 20% of college graduates know that James Monroe is called the "Father of the Constitution"? Students resort to calculators when asked to perform division problems? Shocking headlines, for sure. The call for national standards arose partly from such headlines.

Most countries have a core curriculum, although the curricula vary in level of detail and implementation requirements. In the United States, though, each state, not the federal government, is charged with overseeing schools. Under No Child Left Behind (NCLB), each state developed its own standards to measure student progress against set criteria. However, the quality of those standards and how student proficiency and school success were measured varied greatly. The Fordham Institute wondered how schools in different states could have nearly identical national test scores, yet one be labeled as healthy and another as failing (Brown Center, 2012).

As of this writing, the new Common Core State Standards (CCSS) for mathematics and English language arts have been adopted by forty-five of the fifty United States (a forty-sixth, Minnesota, adopted the English but not the mathematics standards). As with any sweeping reform, the CCSS have fans and enemies—and multitudes of educators who are swamped with the work of implementation are too busy with "how" to debate the "why."

Within this huge initiative are many, many polarities, including the following:

Local power AND Federal Power

Breadth AND Depth

Test Success AND Mastery of Concepts

Schooling for Career AND Schooling for Learning's Sake

Part (each student) AND Whole (the education system)

As unproductive as we've seen ignoring polarities can be, equally unproductive is lumping several together while looking at a major issue, initiative, or ongoing difficulty. Therefore, in this chapter we're going to focus on just one of the values clashes embedded in the adoption of the CCSS.

SEEING THE POLARITY

At one pole, we'll examine the values behind "standardization." Bill Gates, whose foundation supports and has committed resources to developing assessments tied to the CCSS, told a *Wall Street Journal* reporter, "It's ludicrous to think that multiplication in Alabama and multiplication in New York are really different. . . . In terms of mathematics textbooks, why can't you have the scale of a national market? Right now, we have a Texas textbook that's different from a California textbook that's different from a Massachusetts textbook. That's very expensive" (Riley, 2011).

At the other pole are those who value "customization"—the schooling ideal of treating every child as an individual to nurture his or her unique gifts. Brooks and Dietz (2012) declare, "The homepage of learning isn't on the Common Core State Standards Initiative website—it is in the minds of individual students, supported by their teachers" (p. 65).

Note that the benefits of standardization fit with a general bias in the United States toward efficiency and objectivity (see page 231 in Chapter 12 for a full discussion of the basis for this statement and the equally valuable alternative). And when one set of values "wins," everyone loses. The mapping process, or some tool to ensure that the values of customization are included, is essential to successful implementation of the Common Core.

MAPPING THE POLARITY

Thus, we have ongoing tension between the Standardization pole, ensuring that students all receive the same basic education, and the Customization pole, ensuring that individual student needs are met. Let's start with "meaningful diploma" as our *greater purpose statement*. While the phrase could be interpreted in many ways, it incorporates the drive of standardization to ensure that graduates can support themselves financially and the desire of customization to ensure that they value and embrace the education they receive. The discussion might thus appeal to both utilitarian values and the benefits of uniqueness.

The *deeper fear* is once again student failure. If democracy rests on the foundation of a well-educated citizenry, then we depend on our public schools to deliver an education to every student.

Let's look at what each side values.

POSITIVE RESULTS OF FOCUSING ON STANDARDIZATION

Right now, this pole is being emphasized in the United States by the adoption of the CCSS. Again, entire books and websites address this polarity. What follows is a synthesis of the various positions being expressed. The full map can be found at the end of this chapter on pages 126–127.

1. High school diploma requirements equate to graduates having learned the standardized content required by colleges and employers.

The CCSS were developed by asking colleges and employers about the knowledge and skills they expect high school graduates to have and working backward to ensure that a high school diploma indeed incorporates this learning. The goal was ensuring that graduates were qualified for jobs that could provide family-sustaining wages, benefits, and opportunities for advancement.

For example, employers and university faculty valued writing coherent arguments that rely on relevant texts more than they valued writing narratives. The CCSS thus shifted instructional focus to working with nonfiction, informational texts and away from personal narratives and creative writing.

Note, though, that the CCSS call for content literacy, meaning that science and social studies course work are also part of literacy instruction. Within language arts courses, there will still be room for the study of literature, creative writing, and narrative writing as long as other content area teachers cover the skills needed for close reading of informational text and emphasize persuasive and other forms of writing called for in the standards.

2. Standardization allows for economies of scale for textbooks, assessments, lessons, support materials, teacher training, and professional development.

When every state had separate standards, textbook companies released different editions of many texts. Further, each state developed its own high-stakes tests and databases with sample questions. The CCSS should produce some economies of scale.

For example, with funds from Race to the Top Assessment initiative, five organizations are developing common assessments that all participating states will be able to access, along with a large bank of sample items. The Partnership for Assessment of Readiness for College and Careers (PARCC) includes twenty states, and the Smarter Balanced Assessment Consortium includes twenty-five states. Representatives from K–12 education, universities, communities, and state governments are working together to develop a series of assessments that

> builds a pathway to college and career readiness for all students,
>
> creates high-quality assessments that measure the full range of the Common Core State Standards,

supports educators in the classroom,

makes better use of technology in assessments, and

advances accountability at all levels. (PARCC, 2012)

3. The CCSS allow for efficient measurement and comparison to ensure that all students receive the content they need.

The content that students are taught at each grade level hasn't been consistent from state to state, school to school, or classroom to classroom—and students in high-poverty schools generally receive less, in terms of both the amount covered and the level of rigor. Proponents of the CCSS hope that implementation will guarantee a progression of knowledge and skills for every child. Schmidt and Burroughs (2012) point out that students cannot learn concepts to which they are never introduced, a particularly troublesome problem in mathematics. They take issue with those who claim that, since state standards have failed to equalize the quality of content students are taught, the CCSS will also fail to do so. "This claim seems to assume that the content taught at a particular grade in any given year is essentially the same in any classroom in the state" (p. 56). And of course that has not been true.

While implementation will affect whether students receive the curriculum suggested by the CCSS, it will definitely make it easier to compare student progress. Under the current system, students in some states showed significant progress on state assessments, yet results on the National Assessment of Educational Progress remained flat. Further, some states showed significant progress, but further investigation revealed that they had changed the cutoff marks for proficiency or the nature of the test. Proponents of standardization point out that if students are competing for the same college and career slots, then they should be confident that, for example, being proficient in math in New York and in California means the same thing.

4. The CCSS with their incorporation of rigor and processes ensure that a student's education will involve both content and processes.

From the start, writers of both the literacy and mathematics standards emphasized balancing knowledge, application, and "twenty-first-century skills" such as problem solving, analysis, and persuasion. Note that *Content AND Process* is another polarity embedded in this issue; people at each pole claim that their approach ensures that students gain both, but an overfocus on either pole will affect this embedded polarity as well.

In the CCSS mathematics standards, eight "standards of practice" are included:

1. Make sense of problems and persevere in solving them.

2. Reason abstractly and quantitatively.

3. Construct viable arguments and critique the reasoning of others.

4. Model with mathematics.

5. Use appropriate tools strategically.

6. Attend to precision.

7. Look for and make use of structure.

8. Look for and express regularity in repeated reasoning. (CCSS, 2012b, pp. 7–8)

The language arts standards define the meaning of literacy to include a broad range of skills, not just text decoding and writing:

> Students who meet the Standards readily undertake the close, attentive reading that is at the heart of understanding and enjoying complex works of literature. They habitually perform the critical reading necessary to pick carefully through the staggering amount of information available today in print and digitally. They actively seek the wide, deep, and thoughtful engagement with high-quality literary and informational texts that builds knowledge, enlarges experience, and broadens worldviews. They reflexively demonstrate the cogent reasoning and use of evidence that is essential to both private deliberation and responsible citizenship in a democratic republic. (CCSS, 2012a, p. 3)

5. All students need a breadth of knowledge in content areas in order to analyze and apply it.

Typically, children from middle- and upper-class homes enter school with a larger vocabulary and more of the basic knowledge that is valued in our culture than do children from more impoverished environments. This can put low-income students at a considerable disadvantage for academic work. Hirsch (2001a) articulates that students will benefit from specific topics, by grade, that prepare them for the next level. His organization, Core Knowledge, believes that these topics should be ones

> that have the greatest potential for developing general competence and narrowing the test-score gap between groups. We made an inventory of the knowledge that is characteristically shared in American society by those at the top of the socioeconomic ladder. That turns out to be the knowledge take for granted in American society—in college classrooms, in conversations with strangers, and in books and newspapers addressed to the general reader. Since that knowledge is taken for granted and not explained, ignorance of that assumed knowledge will seriously handicap those who lack it.

In other words, while of course students need to analyze, interpret, and create with information, there is still a definable body of knowledge that students need to master. Standards support that goal.

NEGATIVE RESULTS OF OVERFOCUSING ON STANDARDIZATION TO THE NEGLECT OF CUSTOMIZATION

Other educators, while not necessarily against the standards, are very concerned about how they might be implemented. As with all systems involving polarities, overfocusing on one pole brings the downside as well as the positive results from that pole. Below are possible outcomes from CCSS implementation if this polarity isn't leveraged.

1. Businesses and politicians are deciding what is best for students.

The basis of the standards, working backward from what postsecondary education and employers want, raises two concerns. First, there are concerns that the standards for the youngest students, kindergartners through third grade, may not be age appropriate. Some early childhood development experts are wary of de-emphasis of the valuable role of play in learning. They also question whether the CCSS might be used to delay kindergarten entry if children do not meet certain benchmarks.

Second, there are questions about the actual content of the standards. For example, analytical writing and persuasive writing are given far more emphasis than narrative writing. Critics question whether this emphasis will motivate all students; they point to *Freedom Writers* and other success stories where personal writing catapulted students toward success.

Granted, narrative writing has seldom been taught well. "How I Spent My Summer Vacation" or "My Favorite Number" essays have little long-term value. But narrative writing that crafts events to make a point *is* valued in business circles; consider books such as *Good to Great* (Collins, 2001) or *The Tipping Point* (Gladwell, 2000), for example. Further, cultures such as Native American nations use storytelling as a primary tool for conveying wisdom and values. In *Our Stories Remember* (2003), Joseph Bruchac summarizes:

> Our stories always serve at least two purposes. They are told for the sake of entertainment itself (helping us, as Maurice Dennis, an Abenaki elder, put it to me, "survive another winter") and because that which is entertaining will be listened to and remembered. The second purpose of stories is to teach, to educate about things one needs to know, to guide people toward proper behavior, to show the results of good behavior, to warn about the consequences of ill-considered or selfish actions. It was that way; it is still that way. (p. 52)

Standards, then, trigger diversity and social justice issues even as they are seen as a solution to the very same problems. Brooks and Dietz (2012) point out that diversity is at risk if there is only one set of standards, approved textbooks, and assessments.

2. Standards lead to concerns over coverage of curriculum and limit teacher discretion to meet student interests and needs.

We know that children develop at different rates and have different interests. One of the biggest difficulties with common standards is that because of them, schools strive to push children through the curriculum at the same pace, especially if schools—and teachers—are being judged by performance against those standards.

While the Common Core decreased the number of standards over what existed before in many states, most of the educators I've spoken with believe that there are still too many standards to cover in a school year, especially for students who struggle in any way. Because one of the biggest predictors of school success is having a guaranteed and viable curriculum (Marzano, 2003), having too many standards is a major red flag.

In one district, teachers were told exactly which page of the mathematics curriculum their middle schoolers were to start on and that teachers would be held accountable for following that guideline, regardless of what pretest results showed. This would "accelerate" student learning, whereas if teachers spent time reviewing prior knowledge, time would be wasted on "remediation." The result? Students fell *further* behind because of the great numbers who didn't pass the very first unit of the year. The teachers had to back up, teach the requisite knowledge, and then reteach the grade-level topics students hadn't grasped. No one meant for more students to fail; rather, the standards didn't match the learning needs of those particular children.

This is a typical paradoxical result of ignoring one pole; in this case, ignoring the needs of a specific group of students with the intention of avoiding remediation led to a downward spiral of more remediation.

What is interesting, though, is that even the Gates Foundation has a goal of 80% of students, not 100%, reaching "college/career ready" proficiency by 2020. Is this acknowledging that the CCSS won't work for 20% of our students? Or that the changes will take even more time and effort to have a real impact?

3. Standards result in an emphasis on test preparation.

In its report on possible outcomes from CCSS implementation, The Brown Center (2012) states,

> The push for common education standards argues that all American students should study a common curriculum, take comparable tests to measure their learning, and have the results interpreted on a common scale, with the scale divided into performance levels to indicate whether students are excelling, learning an adequate amount, or falling short. Past experience with standards suggests that each part of this apparatus—a common curriculum, comparable tests, and standardized performance levels—is necessary. No one or two of them can stand alone for the project to succeed. (p. 7)

Teachers know that the CCSS provide room for creativity and individual approaches to a topic, but school schedules very well may not. One teacher summarized how she and her colleagues felt. "You can *say* we can provide multiple pathways for learning and should spend more time on concepts when students don't understand something, but come test results, I'm going to be asked, 'Did you cover everything?' not 'Did they understand everything?'"

As we saw in Chapter 3, an emphasis on test preparation has led to a narrower curriculum, loss of recess time, and less instruction in the arts and physical education, especially in high-poverty schools.

4. Tests seldom capture twenty-first-century skills, at least not with efficiency.

While the consortiums working on the common assessments initially promised to assess more than fact-based learning, as I was writing this chapter, the Smarter Balanced Assessment Consortium announced that it was reducing the number of performance assessment items to just one each for the math and reading tests. Performance assessments include essay writing and more complex mathematics items where students need to show their reasoning. With just two such items in total, they estimate that the tests will take about seven to eight hours, versus up to nearly fourteen hours for the original drafts that included more complex items (Gewertz, 2012).

States that previously tried performance assessments already discovered the difficulties of assessment time, grading consistency, preparing students for the assessment formats, and so on. While the CCSS were developed with the idea that higher-level thinking would be assessed, doing so through standardized tests can be extremely difficult, costly, or both.

In his classic management article "On the Folly of Rewarding A, While Hoping for B," Steven Kerr (1995) points out how often we reward or punish the wrong behaviors. In the case of the CCSS, while the sample test items often require some reasoning rather than factual recall or calculations, they are still multiple-choice items. Measuring the knowledge students have learned and basing teacher evaluations on those test scores while hoping for higher-level thinking is as much a folly as the examples Kerr gives: rewarding short-term profits while hoping for long-term growth, rewarding professors for publishing research while hoping they'll concentrate on pedagogical excellence, and so on.

5. Students may not have the chance to explore fine arts, hands-on trades, or other areas that could become the basis for careers.

Especially in schools with high percentages of struggling students (usually those with the highest percentage of students eligible for free/reduced lunches), the temptation will be to focus instruction on what is being measured. One solution, especially to ensure emphasis on the science and technology education necessary to develop a competitive workforce, is to create standards and tests for more content areas. Opponents, though, cry that students are already tested too much.

Step into the shoes of an eleven-year-old I was tutoring. She'd been excused from her extra hour of mathematics class to work with me for a day. At the end of her session I asked, "Where do you go next? I'll write you a pass." "I've got Reading Helps now." I did a quick calculation in my head; that meant she had six straight periods of core academics in a six-period day. I said, "Gosh, you must be working hard with that schedule." "Yeah," she replied. "I don't get to do anything fun, not even Spanish."

At eleven years of age, what would be your school attitude without music or art or physical education or a foreign language? When I've polled parent groups, few are reluctant to admit that middle school was made bearable by cooking and band and all the other "fluff" classes that let us use different parts of our brains!

POSITIVE RESULTS OF A CUSTOMIZED APPROACH TO EDUCATION

Let's turn to the values of those who question the value of common standards and prefer a more customized approach to education.

1. Customization allows children to graduate ready to make the most of their unique gifts and talents.

Let's be honest: Weren't you far more attracted to some careers than others? Aren't there occupations you *know* would make you miserable? Some students are wired to take far more interest in STEM courses and careers, others in hands-on craftsmanship, and still others in the fine arts. If schools don't expose students to all areas, some children may never find their gifts.[1]

In a blog titled "Common Sense vs. Common Core: How to Minimize the Damage of the Common Core," Yong Zhao (2012), who was born and educated in China and is now associate dean for global education, University of Oregon, pleads with parents and educators:

Don't cut arts, music, sports, recess, field trips, debate teams, or other programs in order to align with the Common Core. Nothing is more core than a child's interest and passion. A well-balanced, broad curriculum that meets the needs of each child is a much better bet for your children's future than one devoted to two subjects standardized and prescribed by people who have no knowledge of your community or your children.

I had the privilege of visiting a technical high school that was owned by five school districts. Businesses in the area supported the school, hoping to foster homegrown talent, and every facility was up-to-date. Students learned to work with the high-tech electronics of new cars, build and weld with the latest equipment, cook in modern industrial kitchens modeled after gourmet restaurants, and work on the most advanced computer systems available. A couple of students were already making five-figure

---

1. For a summary of research on personality types and occupational choice, see page 236.

incomes through their graphic design work. Others had won culinary competitions or secured paying apprenticeships.

As I toured the carpentry area, the students talked about how easy it was to learn mathematics in such an applied environment. "Our teachers tell us, 'If you don't understand fractions and angles and ratios, your roofs will collapse!" They were mastering a broad yet specialized domain of mathematics, not a general array of standards, and would be well prepared for their chosen careers.

2. Customization allows for discretion based on teacher expertise, local culture, and community involvement.

While math may be math and 2 + 2 = 4 in Massachusetts and in Nevada, the norms for instruction, discourse, independent thinking, sharing opinions, and many other factors vary from culture to culture, even within the fifty states. Further, when we avoid textbooks that fit a common set of standards, teachers can explore collaboratively how materials about local history, customs, and events might be used to meet learning targets. Here are some examples:

> I saw a powerful transformation in a Native American classroom when they studied the 1973 seizure of Wounded Knee, South Dakota, by about 200 Oglala Lakota and American Indian Movement members. The students *knew* warriors who had been involved.

> A science teacher combined research, writing, and environmental science by having students develop and carry out projects to improve the neighborhood surrounding the school.

> A math teacher had students calculate whether their classrooms met the district's regulations regarding square footage per student.

Standardization doesn't preclude such location-specific lessons, but districts and schools often welcome and encourage the efficiency and safety of recommended curriculum.

Returning to the topic of the types of writing emphasized, while I can't speak for their elders, the information I've read indicates that Native Americans might consider a fiction book such as National Book Award winner Louise Erdrich's *The Birchbark House* a more appropriate way to teach non-Indian children about their culture than nonfiction texts. When we devalue narrative, are we devaluing cultures? Lisa Delpit (1995) points out the balancing act as we try to help students from the working class and from other cultures learn the norms and discourses of power.

I also do not believe that we should teach students to passively adopt an alternate code. They must be encouraged to understand the value of the code they already possess as well as to understand the power realities in this country. Otherwise they will be unable to work to change these realities. (p. 40)

3. Customization allows students to grow at their own pace.

The knowledge gap between kindergartners from well-to-do households and impoverished households is significant, and a predictor of school success. As discussed above, the CCSS solution is more, earlier, to ensure college/career readiness. In contrast, remember that in Finland, while preschoolers are definitely involved in literacy activities, formal literacy instruction does not begin until children are seven years old.

I need to point out one glaring example from a licensed teacher who home-schooled her own children. Her oldest child easily mastered reading at age six, but her second child didn't want to sit still and couldn't seem to make sense of the connections between sounds and letters, even though he could name them. Knowing that reading readiness is often delayed for boys, she set the materials aside for six months. When she pulled them out again, he caught on quickly. In fact, he was plowing through *Hardy Boys* books within a few months; note that the original books in the series are actually written at about a fourth-grade level. He loved to read. In standardized public schools, no such six-month respite is possible.

Teaching students at their own pace keeps them in that zone of proximal development, where their ability matches the materials, leading to flow rather than frustration!

4. Customization embeds twenty-first-century skills.

When students are more involved in designing their own pathways for learning, they develop the kinds of planning, questioning, and inquiry skills employers seek. This is different from the Common Core emphasis on standardizing the knowledge and skills desired by colleges and employers. Tony Wagner (2006) investigated what corporate executives were really looking for in graduates. One told him,

We can teach the technical stuff. But for employees to solve problems or to learn new things, they have to know what questions to ask. And we can't teach them how to ask good questions—how to think. The ability to ask the right questions is the single most important skill. (p. 2)

Think how designing one's own learning projects helps develop these skills!

While the CCSS definitely makes possible this kind of learning activity, teachers need significant time for planning. Again, the danger is that if the related tests cover more content knowledge (standardization) than process and performance skills (customization), we will be "rewarding A while hoping for B."

5. Customized education is more likely to produce excitement about learning, which is key to academic success.

With estimates that current graduates will most likely change careers three to seven times in their lives, ensuring that students know how to learn and enjoy it is key to their future success. We simply can't teach them all they need to know no matter how "college and career ready" the CCSS promise to make them. Customization allows teachers to try a wide repertoire of topics, strategies, and environments to "turn on the lightbulb" for each student.

Many of the most successful "alternative schools" that educate students who have failed in our regular school system employ project-based learning. Students, with the aid of mentors, design lengthy projects that help them tap into their own skills and passions while meeting graduation requirements. Students have learned to run a recording studio by working with a music store owner, studied child development while being mentored at a day care center, developed historical research skills from working with firefighters and investigating the history of the development of their equipment and techniques, and more (Clarke, 2012).

John Clarke, who serves as a mentor for a program in Vermont, commented that test scores seldom help struggling high school students develop an interest in learning.

> High school students are not noted for their compliance with adult demands—and many students have learned over the years that they won't achieve success or receive positive recognition by sitting in a classroom, so they stop trying and grow increasingly resentful of imposed limits on their choices. (p. 64)

He notes that it is often a random experience or a book or movie a student happens across that "helps that kid separate 'what has always been' from 'what could be'—and experience renewed energy to continue" (p. 64).

NEGATIVE RESULTS OF OVERFOCUSING ON CUSTOMIZED EDUCATION TO THE NEGLECT OF STANDARDIZATION

While the preceding results contribute toward our GPS of a meaningful diploma, again as with all polarities, an overfocus on customization will also bring its downside. Here are some sample negative outcomes.

1. Students graduate without specific content knowledge and skills that colleges and employers say they need.

Without any articulated standards or benchmarks, chaos can reign. Students might pursue their own interests while ignoring crucial knowledge. And teachers may concentrate on their favorite areas. This is certainly a real danger if there are no common expectations for what it means to earn a high school diploma.

2. We can't compare student achievement across schools.

In a report called *The Proficiency Illusion*, the Fordham Institute made the case that with different proficiency standards, and different learning targets altogether, one can't compare student learning across states. The more student learning programs are customized, the less one is able to compare school effectiveness even within the same state, district, or school (Cronin, Dahlin, Adkins, & Kingsbury, 2007). Proponents of standards point out that this makes it difficult to identify the most effective educational practices and introduce them in places where students are falling behind.

3. Students aren't able to track progress toward gaining the knowledge and skills they need for chosen education or career paths.

Before NCLB, the first indicator parents and children might have had that their education had been an inadequate preparation for college was their initial ACT or SAT score. Especially if one agrees that there is a specific body of knowledge that acts as a "gatekeeper" to success in a given culture, then knowing whether one is on track in acquiring that knowledge seems very necessary.

In her novel *Catalyst*, Laurie Halse Anderson (2002) tells the story of Kate, a bright girl who is determined to go to MIT, as did her deceased mother.

She pursues her passions for science and mathematics relentlessly but does the minimum in her humanities coursework. Even though a few of her teachers warn her, she assumes that her perfect math SAT score will make up for her not-so-perfect English score. It doesn't; Kate's life falls apart when MIT rejects her. While Kate in the novel benefits from rethinking her priorities, in real life, such one-sidedness has had deeper consequences for many.

4. Customization is expensive and time-consuming.

With economies of scale as one of the driving factors behind the CCSS, it shouldn't be a surprise that the inefficiencies of customizing education is one of the biggest strikes against this pole.

In the 1990s, Minnesota began its work with standards with a two-pronged approach, partly to incorporate performance standards and partly to allow students to demonstrate learning in many ways. In addition to basic skills tests for literacy, mathematics, and writing that students had to pass in order to graduate from high school, Minnesota developed "Profiles of Learning." These were cross-disciplinary, performance-based assessments that were designed to require deeper levels of understanding on twenty-four standards.

Note that this attempt at customization still involved standardization. While districts could design their own assessments, the Minnesota Department of Children, Families and Learning developed about 150 sample packages. Examples included preparing a position paper and presenting it to a community group involved in decision making or conducting a historical and ethnographic study of a workplace or community institution. These high school packages took three to six weeks of course time to complete. The directions for one of the sample packages were sixty-five pages long. Teachers reported significant decreases in job satisfaction due to the planning and grading time involved; some packages took upwards of an hour apiece to grade. Parents complained that many of the packages seemed like busywork. The entire effort was overturned by the legislature before a single graduating class had been assessed. Failed efforts like this make it easy to build a case for straightforward standards and assessments.

5. Students come to believe that schools, not they themselves, are responsible for ensuring they graduate.

When customization becomes the norm, students may expect that every aspect of learning will be engaging. This can have several side effects:

- Without clear standards, assignments can quickly turn into creative or engaging events that fail to embed, or meet, solid learning goals.

Many teachers have told me that working with their state standards helped them realize that many of their favorite lessons or projects didn't result in much learning even if students enjoyed them.

- If students (and parents) believe that learning should follow a child's interests and passions, then they may mistake the hard work of mastering a skill or becoming an expert as work that is too boring and therefore not worthy of their time. They may not realize, for example, that becoming a fashion designer requires mathematics skills or that real writers revise and revise and revise.

- Learning gets "dumbed down" so that students don't have to struggle too much.

Think way back to Pete's team in Chapter 2. Customization requires leveraging the polarity of *Student Responsibility AND Educator Responsibility.*

TRANSFORMING THE POLARITY

Note how, having experienced the downside of customization, it would be easy to think of the upside of standardization as the "solution." Yet if we do this to the neglect of the customization pole in implementing the CCSS, we will get its downside as well.

Both "sides" might draw on the quote from Winston Churchill, "Those who fail to learn from history are doomed to repeat it." The United States has several years of experience with state standards that it can study to improve its chances of success with national standards. We've also tried a customized approach, with failed "open school" initiatives in the 1970s as prime examples.

Early Warnings of Overfocusing on Standardization to the Neglect of Customization

A. Increase in time spent on test preparation for specific content.

B. Increase in teacher questioning and assessment for facts versus those that require reasoning, analysis, or synthesis.

C. Increase in including teacher progress on pacing schedules in their evaluation.

D. Decrease in controversial issues in curriculum such as racism and immigration—multicultural teaching pushed out.

E. Increase in test and curriculum companies, not educators, determining what is taught and assessed.

Early Warnings of Overfocusing on Customized Education to the Neglect of Standardization

A. Increase in percentage of college freshmen needing remedial classes in college.

B. Decrease in students finishing high school in four years.

C. Decrease in teacher adherence to an articulated vertical curriculum that guarantees students a basic education.

D. Increase in graduation requirements that students can easily fulfill well before year twelve.

E. Decrease in percentage of students who take higher-level courses in all core content areas.

STEPS TO MOVING BEYOND POLARIZATION

The CCSS *are* being implemented, so this is a perfect environment for considering how to incorporate the values of the customization pole in order to avoid the vicious cycle that an overfocus on standardization could bring on. Implementing the CCSS won't be easy. Killion (2012) warns that short-term results cannot be the focus.

> Implementing Common Core Standards requires a long view, one that extends out at least a decade or more. Planning for implementation must include rigorous, ongoing assessment of how each action contributes to the goal of every student being college and career ready. It must include regularly scheduled opportunities, at least annually, to redefine the problem, solutions, and implementation strategies based on data. It requires that the plan not constrain adaptations that are needed to achieve results in circumstances with unique needs. Most importantly, it requires increased focus on professional learning among those responsible for implementing the change.

Further, we need to keep a laser focus on the fact that the CCSS haven't actually been tested. Many researchers do not believe that standards have any power to improve student achievement; after all, we've had state standards for years, yet scores on the National Assessment of Educational Progress have remained relatively flat. There is no correlation between which states have had the most rigorous standards and where students make the most progress (Brown Center, 2012). Why would we expect that common standards would have any more influence on actual student learning?

Remember the school superintendent from *Hard Times?* We've tried this reform before, and the pendulum swings back when the cycle gets too vicious. If we don't learn from past reform troubles, we're doomed to repeat them. Leveraging this polarity is in itself an *action step* to ensure this doesn't happen.

HIGH-LEVERAGE ACTION STEPS THAT ACCESS THE UPSIDE OF BOTH POLES

A. Develop alternative authentic assessments.

Remember that the consortiums responsible for developing assessments for the CCSS are already cutting back on performance items and are admitting that tests used to track progress may not be useful for informing instruction. This opens a dangerous window for the tests to become too oriented toward facts and procedures. If testing time and costs prevent the inclusion of the kinds of rich tasks that ensure our students are also learning higher-order skills, then efforts must continue on alternative ways of making sure we are measuring these, perhaps at the school level rather than the national level. Littky (2011) pleads,

> The new core curriculum and dependence on standardized tests will only make it harder to improve the schools and systems that educate our youth. I am all for accountability, but as long as we use inaccurate measures of students' growth, we will never truly improve the way we educate our youth. We measure what we value. If we believe that curiosity, moral courage, application of knowledge, and perseverance are as important as reading, writing, and speaking, then let's create schools that allow students to learn those qualities, and let us measure them. (p. 109)

B. Establish clear goals or concepts to be taught, but allow multiple paths for reaching those goals.

A huge temptation with CCSS is standardizing more and more of how teachers run their classrooms. We have yet to find a silver bullet in education, but that hasn't stopped policymakers from assuming that what worked well in one place will work just as well in every environment. The failure of the Reading First initiative, where billions of dollars were poured into schools to implement supposedly research-based methods yet resulted in minimal improvement in literacy, is one of the more recent examples.

Setting clear standards and goals, yet allowing multiple pathways, can avoid the traps of standardizing everything by allowing teachers to customize content to meet the interests and talents of individual students, local issues, their own passions, and more.

C. Invest in professional development needed for teachers to effectively teach content and process standards in differentiated classrooms.

When Schmidt and Burroughs (2012) surveyed teachers, they found that less than half of elementary teachers felt prepared to teach the CCSS. Extensive teacher training will be required, as Killion (2012) indicates, to assist teachers so that lessons

- target the standards,
- incorporate twenty-first-century skills of independent learning, inquiry, collaboration, reasoning, and problem solving,
- differentiate for student ability, learning needs, interests, and culture, and
- build in formative assessments that inform instruction.

Of course, these abilities have always been at the heart of what helps students learn—and all but the first are required to deliver an excellent customized education as well.

Studies of professional development indicate that the kind of professional development for teachers to master these skills would involve at least forty to one hundred hours of training, be content focused, bring teachers from the same school together for collaboration, and actively engage them. Even when these criteria are met, the size effect on student achievement is small (Loveless, 2012). In other words, investing in the CCSS needs to go far beyond curriculum and assessment.

D. Limit standards to the number that can reasonably be taught, with clear agreement on power standards that are enduring, leverage-able, and essential.

Refer back to the need for a viable curriculum. This is essential for the CCSS, especially since the assessments connected with them will be used to determine who graduates and how teachers are evaluated in many states. The tendency of many schools to focus on standardization alone makes it very important to develop a guaranteed and viable curriculum to support Customization AND Standardization.

ACTION STEP THAT SUPPORTS THE UPSIDE OF STANDARDIZATION

E. Focus on learning, not on tools.

Alberti (2012) points out that the tendency is to rush to purchase new curriculum, software, programs, or other tools to support the changes before we understand at a deep level what the changes really mean. She suggests focusing on a few key shifts in the standards first, learning how to best help students acquire the new learning and skills they encompass so that we can concentrate on what might have the biggest impact even as we experience how the CCSS will change our classrooms. These include the shift to more informational texts, building academic vocabulary, basing writing on texts, and using the mathematical processes.

ACTION STEP THAT SUPPORTS THE UPSIDE OF CUSTOMIZATION

E. Ensure that programs allow for development of talent diversity.

Whether we pass laws to ensure that all students learn about the arts, fitness, computer programming, cooking, woodworking, and so on, or create schools where students are truly encouraged to try as many areas as interest them, and continue to engage them even as they master the CCSS, we need to make sure that dancers know they are dancers, inventors know they like to tinker, writers find their voice, budding pediatricians know there is a soft side to sciences, and so on.

Consider the following "gedanken experiment," a tool physicists use to test theories by imagining apparatus or circumstances, as Einstein did for the theory of relativity:

What would you have wanted as a child?

A focused curriculum handed to you or one that made room for your interests?

Six hours of academics or academics balanced with arts, music, and a chance to learn how to wire a house or make a pie or invent a new kind of fuel or imagine a universe?

Test prep or projects that challenged you and allowed you to showcase your unique talents?

The point of a gedanken experiment is that you can "see" the truth when more formal research isn't helpful. We don't need research; our

Polarity Thinking Map for Learning Standards

Meaningful

Action Steps

A. Develop alternative authentic assessments.

B. Establish clear goals or concepts to be taught, but allow multiple paths for reaching those goals.

C. Invest in professional development needed for teachers to effectively teach content and process standards in differentiated classrooms.

D. Limit standards to the number that can be reasonably taught, with clear agreement on power standards that are enduring, leverage-able, and essential.

E. Focus on learning and not on tools.

Values = positive results from focusing on the left pole

1. High school diploma requirements equate to graduates having learned the standardized content required by colleges and employers.

2. Standardization allows for economies of scale for textbooks, assessments, lessons, support materials, teacher training, and professional development.

3. The CCSS allow for efficient measurement and comparison to ensure that all students receive the content they need.

4. The CCSS with their incorporation of rigor and processes ensure that a student's education will involve both content and processes.

5. All students need a breadth of knowledge in content areas in order to analyze and apply it.

Focus on Standardization   and

Early Warnings

A. Increase in time spent on test preparation for specific content.

B. Increase in teacher questioning and assessment for facts versus those that require reasoning, analysis, or synthesis.

C. Increase in including teacher progress on pacing schedules in their evaluation.

D. Decrease in controversial issues in curriculum such as racism and immigration—multicultural teaching pushed out.

E. Increase in test and curriculum companies, not educators, determining what is taught and assessed.

1. Businesses and politicians are deciding what is best for students.

2. Standards lead to concerns over coverage of curriculum and limit teacher discretion to meet student interests and needs.

3. Standards result in an emphasis on test preparation.

4. Tests seldom capture twenty-first-century skills, at least not with efficiency.

5. Students may not have the chance to explore fine arts, hands-on trades, or other areas that could become the basis for careers.

Fears = negative results from overfocusing on the left pole to the neglect of the right pole

Student

Source: Map template copyright by Polarity Partnerships, LLC.

Diploma

Values = positive results from focusing on the right pole

1. Customization allows children to graduate ready to make the most of their unique gifts and talents.

2. Customization allows for discretion based on teacher expertise, local culture, and community involvement.

3. Customization allows students to grow at their own pace.

4. Customization embeds twenty-first-century skills.

5. Customized education is more likely to produce excitement about learning, which is key to academic success.

Focus on Customization

and

1. Students graduate without specific content knowledge and skills that colleges and employers say they need.

2. We can't compare student achievement across schools.

3. Students aren't able to track progress toward gaining the knowledge and skills they need for chosen education or career paths.

4. Customization is expensive and time-consuming.

5. Students come to believe that schools, not they themselves, are responsible for ensuring they graduate.

Fears = negative results from overfocusing on the right pole to the neglect of the left pole

Failure

Action Steps

A. Develop alternative authentic assessments.

B. Establish clear goals or concepts to be taught, but allow multiple paths for reaching those goals.

C. Invest in professional development needed for teachers to effectively teach content and process standards in differentiated classrooms.

D. Limit the standards to the number that can reasonably be taught, with clear agreement on power standards that are enduring, leverage-able, and essential.

E. Ensure that programs allow for development of talent diversity.

Early Warnings

A. Increase in percentage of college freshmen needing remedial classes in college.

B. Decrease in students finishing high school in four years.

C. Decrease in teacher adherence to an articulated vertical curriculum that guarantees students a basic education.

D. Increase in graduation requirements that students can easily fulfill well before year twelve.

E. Decrease in percentage of students who take higher-level courses in all core content areas.

minds can tell us that we need to make the most of the CCSS by unleashing the positive power of this polarity.

REFLECTION

1. Has your team worked with the concept of "power standards," identifying those that are enduring, can be leveraged for other learning, and are essential for the next level of instruction (Reeves, 2005)? The idea is to narrow what is to be taught so that all students can master these power standards within the school year—a "guaranteed and viable curriculum." Work collaboratively with the grade-level standards in a content area and apply these criteria. Often, this exercise provides both focus and a sense of efficacy that there will be time to cover the essentials.

2. The four major issues covered in Chapters 3 through 6 all involve polarities related to Part (freedom, uniqueness, initiative, customization) AND Whole (equality, connectedness, synergy, standardization). These are always part of distribution systems such as education and other public goods. Can you think of other "solutions" in education that aren't working because they are actually part of these polarities?

Part III

Putting the SMALL Polarity Thinking Tools to Work

7 Introducing Polarity Thinking to Your Team

Are there issues, dilemmas, or disagreements that keep returning to the table in your learning community? *All* the following examples can be considered through the lens of polarities:

> Should students be penalized for turning in assignments after the deadline?
>
> Is allowing students to retake tests a good policy?
>
> When should students be sent to the office because of behavior problems?
>
> Should all teachers be using the same lesson plans?

These may bring to mind at least a dozen other topics you've heard discussed in district offices, the teachers' lounge, and elsewhere. While Part II showed how polarity thinking can help us sort out some of the most puzzling policy issues of our time, Part III provides tools that you can start using immediately for these day-to-day dilemmas and for bigger strategic decisions as well.

Note that working with these tools involves another universal polarity, that of *Training for Work AND Doing the Work.* As shown in Figure 7.1, too little time spent studying how polarities work can result in mistakes that undermine the processes. Yet getting started with polarities means reclaiming energy currently being lost on trying to solve problems that are actually polarities. These next chapters are designed to allow you to use polarity thinking well right away. Several tools can help you facilitate effectively and thus learn by doing the work.

Figure 7.1 Learning AND Doing Polarity

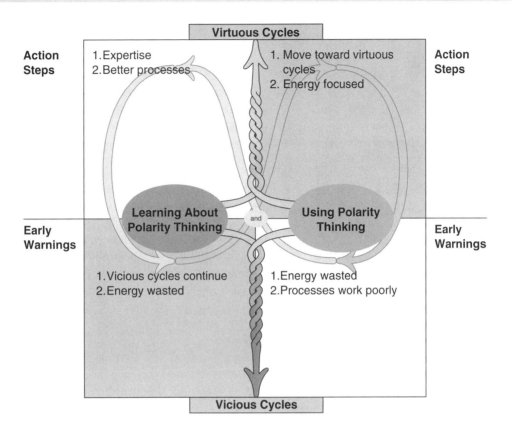

Source: Map template copyright by Polarity Partnerships, LLC.

ACTIVITY 7.1: A FORTY-FIVE-MINUTE INTRODUCTION TO LEVERAGING DIFFERENCES

The first item in your toolkit is a presentation, complete with activities, to introduce your learning community to working with polarities. The following slides with facilitation instructions are available at www.corwin .com/positivepower. *Note: This is written as a script. Many presenters, though, will feel more comfortable using their own words to convey the ideas.*

Objectives:

- To introduce a team to the three main steps of the Polarity Approach to Continuity and Transformation (PACT)
- To provide a concrete experience by mapping a common polarity

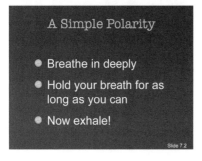

Materials:

- Projector and screen, flipchart markers, chart paper. Prepare four chart pages, labeling them with one each of the following:
  - Positive results of caring for self
  - Positive results of caring for others
  - Negative results of overfocusing on self to the neglect of others
  - Negative results of overfocusing on others to the neglect of self

- Place these around the room in an arrangement that imitates the four quadrants of a polarity map.

Note: The slide presentation contains a blank polarity map. Some groups input all the data from the four flipcharts on the Care of Self AND Care of Others exercise. The map can then be used to capture the group's ideas for action steps in the last segment of the exercise.

1. Introduction

[Slide 7.1] Have you noticed how often we discuss the same issues over and over? Or we implement a strategy, only to change it the next year? Today, we're going to look at a set of tools that will help us recognize when we need to solve a problem AND when we're dealing with an ongoing tension where there are two truths that need each other over time.

[Slide 7.2] Let me give a quick example. Breathe in deeply. Keep breathing in. Now hold your breath. Hold it. *Note: Hold your own breath for at least five seconds.*

Now exhale!

[Slide 7.3] Which is better? Inhaling or exhaling? Neither, right? Our bodies need both—and they're interdependent. Inhaling and exhaling are an example of a polarity.

Note that inhaling and exhaling are an energy system. [Slide 7.4] We can illustrate it with an infinity loop. When we were holding our breath, our bodies started signaling "Too much carbon dioxide!" so we exhaled. Pretty soon our bodies demand that we inhale to get more oxygen. That's how polarities work. Each pole makes a valuable contribution to the system. And each pole has its

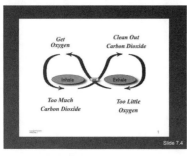

limits. These limits become pronounced when we overfocus on one pole to the neglect of the other, as you experienced with inhaling just now.

You've worked with polarities your whole life: Individual AND Community, Tradition AND Change. [Slide 7.5] This book, *Unleashing the Positive Power of Differences,* looks at how these tools can frame some of the big issues in education, such as meeting children's academic needs AND children's other needs. And helping students master math algorithms AND creatively solve math problems. Plus, there are tools for helping teams formulate a plan on local issues such as how we collaborate, lead, make curriculum decisions, and so on.

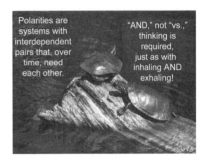

So let's clarify just a couple definitions and then dive into trying out a tool. [Slide 7.6] Polarities are interdependent pairs that, over time, need each other. Just like these turtles here. Yes, they can trade off being at the tip of the log, and one can even disappear for a while into the water, but over the long term they need each other. They require "and" instead of "versus" thinking. Note that some issues *do* require versus thinking; often, they're problems that can be solved once and for all. We're dealing with messier systems here— polarities that require a different way of thinking.

[Slide 7.7] Why do we care about polarities? Because we can reclaim all the energy that's wasted on arguments, resistance, policy swings, and so on, if we learn to start with three steps that organize our collective wisdom. We need to *see* the polarity, *map* the results of focusing on each pole, and *leverage* the energy of both sides to move us all toward a greater purpose. Let's see what each one of those steps involves.

[Slide 7.8] Step 1 is seeing the polarity. How do we know whether something is a problem to be solved once and for all or a polarity where we need to identify the value of each position? Four key questions can help us decide:

- Is it ongoing? Like breathing?
- Are the alternatives interdependent? Like inhaling and exhaling?
- Over time, are both poles or solutions needed?
- Finally, if we focus on only one upside, will we eventually get that

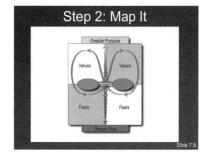

pole's downside as well and thus undermine what we'll term our *greater purpose statement* or GPS?

[Slide 7.9] Step 2 is *mapping* the polarity system. Now we've embedded that infinity loop within a map that helps us better understand each pole. We identify a GPS—the motivation that convinces people at each pole that working together will be worth the hard work involved. We also identify a *deeper fear*—what might happen if we fail to work together. Then we identify the positive results, or values, of each pole. And we identify the fears, or negative results of overfocusing on each pole to the neglect of the other.

The map helps us consider how we got to where we are. What policies, decisions, or viewpoints influenced our current approach to these issues and any current issues?

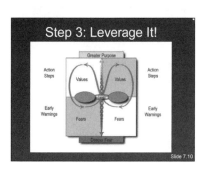

[Slide 7.10] Finally, in Step 3, we *leverage* the polarity to get as much of the positive impact of each pole as we can. To do this, we identify *early warning signs* that we can measure. These will let us know if we're focusing too much on one of the poles. And we develop *action steps*, the strategies and practices we can implement to get the best of each side. Our goal? To use those action steps to stay in a virtuous cycle, as shown here with the infinity loop mostly encompassing the upper half of the map. We're trying to avoid a vicious cycle that would spiral us down toward our fears. And here's an important truth: If we overfocus on a pole, we get the downside of *both* poles. That's why the process for leveraging polarities is worth the work.

[Slide 7.11] Before I get you up on your feet to map a polarity, let's look at one more example: *Activity AND Rest.* We all know we need to be both physically and mentally active. It adds energy to everything we do. But we also need rest. Let's say that we choose to exercise as an action step for

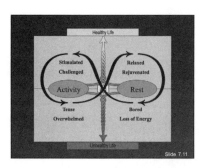

gaining the upside of the activity pole. Turn to a partner. Come up with one positive result from exercise and one from rest. Then list a negative result from too much exercise and one from too much rest. [Allow people to brainstorm for about ninety seconds and then ask for some examples].

I had you complete that little exercise to clarify that we're familiar with polarities. However, recognizing them and handling them well are two different things, aren't they? We all know people who overtrained, injured themselves, and had to take a break from their favorite sport *and* we know others who get too little exercise and have trouble climbing a set of stairs. Let's walk through the full process for another familiar polarity to see the power of transforming how we work with it.

2. Exercise: Care of Self AND Care of Others

[Slide 7.12] In just a moment I'll ask you to move to one of the flipchart papers around the room. Because we're all in a caring profession where the focus is on meeting the needs of children, leveraging *Care of Self AND Care of Others* can be difficult, can't it! We're going to work together to map the positive results and negative results of focusing on each pole. You can choose any place to start, but try to form equal-sized groups. In your groups, you'll have two minutes to brainstorm items for your chart and record them. Choose someone to record who is willing to report to the larger group. Any questions?

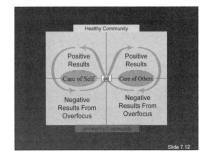

Instructions for the Rest of the Exercise:

1. After each group has finished brainstorming, ask everyone to gather around the chart for Positive Results of Care of Self. Ask someone from that group to read the items. Comment that the rich list of positive outcomes draws people toward this pole. However, as wonderful as it all sounds, if we overfocus on any pole, we get its downside.

2. Have the group gather around the Negative Effects of Care of Self and have someone from the group read the chart. Ask how the group feels after hearing the list. Comment that we often then see the other pole as the solution—here, Care of Others—because it is the natural self-correction in an interdependent system.

3. Move to the Positive Results of Care of Others. Ask someone to read the group's items. Again, comment that an overfocus will always bring the downside.

4. Move the group to the Negative Effects of Care of Others and have someone read the group's list. Comment that once again the opposite pole can seem like a solution. With or without care, we will continue to move through the infinity loop. Circumstances change where we need to be, such as when a family member is sick or if we ourselves are sick. However, fighting between the poles as if

they are an either/or choice or choosing one pole as a solution will lead to a vicious cycle where too many people have unmet needs!

5. Ask everyone to form a circle. Have the four recorders bring the charts with them and stand in the middle, in their proper "quadrants," back-to-back and facing the outside of the circle.

6. Ask the two "negative results" recorders to read their items one by one, alternating and taking a step toward the bottom of the circle each time they read one. State that you're having them demonstrate the spiraling down of a vicious cycle.

7. Then ask the two "positive results" recorders to do the same, stepping toward the top of the circle. State that you're having them demonstrate the power of determining the action steps that will capture the best of both poles.

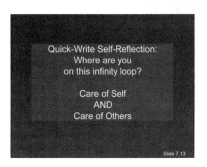

8. Ask participants to return to their seats. [Slide 7.13]. Have them do a quick-write on where they'd place themselves on the infinity loop of Care of Self AND Care of Others. How well are they handling this polarity? Are they moving toward the upside or downside of a pole? Are they in a virtuous or vicious cycle? Give them a couple of minutes and then ask for brief comments about their reflections.

9. Split participants into two groups. Have one side brainstorm measurable early warning signs of overfocus on care of self and record them on a piece of flipchart paper while the other group does the same for overfocus on care of others.

10. Finally, ask everyone to talk with a partner about action steps your learning community might take to help everyone better manage Care of Self AND Care of Others. Record these on flipchart paper. Or enter them, and the early warning signs, into the map provided at the end of this chapter (available at www.corwin.com/positive-power.).

3. Closing Remarks

We'll be employing these tools again and again to try to use our limited collaborative time as well as we can. When we choose to work with polarities and see two points of view, we expand our own knowledge of an issue, we better understand how someone else can hold a different opinion, and we can find far more common ground and ways of working together than we suspected were possible. We can even use these tools to help our students think at higher levels. [Slide 7.14] As F. Scott Fitzgerald put it, "The test of a first-rate intelligence is the ability to hold two opposed ideas in the mind at the same time, and still retain the ability to function" (*Columbia World of Quotations*, 2013). We can leverage our collective intelligence by using polarity thinking to create better policies, strategies, and processes for our students and ourselves.

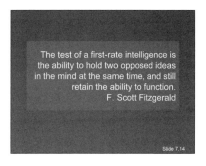

REFLECTION

1. This introduction is fairly straightforward, but the following actions may help ensure that you and your learning community are ready. Which ones might benefit you?

   ○ Reread Chapters 1 and 2 to review the basic concepts of polarity thinking

   ○ Use the slides to explain polarity thinking to a peer who is unfamiliar with the concept. What questions does he or she raise? Are you ready to answer them?

   ○ Practice creating a Care of Self AND Care of Others map on your own to better familiarize yourself with the process. You'll also be better able to prompt any group that isn't sure of the directions.

2. I chose Care of Self AND Care of Others as a starting place because teaching is a helping profession and many educators struggle to leverage this polarity well. Participants can develop a good map from their own experiences; it requires no research or outside resources. However, some groups may wish to tackle an issue that is more closely related to their own current goals or dilemmas. Feel free to do so, but consider the following:

   ○ Does it require significant content knowledge? Often, it is difficult to pay attention to a new process if the content is also new or complex.

   ○ Is it controversial? Beginning with a neutral polarity can help people grasp the usefulness of the tools instead of worrying about outcomes from the process.

   ○ Can it be done relatively quickly? If your group is unfamiliar with one or both of the poles or with how a polarity applies to them, it may take longer to map.

   ○ Have you been focusing on one pole? If, for example, your organization has spent considerable time recently in training on professional collaboration and that training was well received, group members may struggle to articulate the positive results of independent work for the polarity Independence AND Collaboration.

Polarity Thinking Map

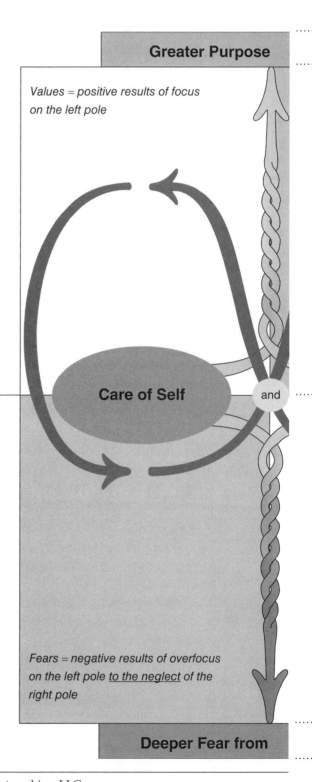

Action Steps

How will we gain or maintain the positive results from focusing on this left pole? What? Who? By when? Measures?

A.

Early Warnings

Measurable indicators (things you can count) that will let you know that you are getting into the downside of this left pole.

A.

Greater Purpose

Values = positive results of focus on the left pole

Care of Self   and

Fears = negative results of overfocus on the left pole to the neglect of the right pole

Deeper Fear from

Statement (GPS)

Values = positive results of focus on the right pole

Action Steps

How will we gain or maintain the positive results from focusing on this right pole? What? Who? By when? Measures?

A.

and — **Care of Others**

Early Warnings

Measurable indicators (things you can count) that will let you know that you are getting into the downside of this right pole.

A.

Fears = negative results of overfocus on the right pole <u>to the neglect</u> of the left pole

lack of optimization

8 Guiding Your Team Through Polarity Thinking

O ne of my favorite differentiation strategies for mathematics is finding tasks that are rich enough to require collaboration *and* that can be approached in multiple ways. If carefully chosen, these tasks allow students with different levels of knowledge to engage at their own level of understanding. Frequently, students are successful with such problems when they first work with others of similar ability and then participate in a discussion about approaches that other groups used (Fosnot & Dolk, 2002).

During the break at a workshop where I'd introduced this strategy, two teachers approached me and said, "We've been told that we must *always* use heterogeneous groups so that our struggling students can benefit from high-level thinking. Are you saying that grouping by ability is a good practice? It was so much easier to teach when we did that."

I asked whether in the past their "low" groups had been given different tasks. "Of course—they couldn't do the harder ones on their own. Now we are supposed to 'scaffold,' but that means all our attention goes to guiding some students through work that's over their heads."

I used the age-old pizza/fractions problem to explain multiple points of entry. "If students only know about sharing fairly, they can solve it through the idea of 'One for you, one for me, one for you . . .'" and so on. If they know how to divide fractions, they can solve it using a more advanced strategy. In a heterogeneous group, those who know how to divide fractions will most likely take over. In homogenous groups, each group can do rigorous problem solving at their level of understanding.

"But you can't stop there. A teacher has to carefully choose which groups will present their solutions, and in what order, so that everyone is exposed to more complex thinking. Further, it takes practice—as long as six weeks of guiding these discussions—until students are comfortable asking clarifying questions, admitting that they don't understand something, and helping their classmates analyze how mistakes were made. It isn't ability grouping versus mixed-ability grouping; it's creating structures that gain the benefits of both ways of grouping."

I've seen this all too often. Schools that used to group by ability experienced the downside of tracking, such as labeling, elitism, or "lower" students becoming bored with repetitive work. They decide to end tracking and do away with all forms of homogeneous grouping in the process. Without extensive training in differentiation and built-in opportunities for students to reach mastery at different paces, both of which would involve at least some homogeneous grouping, the school will eventually experience the downside of heterogeneous grouping. And some homogeneous grouping will be seen as the "solution."

Chances are that you've been part of a discussion on this tough issue. How, or whether, we group students is often approached as a problem to solve when in fact it is just one question in the midst of a set of universal polarities that affect many aspects of education. These include the following:

Part AND Whole

Individual AND Community

Focusing on the Needs of All Students AND Focusing on the Needs of the Subgroups

Freedom AND Equity

Uniqueness AND Connectedness

Homogeneous Grouping AND Heterogeneous Grouping fits right in. Any of these let us look at the needs of all students, whether they are succeeding, struggling, or somewhere in the middle. How do we meet individual needs within a system that must also work for the good of all and that has limited resources? Treating it as a problem to solve often quickly brings the negative results of overfocus on one pole, doesn't it! The rest of this chapter provides an exercise for mapping and transforming this issue. Although a sample map is included at the end of this chapter, your site will most likely benefit from building its own—especially the early warning signs and action steps—to fit your particular circumstances. This exercise can be used for other polarities as well.

THE FULL PACT PROCESS

In building full maps that leverage key polarities, you will want to use the full five-step Polarity Assessment for Continuity AND Transformation (PACT) process. In the last chapter, *assess* and *learn* were wrapped in with *leveraging*, but the process becomes even more powerful when you consciously take time with these steps: see, map, assess, learn, *and* leverage, the SMALL process, defined back on page 14.

Steps 3 and 4, assess and learn, involve considering how well your team or organization is currently leveraging the polarity. Appendix A is a case study that illustrates how a formal, automated assessment, with twelve to fifteen questions, can be used.

Or the instructions below include a quick "arrow method" to assess how people view your team's current leveraging of this polarity. Is it a virtuous circle, or is it more out of balance? The quick-write process on page 136 (Chapter 7) can also ready participants for a constructive assess/learn discussion.

ACTIVITY 8.1: MAPPING BY MOVING THROUGH A POLARITY

Objectives:

- To provide a model map for a very practical issue that teachers face all the time.
- To introduce another methodology for mapping and transforming a polarity for the issues that are currently most acute for your learning community. The instructions walk you through this particular polarity, but the process can be used for many, many polarities of your own choosing.

Time Frame:

Allow at least sixty minutes to map the positive and negative results of each pole and identify early warning signs. Developing valuable action steps may or may not involve researching strategies.

Note: This exercise assumes that participants have already worked through the introduction to polarities provided in Chapter 7.

Number of Participants and Adjustments for a Larger Group:

Ideally, participants will work in four groups with three or four people in each group. If your group is larger than sixteen, plan for building more than one map—four groups working on one map and the other four groups working on the second map.

Materials Needed:

Flipchart paper and markers

For each map . . .

- Prepare four charts using large sheets of chart paper with one each labeled as follows:

  1. Positive results of homogeneous grouping

  2. Positive results of heterogeneous grouping

  3. Negative results of overfocus on homogeneous grouping to the neglect of heterogeneous grouping

  4. Negative results of overfocus on heterogeneous grouping to the neglect of homogeneous grouping

- Arrange the room so that each titled sheet of chart paper can be posted on a wall, with the first sheet, "Positive results of homogenous grouping," on the far left and the fourth sheet, "Negative results of overfocusing on heterogeneous grouping to the neglect of homogeneous grouping," on the far right (see the following diagram). Allow space for participants to "move through" the mapping process. For example, if, with two dozen people, you'll be creating two maps, on one wall of the room have a set of four sheets of titled chart paper and on the other wall have an identical set of four sheets of titled chart paper. Use flipchart stands and round tables as substitutes if the wall space is not available.

Facilitation Instructions:

1. Positive results of homogeneous grouping	2. Positive results of heterogeneous grouping	3. Negative results of overfocus on homogeneous grouping to the neglect of heterogeneous grouping	4. Negative results of overfocus on heterogeneous grouping to the neglect of homogeneous grouping

1. Introduce the topic of Homogenous AND Heterogeneous Grouping by citing an example that will be familiar to your group where you've seen a policy swing on this issue. Examples include inclusion and pullout programs; policies that involved tracking students; reading ability groups of the past that had names such as Owls, Robins, and Bluebirds; switching from a variety of high school elective English classes to English 9, 10, 11, and 12; and so on.

2. Explain that there are five steps to leveraging a polarity and that you will be walking through each of the steps (consider listing these steps on a whiteboard or chart):

   Step 1: See it

   Step 2: Map it

   Step 3: Assess

   Step 4: Learn

   Step 5: Leverage it

3. *Step 1: See it.* Let the group discuss the four questions that help determine whether the issue is a problem to solve or a polarity that needs transformation.

   a. Is it ongoing? Have we seen practices swing back and forth?

   b. Are the alternatives interdependent? Like inhaling and exhaling?

   c. Over time, do we need both solutions?

   d. Have past attempts to deal with this issue led to frustration, anger, divisiveness, and wasted time?

4. *Step 2: Map it.* Divide participants into groups of three or four in any manner you wish and assign each group one of the four titled flipcharts as a place to start. Give the following instructions.

   a. Each group will have a chance to add to each sheet/quadrant of the polarity map.

   b. They will spend two minutes at each quadrant station, brainstorming potential results in that quadrant, adding to the lists begun by other groups. You will signal when the time is up. All groups will move to the next chart at the same time.

c. They will move through the charts in the number in which they are ordered, with the group starting at "4. Negative results of overfocus on heterogeneous . . ." moving to "1. Positive results of homogeneous" and so on.

d. When all the groups have had a chance to work at each station, they will remain at their last station and, using a new piece of chart paper, develop a list of the four or five most important ideas that seem to capture the themes of the majority of the statements, combining or rewording as necessary.

e. Post the four final charts on one of the walls so that the polarity map is replicated with each quadrant in its proper place. Post a

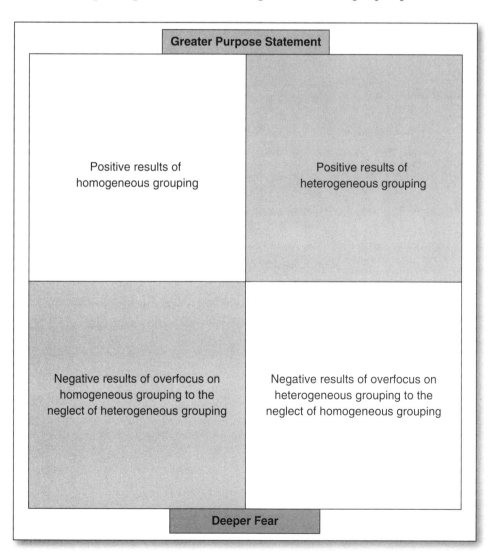

half-sheet of blank chart paper at the center top of the polarity map and label it "Greater Purpose Statement" and a half-sheet of blank chart paper labeled "Deeper Fear" at the center bottom of the map (see the diagram on the previous page). Alternatively, you can capture the information in a presentation slide such as the one given in the Chapter 7 presentation slides available at www.corwin.com/positivepower.

f. *Deeper fear.* Ask participants to turn to a partner and discuss the question, What is our deeper fear about this issue? What are we afraid might happen if students aren't grouped in an optimal way, whatever we decide that might be? Record their ideas on the deeper fear sheet. With groups larger than a dozen, ask everyone to share their ideas at their tables and then facilitate a large-group discussion, consolidating the ideas into statements that can be written on the deeper fear chart.

Note: My suggested deeper fear is "Some students' needs aren't met." Feel free to start by suggesting this to the group and asking for modifications, if you have concerns about time. Push to avoid generalities like "full potential."

g. *Greater purpose statement.* Use the same process for identifying a greater purpose statement (GPS). Remind the group that the GPS identifies, "Why is it worthwhile for us to work together when we have differences of opinion on this issue?" You may also use my suggested GPS (or your own version), "Meet Needs of Diverse Learners," if your time is limited. If you decide to provide a GPS, have participants do a two-minute quick-write about their reaction to the GPS. Then ask if any phrasing changes or concerns come to mind. Building buy-in for the GPS often helps increase enthusiasm for the mapping process and commitment to the final map. Record the finalized greater purpose statement(s) on the chart labeled "Greater Purpose."

Note: Sometimes while creating the content of the four quadrants, groups will notice that the same phrase will be included in both of the top two quadrant sheets, such as, "Some students challenged to learn," or the bottom two quadrant sheets, such as, "Some students bored by instruction methodology." When you see the same or a similar idea in both the top two sheets, consider that as a hint to the group that the greater purpose might be the statement that is contained in both of those quadrants—for example, "Students challenged to learn." The same would be true of similar statements in the bottom two quadrants, indicating a common deepest fear—for example, "Instructional methodology fails to engage students."

h. Discuss the "map it" step using some or all of the following questions:

    i. For which quadrants was it easiest to develop the content? For what reasons?

    ii. For which quadrants was it most difficult to develop the content? Again, for what reasons?

    iii. What insights did you gain about student groupings as you completed the four sheets?

    iv. Would it have been better to create the greater purpose and deepest fear statements before generating the content of the four quadrants? Explain your response.

    v. What questions or concerns do you have about mapping a polarity?

5. *Step 3: Assess where you are.*

a. Draw the infinity loop on the charts showing how groups move from one chart to the next (see diagram below).

b. Ask your group to consider the following questions as a way of assessing your group's progress in leveraging the Homogeneous Grouping AND Heterogeneous Grouping polarity:

    i. *Arrow assessment.* Where is your learning community/ building/district on the infinity loop of this polarity—more toward heterogeneous or homogeneous grouping? Think about where you would place a "trend arrow" within the infinity loop right now. Would it be trending from the downside of the heterogeneous toward the upside of homogeneous or from the downside of homogeneous to the upside of heterogeneous? Is it more of a virtuous cycle, getting the upside of both, or a vicious cycle due to an overfocus on one pole to the neglect of the other?

    ii. Would different stakeholders choose different positions on the infinity loop? For example, parents of gifted students? Parents of students with special needs? Classroom teachers? Specialists? Administrators? The students? *Note: Consider having participants form groups such as administrators, classroom teachers, specialists, paraprofessionals, and so on. Give each group an index card on which you've drawn an arrow. Have them come to consensus and then place their arrow on the infinity loop on the wall.*

    iii. Where were we last year, two years ago, five years ago?

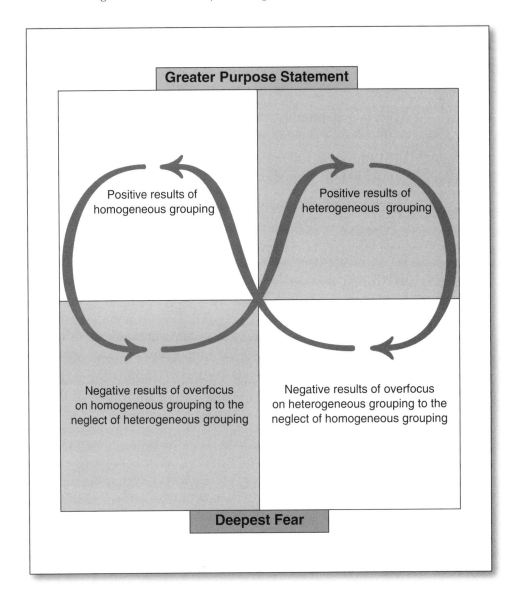

c. Discuss the anticipated flow from one pole to the other and consider it a healthy self-correction. If your team is new to working with polarities, framing this reality may be useful with comments similar to the following: Because this is truly a polarity, classrooms, schools, and other systems experience movement through the infinity loop. For example, if when overfocusing on heterogeneous grouping, teachers insist that all students are always reading the same books, eventually a certain percentage of students or parents will request independent study or literature circles, moving the system more toward homogeneous groups. If a class emphasizes homogeneous groups, eventually the feeling of community dwindles without shared experiences or because of hints of elitism. We either continue to solve these "problems" as they arise, or we consciously plan to get as much of the upside of both poles as we can. For example, we might see in the same classroom some materials being used by all students and some materials being used to match individual students' abilities and interests. Our goal with this step is to learn from where we've been and how we got to where we are to leverage what will work best for us and avoid what could spiral us down toward our deeper fear.

6. *Step 4: Learn.* Use the following questions to discuss how your group can learn from your past and anticipate the future:

   a. Considering our last discussion where we assessed our current position, what policies, strategies, or beliefs moved us to where we are on the infinity loop?

   b. Have we overcorrected? Undercorrected? What is working? What needs to change?

   c. How can we achieve some of the benefits of the other pole while holding on to some of the good aspects of the pole we are now embracing?

   Building this common understanding of the present allows groups to strategically plan to anticipate the downsides of each pole and take actions to capitalize on the benefits of each pole.

7. *Step 5: Leverage.*

   a. Cut two sheets of chart paper vertically in half. Label two of the sheets "Early Warning Signs" and the other two sheets "Action Steps." Post the sheets on the wall according to the diagram that follows.

      Alternatively, cut chart paper into strips, a half dozen strips per sheet. Have participants write their ideas for early warning signs and action steps on these strips so they can be posted on the wall and moved to reflect similarities or priorities.

   b. *Early warning signs.* Brainstorm early warning signs that might indicate one pole is being overemphasized to the neglect of the

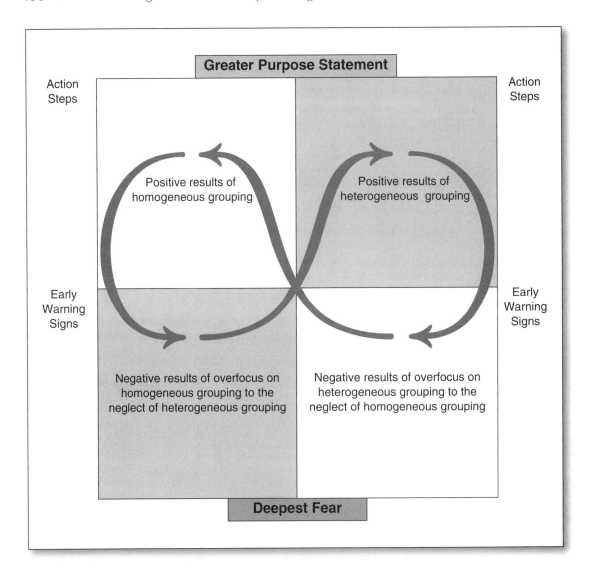

other. Record suggestions on each of the early warning signs charts. Examples might include the following:

➢ Teacher evaluation of quality of individual work and group work

➢ Teacher measures of group effectiveness

➢ Increased number of students off-task during group work time

➢ Increased number of students complaining about having to work in groups with the same students

➢ Students "sneaking" into other groups

> ➢ Increased complaints or requests from parents about groupings

> ➢ Observations of how students form groups of choice

> ➢ Percentage of students engaged during all-class discussions and small-group discussions

Some teams appoint "canaries" for each of the early warning signs charts. These individuals are charged with speaking up when they think more and more of the early warning signs are appearing, suggesting a need to move toward the other pole.

c. *Action steps.* Tell the group that you'd like to close with a five-minute all-share brainstorm on possible action steps they're aware of that might increase the positive results listed in each of the top two quadrants. Ask people to share ideas with a partner for just a minute and then ask for ideas from the group. Ask for action steps for each pole, listing them on the designated charts, and then for "high-leverage" action steps that support the upside of both poles, listing them on the greater purpose chart; the strategy for rich mathematics problems explained in the opening story of this chapter is one such actionable item. *Or have them record ideas on strips of paper. Alternatively, capture all the ideas in the blank polarity map slide included in the Chapter 7 presentation slides, available at* www.corwin.com/positivepower.

8. *Close.* Share the next step in the process. As noted at the beginning of the exercise, solidifying your action steps into a workable plan for moving forward will most likely take more than one meeting. Be ready to tell the group who will be involved (or ask for volunteers), what will happen next, and when it will happen.

Alternative Process: Instead of one, place four pieces of chart paper at each station. Write the labels for each station, as listed on page 143, on small sheets of copy paper and post those at each station. Then, have each group capture its ideas on a separate piece of chart paper. Before group members leave a station, they place their sheet at the bottom of the stack so that the next group sees only a new, blank sheet.

Then, have the groups move through three stations. When they move to the fourth station, give one of the following assignments:

● Draw an image that summarizes the flipcharts for that pole. This accesses different parts of the brain than writing and can provide fresh insights as well as new energy for the process.

- On the last piece of chart paper, summarize the writings of the other groups in about five key statements. Note that the entire group, or a follow-up committee, will take more time with all the charts to ensure that the wisdom of the group is captured, but this process provides a manageable number of items for the next step in the process.

Both processes work well; while participants often find it easier to brainstorm when they can build on the ideas of others, having each group start over often results in more diverse ideas. If your team continues to use polarity mapping, mixing up the processes keeps the mapping process fresh.

FROM MAPPING TO A SUSTAINABLE PLAN

The key to transforming this polarity is identifying and implementing solid, doable action steps. This may require researching what is working elsewhere, asking experts in the field, or encouraging teachers to share their own best practices. In fact, teachers may be far more willing to share once the topic is identified as a polarity rather than an issue where there is a "right" and "wrong" approach. Here are a few principles for developing your action steps:

- *Identify criteria for choosing.* Possibilities include the following: Is time for training and practice available for action steps such as rich math tasks that require changes in teaching practice? Do you have adequate funding to implement it well?
- *Account for the learning curve.* Remember, incorporating more of the upside of either pole involves a learning curve; if your plan doesn't take this into consideration, cries of "This isn't working" may quickly send people back toward their more familiar pole!
- *Check for buy-in.* Often, community members who are most concerned about an action step have good reasons. Seek them out and use their concerns to reexamine your implementation plans. Also, consider Chart 12.12, on page 242, and the lens of teacher learning styles. Does your action step meet their needs?
- *Revisit the plan.* Few polarity maps are once-and-for-all documents. Set a date for revisiting the early warning signs and the action steps you are taking.

The overall goal is to create a tool, your map of this polarity, that reminds stakeholders of the values involved in each pole, the greater purpose that makes working together essential, and the path for leveraging both poles to gain from actions that work best for everyone.

REFLECTION

1. Consider mapping this polarity with three or four colleagues who are unfamiliar with the process, using poster paper and moving through the infinity loop as you add to the charts. Ask for feedback on where they needed more instructions or information on the purpose of the activity. This will give you a sample map to draw on as well as a chance to practice facilitating the process.

2. Before using the process with your full team, consider the following:
   - Do you know of conflicts around the issue you are mapping? If so, acknowledging the values and fears of each side at the start of the process often leads to buy-in. Mention a specific incident or policy swing and the merits of each side and emphasize that this process is designed to help people see the value of each position. Again, this activity assumes you have already led your team through the introduction to polarities provided in Chapter 7.
   - Map the known positive and negative results of each pole in your own community as part of your preparation. Share any that might create openness to the process, but don't share them all; allow participants to recall them during the mapping process.
   - Consider your facilitation skills and whether you might work with a cofacilitator. Having a second person to mingle with the groups and answer questions can be very helpful.
   - Make sure you are clear about your purpose for working through the SMALL mapping process—that is, whether you are highlighting the issue so that individuals and teams can make more informed decisions about grouping or working to create a set of strategies to better leverage this polarity.

Polarity Thinking Map for Grouping Students

Action Steps

A. Provide enrichment opportunities to all

B. Identify resources outside the school

C. Develop flexible scheduling blocks for regrouping students as needed

Values = positive results from focusing on the left pole

1. Allows for depth, common focus
2. Students build peer friendships
3. Teachers can develop expertise for different student needs
4. Teacher planning time reduced; narrower band of rigor, needs
5. Students benefit from learning through their own styles and interests

Homogenous Grouping

and

Early Warnings

A. Increase in students staying in same "track."

B. Increase in students' resistance to pullout instruction.

C. Decrease in evidence of student acceptance of differences.

D. Decrease in student efficacy.

1. Lack of multiple perspectives, empathy
2. Elitism, reinforcement of stereotypes
3. May need multiple teachers, more transition time
4. Contributes to fixed-ability mind-set, traps of tracking
5. Decreased motivation

Fears = negative results from overfocusing on the left pole <u>to the neglect</u> of the right pole

Some Students'

Source: Map template copyright by Polarity Partnerships, LLC.

Diverse Learners

Values = positive results from focusing on the right pole

1. Diversity of perspectives stretches learning
2. Builds tolerance, collaboration, unity
3. Efficient use of time and resources
4. Emphasis of diverse strengths and learning styles
5. Community built through expectations, common experiences, understanding

Action Steps

A. Train teachers in easily usable strategies
B. Teach students cooperation skills

Heterogeneous Grouping

and

1. Students are not equally challenged
2. Teachers are overwhelmed trying to meet all needs
3. Instruction becomes more teacher centered
4. Some students participate more than others
5. Students and teachers more easily bored

Early Warnings

A. All instruction is standardized.
B. Underperformance by many students.
C. Kids mask their abilities.

Fears = negative results from overfocusing on the right pole <u>to the neglect</u> of the left pole

Needs Not Met

9 Using Polarity Tools to Explore Initiatives and Opposing Experts

It's hard to think of a major issue in education where the experts are all in agreement. Often, magazines and journals such as *Educational Leadership* and the *Phi Delta Kappan* choose a topic and invite educators who hold differing views to submit articles. Readers can often see the polarities and map the values and fears of the different authors.

However, we often read a book or article in isolation, and many authors are writing to explain and support their own positions. If they've identified a situation as a problem, they are probably prescribing a solution. If there's a polarity involved, those who value the other pole will most likely take issue with the author's viewpoint.

I was once tasked with calming down a group of white, urban teachers, who as part of a yearlong professional development program were asked to read an isolated chapter from Lisa Delpit's (1995) *Other People's Children*. They had made it through only a few pages when they reacted negatively to the reading. They were so upset that they asked to leave the program, saying, "They're telling us that we're the problem and that reforming our views and practices is the solution. Well, we've worked our tails off learning about culture and beliefs and how to change our teaching. We are *not* the problem."

The isolated passage they'd read could be mapped as shown in Figure 9.1.

Figure 9.1 A Problem/Solution Partial Map

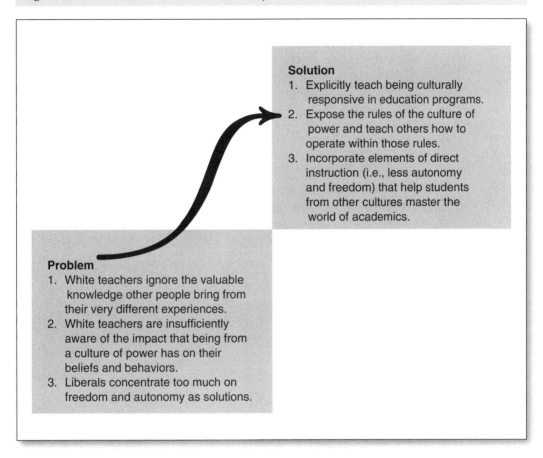

Solution
1. Explicitly teach being culturally responsive in education programs.
2. Expose the rules of the culture of power and teach others how to operate within those rules.
3. Incorporate elements of direct instruction (i.e., less autonomy and freedom) that help students from other cultures master the world of academics.

Problem
1. White teachers ignore the valuable knowledge other people bring from their very different experiences.
2. White teachers are insufficiently aware of the impact that being from a culture of power has on their beliefs and behaviors.
3. Liberals concentrate too much on freedom and autonomy as solutions.

I had read the entire book, so I was able to point out the polarities Delpit addressed in the chapter: *Teaching Processes AND Teaching Skills, Home Culture AND Culture of Power* are two examples. If we remap the section the teachers read with the first polarity in mind, the map might look something like the one in Figure 9.2.

Handing the teachers the chapter with *no* frame of reference increased teacher resistance to Delpit's (1995) overall message. What if instead they'd received a couple of blank maps or maps that named the poles being discussed? The session leaders might have introduced the Delpit chapter by saying, "You know how hard we've worked on active learning strategies. And all of you have sometimes had to go back and explicitly teach some skills. I think this book has some interesting insights as to why many of our students might need more explicit teaching, while at the same

Figure 9.2 Teaching Processes AND Teaching Skills

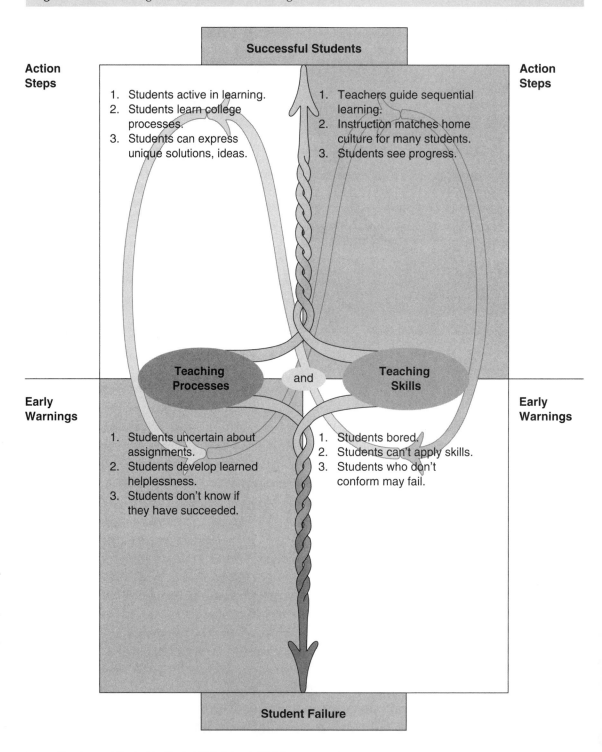

time many educators are pushing for more student-centered practices." Then readers could note the author's positions and complete the map based on their own experiences and other sources. Why take the time? Because if we ignore fears or protests concerning moving away from a pole, we entrench resistance.

Often, we *need* to read authors with whom we disagree; remember our tendency to pay attention only to information that reinforces what we already believe? The lens of polarities can help us pinpoint our objections, listen to the other point of view, and consider where our own fears are keeping us from seeing the upside others value.

Following are two processes for introducing your team to reading key books or articles, or exploring proposed practices or initiatives, with polarities in mind.

ACTIVITY 9.1: READING WITH THE LENS OF POLARITIES

Objective: To practice mapping the positions presented in an article or book.

Materials: Copies of Reading 9.1: "How Do We Help Students Succeed?" (see Appendix B) for each participant; each group will need an extra copy of the reading, one sheet of flipchart paper, scissors, a roll ofcellophane tape or a glue stick, and a few fine-tip markers and chart markers

Time Frame: Forty-five minutes

Facilitation Instructions:

1. Divide participants into groups of three to four people.

2. Give everyone time to read the article.

3. When everyone has finished reading, explain that each group will be cutting the article apart to "map" how the polarities are presented.

   a. Have each group draw a basic polarity map on their chart, as shown in Figure 9.3 (Slide 7.9 of Chapter 7 presentation slides, available at www.corwin.com/ positivepower.). They can label the

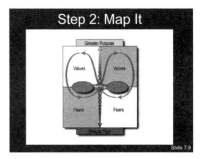

Figure 9.3 Polarity Map Template

poles "Teaching Cognitive Skills" and "Teaching Noncognitive Skills."

b. Ask them to examine the article for lines that support the positive effects of focusing on each of the poles and the negative effects of overfocusing on each pole. As they identify passages relevant to each pole, they are to cut them out and attach them to the relevant quadrant of their map. They can also add any early warnings or action steps suggested.

c. As they finish, ask them to examine the map. Is one pole emphasized to the neglect of the other in the way the author presented the issue? Can they name a greater purpose statement? A deeper fear?

d. Have them use the fine-tip markers to add their own statements to any section of the map they feel is underdeveloped.

4. Have each group trade posters with another group. Ask if they notice any major differences in the maps. Usually, the clippings are posted in similar ways. What catches their interest regarding the additions each group made?

5. Point out that this reading was created to bring together the writings of experts with different viewpoints on the topic of the skills schools need to emphasize for more students to succeed, yet many articles are written from just one viewpoint. And many are written from the standpoint of solving a problem rather than working with a polarity. Ask them to identify individual passages in the article that have this problem-solving flavor. Of the authors mentioned (Tough, Hirsch, Kohn, etc.), which ones might they favor, given their own experiences with these poles? How well is your team leveraging this polarity?

6. Discuss the pros and cons of the article with the polarity in mind. Finish with points of view on whether your team, school, or district is focusing more on cognitive skills or noncognitive skills or whether it seems to be handling the polarity well. What evidence might they give for their positions?

ACTIVITY 9.2: MAPPING ANY ARTICLE

Objective: To use polarities to examine how an issue is presented

Materials: Choose one of the following options:

- Preselect several articles and make copies from which groups can choose one to work with. *Note: working with the original magazines is difficult because the pages of an article are often printed back to back.* Many of the department columns in *Educational Leadership* and *JSD* (*Journal of Staff Development*) are of an appropriate length.
- Choose "pairs" of articles that present two viewpoints on the same topic. Most of the educational magazines that have themes for each issue are great resources for this. Assign each of the paired articles to separate groups.

Each group will need a couple of copies of the reading, one sheet of flipchart paper, scissors, a roll of cellophane tape or a glue stick, and a few fine-tip markers and chart markers.

1. Form groups of three to four participants. Ask everyone to read the article their group has chosen or has been assigned.

2. When everyone has finished reading, explain that each group will be cutting the article apart to "map" how the polarities are presented.

    a. Have each group draw a basic polarity map on their chart, as shown in Figure 9.3 (Slide 7.9 of Chapter 7 presentation slides, available at www.corwin.com/positivepower.)

    b. Ask them to examine the article for lines that support the positive effects of focusing on each side of the poles and the negative effects of overfocusing on each pole. As they identify passages relevant to each pole, they are to cut them out and attach them to the relevant quadrant of their map. They can also add any early warnings or action steps suggested.

    c. As they finish, ask them to examine the map. Is one pole emphasized to the neglect of the other in the way the author presented the issue? Can they name a greater purpose statement? A deeper fear?

3. *If groups were assigned paired articles:* Have the groups meet to compare maps. How do they differ? If the maps are combined, how well do they complete a single map? Is there a common greater purpose statement? Deeper fear? How might a GPS help the authors find common ground? Debrief the exercise with the whole group.

4. *If groups each mapped different articles:* As each group finishes, ask group members to use the fine markers to add to any section of the map they feel is underdeveloped. Have each group describe the core issue presented in the article, answering the following questions:

   a. Was it presented as a problem to be solved, or were two viewpoints discussed? You might refer to the four questions presented on page 133 and on Slide 7.8 in the Chapter 7 presentation slides available at www.corwin.com/positivepower.

   b. Is there a polarity present in the issue, whether it is discussed or not?

   c. Does the author have a clear deeper fear?

   d. Where do they agree or disagree with the author? What did they learn?

Step 1: See it!

- Is it ongoing?
- Are the alternatives interdependent?
- Over time, are both poles/solutions needed?
- If we focus only on one upside, will we eventually undermine our GPS?

Again, Activities 9.1 and 9.2 provide structure for reading with polarities in mind. If we find ourselves strongly agreeing—or disagreeing—with a writer or speaker, we can consider whether polarities are involved and, if so, what experiences, beliefs, or values are causing us to favor one pole over the other.

BOOK STUDY WITH POLARITIES IN MIND

Often, school leaders ask teachers to read books when they wish to shift focus on a policy or issue from one pole to another. Highlighting the polarity before teachers begin reading can accomplish several things.

Second, it provides neutral labels for the "old" and the "new." What if, for example, efforts to improve mathematics had been treated as a polarity from the start with "Mastering Math Skills" AND

"Mastering Problem Solving" recognized as equally valuable by everyone? What kinds of curriculum and instruction might have evolved if effort had been made to consciously strive for the maximum benefits of each pole?

Third, it keeps the focus on both/and thinking rather than either/or thinking. Educators, given the long history of complete reversals in policy, are rightly concerned that a new emphasis will mean tossing out everything connected with the old emphasis. When mapping is used, people can list what they value about current practices from the start. What needs to be kept becomes part of action plans.

ACTIVITY 9.3: INCORPORATING POLARITY MAPPING IN A BOOK DISCUSSION

Objective: To explore the changes an author is suggesting by seeing, mapping, and applying the polarities involved to local issues.

Materials:

- Copies of the book to be studied for each participant. While most books in some way incorporate polarities, some directly address problems that need to be solved and won't lend themselves to this kind of analysis.
- Copies of a polarity map for the book for each participant (see below for information on the completeness of the map).

Facilitation Instructions:

1. In advance, read the entire book. As you read, take notes, using a blank polarity map. You can use a copy of the slide for Figure 9.3 or make your own template.
   - Identify the overall polarity on which you wish to focus. Remember that there may be many, as we saw in Chapter 6 (see page 106), but choosing one makes for clearer analysis.
   - Use two ink colors. In one color, add to the map any points the author makes: values, fears, early warning signs, and action steps for each of the poles. In another color, add your own thoughts as they come to you. If you are reminded of something another author says or a comment you have heard from a team member, record that as well.

2. Decide how much of the map those who will be reading the book might benefit from viewing in advance and how much they might benefit from filling in themselves. Your goal is to increase openness to the author's ideas, not to elicit reactions like those of the teachers to *Other People's Children* in the opening story of this chapter. You could do either of the following:

○ Distribute maps that contain just the polarity on which you would like discussion to focus, naming each pole.
○ Or complete part of the map. The examples that follow (see Figures 9.4–9.6) are *The Book Whisperer* (2009) by Donalyn Miller. The book advocates teaching reading through a student choice reading program rather than traditional basal reading programs or an intervention curriculum. The maps reflect that teachers are often concerned about how to teach required skills when students are reading different books, as well as the lack of support materials when students choose their own books.

The map shown in Figure 9.4 conveys *The Book Whisperer* as a description of problems with reading instruction and Miller's solution. A leader who wishes to incorporate more choice reading into instruction might use this map by asking whether teachers have seen any of the downsides listed for teaching reading skills. *The Book Whisperer* lays out how independent reading can be used for solid instruction, so the book concentrates on the upside of these practices and action steps.

Before reading, you could have teachers brainstorm what they value about their current methods and record them in the "Positive Results From Teaching Reading Skills" quadrant. Listening to their current opinions can reinforce that you see teaching skills and choice reading as a polarity—and in fact *The Book Whisperer* includes strategies for teaching specific standards and skills. Then, ask participants to list action steps that they would want to take to get the upside of free reading AND the upside of skills. What does Miller offer? What ideas do they have?

Alternatively, one could add more to the map, emphasizing that the purpose of reading the book is to concentrate on action steps that apply to your situation. The map in Figure 9.5 could be used for Steps 3 and 4, *assess* and *learn*, before the team reads, to identify and select appropriate action steps.

When using more complete maps like this, encourage teachers to add, rephrase, and otherwise tailor the four "results" lists to best

Figure 9.4 Problem/Solution Map for *The Book Whisperer*

Polarity Thinking Map for Reading Instruction—
The Book Whisperer by Donalyn Miller

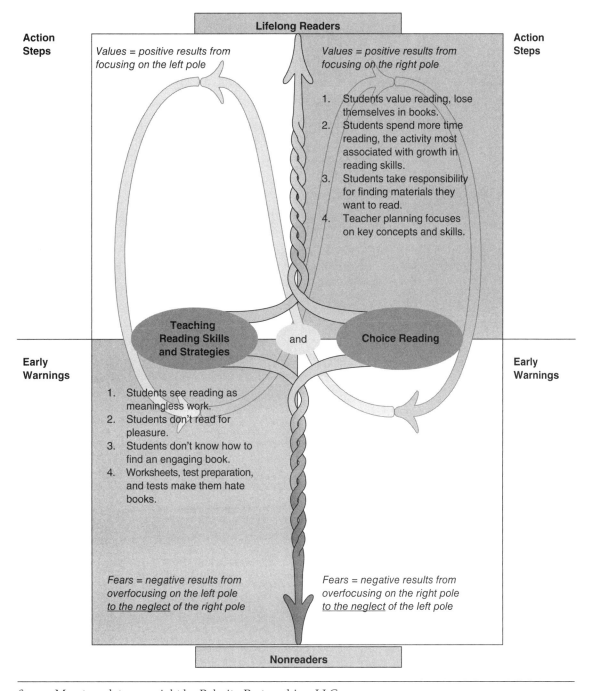

Action Steps

Values = positive results from focusing on the left pole

Action Steps

Values = positive results from focusing on the right pole

Lifelong Readers

1. Students value reading, lose themselves in books.
2. Students spend more time reading, the activity most associated with growth in reading skills.
3. Students take responsibility for finding materials they want to read.
4. Teacher planning focuses on key concepts and skills.

Teaching Reading Skills and Strategies   and   **Choice Reading**

Early Warnings

Early Warnings

1. Students see reading as meaningless work.
2. Students don't read for pleasure.
3. Students don't know how to find an engaging book.
4. Worksheets, test preparation, and tests make them hate books.

Fears = negative results from overfocusing on the left pole to the neglect of the right pole

Fears = negative results from overfocusing on the right pole to the neglect of the left pole

Nonreaders

Source: Map template copyright by Polarity Partnerships, LLC.

Figure 9.5 Polarity Map for *The Book Whisperer* That Includes Current Values

Polarity Thinking Map for Reading Instruction— *The Book Whisperer* by Donalyn Miller

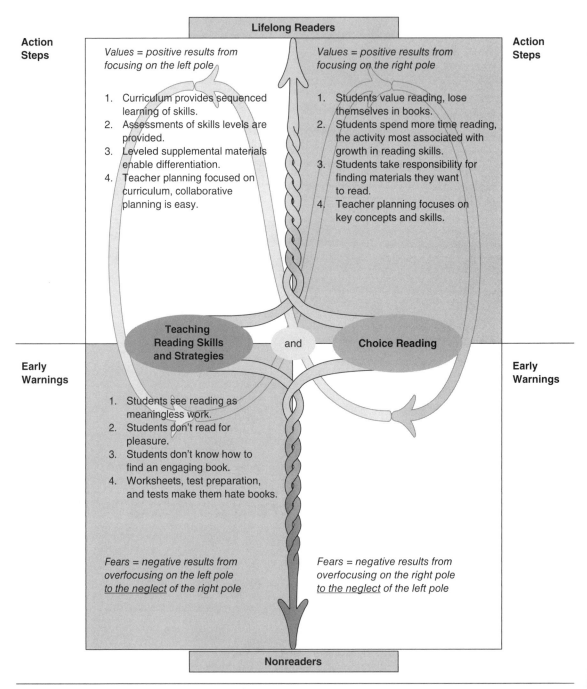

capture the values and fears of their own environment. And they can then add the action steps that they think will most help them move toward the "new" pole supported by the book being studied, as well as the steps that will help maintain the positive results of the current policies or practices that support the other pole.

Note that you can share any portion of the map in advance of reading that you believe will help the readers *see* and *map* the polarity. You could map what you believe people value about current practices and what the author values about the other pole and then fill in together the negative results. You could share how you view the school's current values and negative results from overfocusing on one pole, inviting comments before people begin reading the book. Figure 9.6 shows a complete map, other than the action steps. *The Book Whisperer* is full of action steps for successful instruction through free reading; team members could choose the most important ones for their needs as they read, as well as identify key action steps for the other pole.

Questions to ask as you decide how to create your map include the following:

- Do I anticipate resistance if I try to move our practices toward the pole emphasized in the book we will be studying? Have specific fears already been expressed? How might I use a map to honor those fears?
- Do I know of champions for each pole? Should I invite them into the mapping process before developing what everyone will see?
- Have we planned for implementation? Is our plan realistic when the necessary learning curve is considered? How might that affect how people view the book?

3. Introduce the book study through the lens of the polarity. If school goals or professional development plans already include action steps from your mapping, show how these fit into the map. However, state that one goal of using the polarity process to guide discussion is to ensure that your team's plans and actions leverage it well. Mapping includes everyone's wisdom to identify early warning signs of overfocus on one pole to the neglect of the other, as well as action steps that maximize the positive results that can flow from focusing on each pole.

Figure 9.6 Polarity Map for *The Book Whisperer* for Both Poles

Polarity Thinking Map for Reading Instruction—
The Book Whisperer by Donalyn Miller

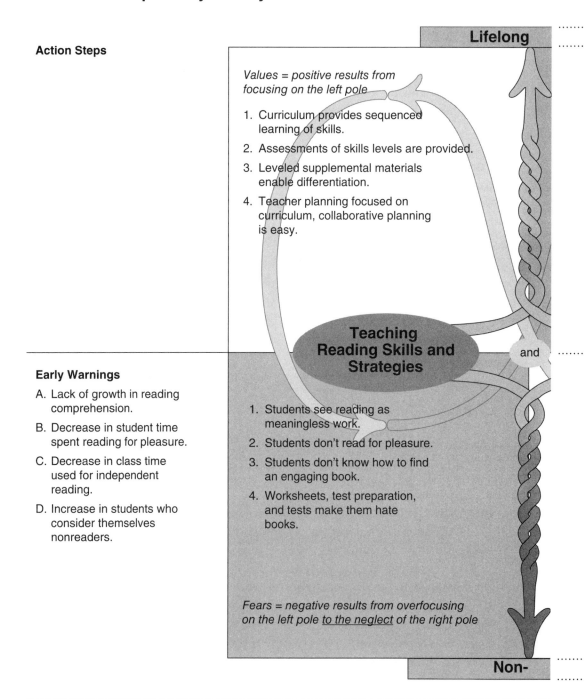

Action Steps

Lifelong

Values = positive results from focusing on the left pole

1. Curriculum provides sequenced learning of skills.
2. Assessments of skills levels are provided.
3. Leveled supplemental materials enable differentiation.
4. Teacher planning focused on curriculum, collaborative planning is easy.

Teaching Reading Skills and Strategies

and

Early Warnings

A. Lack of growth in reading comprehension.
B. Decrease in student time spent reading for pleasure.
C. Decrease in class time used for independent reading.
D. Increase in students who consider themselves nonreaders.

1. Students see reading as meaningless work.
2. Students don't read for pleasure.
3. Students don't know how to find an engaging book.
4. Worksheets, test preparation, and tests make them hate books.

Fears = negative results from overfocusing on the left pole to the neglect of the right pole

Non-

Readers

Action Steps

Values = positive results from focusing on the right pole

1. Students value reading, lose themselves in books.
2. Students spend more time reading, the activity most associated with growth in reading skills.
3. Students take responsibility for finding materials they want to read.
4. Teacher planning focuses on key concepts and skills.

Choice Reading

and

1. Loss of community built by shared texts.
2. Teachers struggle to assess progress on reading skills.
3. Teachers struggle to provide students with appropriate book suggestions.
4. Teacher planning loses focus.

Early Warnings

A. Decrease in student results on accountability tests.
B. Decrease in number of standards teachers have covered.
C. Decrease in teacher knowledge of student reading difficulties.
D. Decrease in number of books students are reading.

Fears = negative results from overfocusing on the right pole <u>to the neglect</u> of the left pole

readers

Encourage people to fill in the rest of the map, adding to your notes, as they read. They might wish to keep a separate sheet of notes for each of the quadrants of the map.

4. For the discussion, choose one of two methods to collect input on the positive and negative results of focusing on each pole:

   ○ Use SurveyMonkey or GoogleDocs or another online tool to compile the results. Ask people to log on and input their notes for each of the four main quadrants on the map. Also ask for measurable early warning signs that came to mind.
   ○ Or collect ideas during your gathering time, using the process explained in Chapter 8. When the groups move to their fourth station, ask them to add any new items. Then, provide another sheet of paper to each group. Ask them to use pictures, not words, to summarize the ideas for the quadrant where they are now standing. This calls on entirely different areas of our brains and often leads to new ideas or understandings. Have each group explain its drawings.

5. Gather early warning signs. Participants could work in small groups to draft and edit measurable markers for each pole.

6. The next step is action planning. If school or team leadership has already developed action steps, demonstrate how these are designed to leverage each pole. If not, ensure that participants understand how solid action steps will be created and implemented, as well as how teachers will be supported.

REFLECTION

1. Think of an education policy or teaching strategy where you witnessed teacher resistance—or that you resisted. Was a polarity involved? Can you map the different positions?

   ○ What "wisdom" were the resisters offering? These are usually the positive results of the pole that is the status quo.
   ○ Why was the change suggested? These are usually the negative results of overfocus on the same pole.

○ What were the fears about the proposed "solution"? These are usually the negative results of overfocus on the solution pole.

○ Finally, what promises were made concerning the change? These are usually the positive results associated with the solution pole.

2. Read an article or book while taking notes in a blank polarity map. Is a polarity involved? What do you notice about the author's arguments from filling in a map?

10

Working With Common Polarities in Education

A teacher gripes about too many meetings. Is he a complainer? Are there too many meetings? Or is the school struggling to leverage the polarity of Autonomy AND Collaboration?

Members of the science department are upset with the district's curriculum coordinator, who purchased and distributed assessments that correlate with student proficiency on their statewide test. Are the assessments inappropriate for your school's students? Are the teachers unwilling to be team players? Or is the district overfocused on centralized decisions to the neglect of building-level decisions?

Being aware of several crucial universal polarities such as these can help education leaders refrain from directing a fire hose at a supposed problem that is in reality a polarity system with interdependent alternatives. In this chapter, we'll look at how these polarities might appear in schools.

As you read, think about ongoing struggles in your classroom, building, or district. Which polarities might be involved? Where might you focus attention on working through the polarity process to make better use of the energy being expended on the issues? At the end of the chapter is a reflection sheet that you can use to record your thoughts about polarities that currently affect your workplace.

AUTONOMY AND COLLABORATION

Autonomy AND Collaboration, Individual AND Team, and *Competition AND Cooperation* are related polarities that affect students, teachers, administrators, parents, and the community at large. Frequently, school systems overcorrect—for example, by moving from a field day with individual competition for ribbons to a field day of exclusively cooperative activities. Consider whether you've seen overcorrection in any of these areas.

In the classroom. While balancing individual student work and collaborative work is an obvious instance of this Autonomy AND Collaboration polarity, others include the following:

- Thinking time. Are students asked to form an opinion, choose a strategy, find a supporting fact, or otherwise think for themselves before a collaborative discussion or tasks begins? Conversely, when an assignment involves working on their own, how often are students allowed to improve their ideas through discussions?
- Do students assess the quality of their own work AND productively help others evaluate and improve their work?
- Are students involved in setting their own goals? What about goals for their team or for the class?
- Are students graded on individual contributions AND team results for collaborative activities?

In a school. Is the Autonomy AND Collaboration polarity leveraged well in professional learning communities? Conflict often arises over whether the stated goals will result in "cookie cutter classrooms" where everyone is teaching the same content in the same ways. Or teachers claim that too many meetings leave little time for developing intriguing instructional plans using their own interests and expertise. Another early warning sign of imbalance is an increase in protests that team meetings are too short to accomplish given objectives.

Schoolwide, to what extent are teachers expected to collaboratively develop class norms or rules? Discipline policies? Grading policies? Where is individuality encouraged or discouraged? Remember, the point of working with polarities isn't to balance things equally, but to ensure that the system benefits from the value each pole adds.

In a district. Review what decisions are made autonomously at the building level. And for what decisions does the district pull together people from various buildings to collaborate? Note that this has a bit different flavor from Centralization AND Decentralization, another common polarity.

This polarity is also sometimes part of professional development decisions. There are economies of scale in collaborating to prioritize topics and hold all-district professional development events, but each building will still have unique needs and want to meet by itself.

TEAM RELATIONSHIPS AND TEAM TASKS

Think about whether enough time is allotted to building relationships before engaging in the work of the team. Unfortunately, with budget pressures and limited time for professional development, schools are prone to overfocusing on the Task pole. All too often, my work with a school begins with conflict resolution, a common result of overfocus on Tasks to the neglect of Relationships.

The lens of *Preparing to Do the Work AND Doing the Work* is a related polarity. With the urgent need to improve student test scores in many schools, it is easy to overfocus on implementation of promising new strategies to the neglect of preparation—with the negative result of failing to understand individual teacher learning needs if they are to implement the strategies well.

In the classroom. Questions that probe how well this polarity is being leveraged might include these:

- Are students supportive and respectful of each other?
- Are collaboration and group process skills and protocols taught explicitly? These are not innate abilities!
- Are students being productive while working in small groups, or are they just talking among themselves?
- Were students involved in setting class norms and expectations?
- Do students enjoy working in teams? Alone?
- Is the necessary work getting done?

In the building. Consider how much time is invested in improving communication, collaboration, or conflict resolution skills—the "Big Cs" of teamwork. Another marker is whether time is allocated for the conversations, celebrations, and other "unproductive" moments that build community. Conversely, are there clear goals for team time and expected eventual results? Or is time often spent in conversations not directly related to team tasks?

In the district. Ask whether a sense of community exists among buildings and the district or whether every building is autonomous. What effort has been made to establish a common identity and purpose? Are there tasks that serve to pull everyone together? Is district leadership a high-functioning team that works well together, respects each person's experience and expertise, disagrees when necessary, and accomplishes its tasks in a timely manner? Or do fellow administrators lack respect for each other and either bully their way through an agenda or fail to accomplish goals, leaving the real work to get done outside the meetings?

CLARITY AND FLEXIBILITY

Many of the issues touched by this polarity affect all levels of education at once. How well is your team, building, or district handling each of these examples?

- Clear goals for students, faculty, administrators, and other stake-holders AND flexibility in how individuals reach those goals
- Clear vertical curriculum (teachers at each grade level know what is being taught at other grade levels) AND flexibility in assignments, resources, and teaching methods used to deliver the curriculum
- Clear homework policies AND flexibility to meet individual student needs
- Clear standards for professional growth AND flexibility in the learning opportunities teachers can pursue to meet the standards
- Clear goals for implementing what is learned in professional development AND room for multiple methods of implementation
- Clear districtwide goals AND differentiated plans for how each building will meet those goals
- Clear Common Core State Standards AND flexibility in how teachers, districts, and states approach those standards.

CONTINUITY AND CHANGE

Literature on organizational change indicates that most significant change efforts take about three to five years to become both effective and sustainable. The research on forming professional learning communities clearly supports this time frame. Yet all too often, we jettison change efforts based on short-term results. Or new leaders believe the myth of "cleaning house" and cancel the priorities of former leaders instead of leveraging *Continuity AND Change.*

Further, *remember that when you shift focus to a different pole, you often get the downside of that pole. Why? Because there's a learning curve. The negative results often appear before people develop enough skills or the systems become strong enough to also show positive results.* The negative results force a swing back to the former pole before one can realistically expect to see positive results!

Think through curriculum adoptions, personnel changes, major initiatives such as professional learning communities, learning standards, accountability tests, grading policies, and so on. How many have been sustained throughout the past five to ten years (continuity) and how many have been recently introduced (change)? Where might the polarity mapping process be helpful?

CONDITIONAL RESPECT AND UNCONDITIONAL RESPECT

We can respect people for what they do (how well they perform) AND respect them for who they are (independent of what they do). When this polarity isn't handled well, people become demoralized, outraged, discouraged, and more. The path to a vicious cycle is quite short. While unconditional respect is often seen as the right of all human beings, attitudes, policies, and even laws can quickly shift to an overfocus on conditional respect. Examples include the following:

- The current furor over teacher evaluation systems discussed in Chapter 4. Belittling teachers and not including educators in creating the systems by which they will be measured are results from an overfocus on conditional respect. How teachers' developmental needs are presented and, if necessary, how they are informed that their jobs are at risk because of their failure to improve both benefit from considering this *Conditional Respect AND Unconditional Respect* polarity.
- Student attitudes toward teachers and vice versa. Do students give teachers respect because they are human beings as well as for what they know and how they teach? Do teachers respect and show common courtesy to students who are behavioral problems—separating the person from the behavior? We can improve our handling of this polarity by having individuals complete Activity 10.1: Demonstrating Respect.
- Student attitudes toward other students. This Conditional Respect AND Unconditional Respect concept is central to bullying prevention.

- All relationships. How do teachers and parents view each other? Teaching and nonteaching staff? District staff and building staff? Teachers and politicians? Teacher unions and government? And so on.

WORK PRIORITIES AND HOME PRIORITIES

In education, this polarity is broader than whether teachers and administrators find their work, including grading papers and answering e-mails, spilling into personal time. Including the whole school community, this polarity touches on homework policies, the school calendar and how vacation days and breaks are scheduled, expectations for parent involvement, the timing of extracurricular activities, transportation options, the availability of help sessions and makeup sessions, and much more.

FOCUSING ON THE NEEDS OF STUDENTS AND FOCUSING ON THE NEEDS OF STAFF

Again, many issues fall under this polarity. Consider the following:

- Is your community or school leveraging well the amount of time, energy, and money allocated for improving student learning compared to the time, energy, and money spent on staff professional development?
- Some buildings overfocus on the needs of staff ("teachers rule"), allowing teachers and other staff members to treat students in any manner the staff thinks is appropriate, including bullying at times.
- Other buildings, districts, and/or communities put such a high value on student test scores that the professional needs of the staff become secondary—overfocusing on the needs of the students. In the worst-case scenarios, we reach our "deepest fear" where staff accuse administrators of always siding with students and parents, while parents and community members make disrespectful comments about staff and the efforts the staff put forth to educate the students.

If we are leveraging the *Focusing on the Needs of Students AND Focusing on the Needs of Staff* polarity, we see the growth of the students dependent on the growth of the staff and vice versa—realizing we cannot have one without the other.

TEACHER AS LECTURER AND TEACHER AS FACILITATOR

Often, school initiatives employ either/or thinking when instruction involves this polarity. I've talked with teachers who were reprimanded for having desks in rows, even though they frequently rearrange them into "group formation." When the "lecturer" pole is the focus, teachers are reprimanded for deviating from scripts. Both/and thinking is more productive; some learning objectives benefit from lecture, but if teachers overfocus on sharing their knowledge and expertise, students may become overwhelmed with information. Or students retreat into admiring the person, laughing at jokes, and politely nodding their heads while their minds have quit working.

Yet we can also overfocus on facilitation. A colleague reminded me of a college professor who relied so much on group discussions and cooperative learning strategies that students thought they were being cheated out of the professor's knowledge that they had paid a hefty tuition to acquire.

OTHER UNIVERSAL POLARITIES

Other key areas in education that may benefit from both/and rather than either/or thinking include these:

- *Centralization AND Decentralization.* Where decisions are made may affect teacher/school, school/district, district/state, and state/federal government relationships and responsibilities
- *School Responsibility AND Societal Responsibility.* Throughout these pages, we've touched on issues that schools need to tackle and issues that schools can't solve on their own.
- *Strict Disciplinarian AND Lenient Disciplinarian.* A variation on the Justice AND Mercy universal polarity, teachers and administrators often judge (and misjudge) each other on how this polarity is handled. Good discipline involves leveraging clarity, consistency, and structure (strict) with responsiveness, adaptability, and creativity (lenient).
- *Fidelity to the Intervention AND Innovation With the Intervention.* An overfocus on fidelity ignores the natural influence of differing teacher strengths, experiences, and interests. However, an overfocus on innovation can strip interventions of key elements necessary for success.
- *Critical Analysis AND Encouragement.* All feedback, to adults and students, benefits from leveraging this polarity well.

Polarities can appear to be at cross-purposes with each other. Focusing on the greater purpose that the poles share helps stakeholders realize how they need each other.

We get excited about the upside of a pole that isn't being honored and all the energy flows toward the "solution." But that solution will soon be the new problem if we don't slow down and ask, "Is this a problem to solve, or are we experiencing the negative results of overfocusing on one pole of an interdependent pair?"

REFLECTION

1. Use Chart 10.1 at the end of this chapter to consider which common polarities may be causing ongoing difficulties in your learning communities. On what issues are there policy swings? Ongoing tension, debate, or infighting? Resistance? Where might polarity mapping make the biggest difference in putting those differences of opinion to use toward a greater purpose?

2. Consider using Activity 10.1 or 10.2 with your team, focusing on one or more of the key polarities you've identified.

   ○ Activity 10.1: Demonstrating Respect both builds an understanding of how respect is being leveraged and demonstrates an effective learning strategy, where individuals brainstorm on large strips of paper that are then incorporated into a "moving outline" with which the group can work to capture the members' collective wisdom.
   ○ Activity 10.2: Point of View Debate provides an engaging debate activity that also demonstrates the benefits of tapping opposite points of view.

ACTIVITY 10.1: DEMONSTRATING RESPECT

Objectives:

- To help students and/or staff understand the Conditional AND Unconditional Respect polarity and leverage it in the classroom. *Note: This activity benefits from learning by doing; have your staff work through the entire activity as a team before using it with students.*

Materials:

- Long strips of paper (either strips of adding machine tape or flip-chart paper cut lengthwise into six strips per page), one for each participant

- Masking tape
- Markers, at least one for every two people
- A large area of table, wall, or window space for sorting the strips
- Two large signs, one labeled "Conditional Respect" and one labeled "Unconditional Respect"

Facilitation Instructions:

1. Provide participants with a specific relationship to consider: teacher-student, student-teacher, student-student, teacher-administration, and so on. Display Slide 10.1 (available at www .corwin.com/positivepower.). Ask participants to write a response to one of the prompts on their strip of paper, using markers, keeping that relationship in mind. Emphasize writing large enough that people can read strips at a distance.

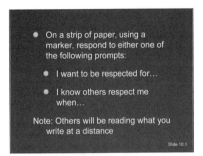

   o I want to be respected for . . .
   o I know others respect me when . . .

2. As participants work, post the two signs, on either a wall or window with space for participants to tape up their responses to Step 1. Position small strips of masking tape nearby that they can use for posting their strips. Or place the signs on tables where the strips can be arranged.

3. Display Slide 10.2 or write the definitions on a whiteboard. Explain to the group the difference between the two forms of respect.
   o Conditional respect is the respect we are given for what we do. We earn it.
   o Unconditional respect is the respect we are given for who we are—teachers, administrators, human beings, students. We don't have to earn it.

4. Ask participants, "Does your statement relate to conditional or unconditional respect? Bring it to the appropriate area." Appoint one or two people to assist posting the strips at each area. Ask them to group together similar ideas.

5. When all the ideas are posted, ask, "If you just look at the number of strips in each area, do we tend to think more about conditional respect or unconditional respect?

6. Work toward building a polarity map by breaking participants into four groups:

   ○ Group 1: Examine the strips posted with Conditional Respect. What are the positive results from focusing on this pole? Record at least five. *Note: These can be recorded on chart paper or added to a master polarity map slide such as the one shown at the end of this chapter, available at* www.corwin.com/positivepower.

   ○ Group 2: Examine the strips posted with Unconditional Respect. What are the positive results from focusing on this pole? Record at least five.

   ○ Group 3: What are the negative results if we overfocus on Conditional Respect to the Neglect of Unconditional Respect? Record at least five.

   ○ Group 4: What are the negative results if we overfocus on Unconditional Respect to the Neglect of Conditional Respect? Record at least five.

7. Post one more sheet of flipchart paper. Use a marker to divide the sheet into quadrants and sketch in an infinity loop so that it resembles the basic quadrants of a polarity map. Tell the group, "Think of this sheet as our polarity map. Where do you think we are on this map? With a marker, draw an arrow that indicates how you think we are moving on this infinity loop: toward the positive or negative results of a pole? More of a virtuous cycle, getting the upside of each pole, or a vicious cycle, getting the downside of each pole?"

8. Brainstorm possible early warning signs for focus on each pole and record them on flipchart paper or polarity map slide (see the map at the end of this chapter, available at www.corwin.com/positivepower). Ask people to consider how they know when disrespect is present. Probe for specificity if the same idea is suggested for each pole, getting at the cause behind the early warning sign.

9. Have people work in small groups to suggest action steps for each pole, as well as any high-leverage steps that would access the upside of both poles. Remind them to include any actions that are already being taken. Collect each group's list.

10. Either before the close of the session or shortly thereafter, inform the group how the possible action steps will be evaluated and selected and how the final map will be shared.

ACTIVITY 10.2: POINT OF VIEW DEBATE

Objectives:

- Understanding how polarities often show up as a conflict between groups with two points of view, both of which think they hold a corner on the solution.
- Demonstrating how two points of view can be combined into a polarity map.
- Experiencing how the energy and time consumed by conflict can be harnessed by a productive framework that acknowledges the wisdom in each point of view.

Materials:

- Enough tables with chairs so that two to four staff members can be seated at each table. Rectangular tables work best but rounds will work.
- Sheets of 8.5″ × 11″ paper with one polarity listed on each sheet of paper. The listed polarities should be ones that staff members find most interesting. For example:
  a. Autonomy AND Collaboration
  b. Centralized Decision Making AND Building-Level Decision Making
  c. Critical Analysis AND Encouragement
  d. Home AND Work
  e. Strict Disciplinarian AND Lenient Disciplinarian
- Sheets of chart paper; tape if not using the self-adhesive type of chart paper.
- Multiple chart markers of two different colors—for example, blue and green or black and brown.
- Timer.

Facilitation Instructions:

1. Around the room, post the signs listing two to five polarities you think your staff might enjoy exploring the most. The activity will work with any polarities.

2. Ask each participant to stand near the sign of the polarity he or she finds the most interesting or challenging, but then ask for cooperation in moving to different ones so that each group has at least four members.

3. Create the debate teams.

   ○ If you have a large number of participants, you can assign more than one group to the same polarities. Each group will be split into two small teams (two to four members) with a similar number of participants on each debate team.

   ○ Within each group, designate one team as "Team A" and the other as "Team B." Tell the A Teams that they will advocate for the pole listed on the left side of their polarity sign. The B Teams will advocate for the pole listed on the right side. For example, given a polarity sign reading, "Autonomy AND Collaboration," Team A will advocate for Autonomy while Team B will advocate for Collaboration.

   ○ Provide all the A Teams with the same-colored markers and all the B Teams with the same-colored markers but in a different color from A Team markers.

4. Provide each team with two sheets of chart paper and ask each team to complete the following. The instructions are on Slide 10.3.

   ○ On the top of one sheet of chart paper, write "Positive results of focusing on [your team's assigned pole] for our building."

   ○ On the other sheet of chart paper, write "Negative results of overfocusing on [other team's assigned pole] to the neglect of [your team's assigned pole] for our building."

   ○ Circulate around the room to make sure the teams are creating their two charts correctly. *Note: You can have these charts prepared for the teams in advance and just let them fill in the names of the two poles.*

5. Ask all the teams to fill in their two charts with content that supports the title of each chart. Tell them the following:

   ○ They will be using these ideas during the debate they are about to have with their counterpart team.

   ○ Avoid letting their counterpart team see their chart.

   ○ They will have about five to seven minutes to create and complete their charts. Allow more time if needed.

6. Arrange the room so that Team A and Team B in each group are seated behind tables facing each other.

   Have each team stick or tape their two sheets to the other team's table hanging toward the floor and facing their team's table.

This should allow both teams to view their individual charts/ notes during the debate without their opponents seeing the content of their sheet.

7. Start the debate this way:
   ○ Tell all the teams the three objectives for the debate [Slide 10.4].

   a. Hold onto your team's point of view.

   b. Get the other team to agree with your point of view.

   c. Have fun!

   ○ Explain that five minutes will be given for the debate.
   ○ Ask all the A Teams to start the debate by asserting one of their points. From then on, the conversation should volley back and forth between the two teams with all members of the team joining the debate.

   a. Team members should use their notes, hanging from their opponent's table, as ammunition for asserting their point of view and disclaiming the other team's counterpoints.

   b. Teams should avoid just reading their lists to each other. There should be an exchange of ideas between the two tables with lots of disagreements.

8. After five minutes is up, bring the debate to closure.

9. Transition the conversation from a debate of two opposite points of view to acknowledging the polarity within the two interdependent opposites.
   ○ Ask each team to remove their debate sheets from their opponent's table and hang them on a wall diagonally opposed to each other so the four sheets now create the four quadrants of a polarity map (see the diagram that follows). The opposing points of view will still be apparent since different colored markers were used by the two different teams.

10. Ask the groups to read together their four sheets in the infinity loop order. Have them draw the loop on the maps if it would be helpful.

11. If different groups debated different polarities during this activity, give the members of the entire staff time to circulate around the room going from map to map reading the polarities they were not involved in debating.

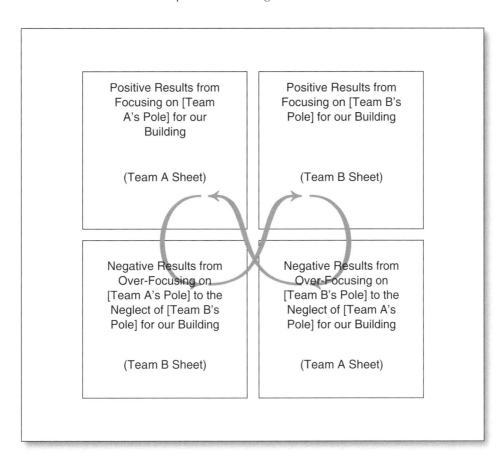

12. Reconvene the entire group and use some, or all, of the following questions to discuss the activity, shown in summary form on Slide 10.5:

   ○ During the debate, did you find yourself discounting the reasons given by your opponents, even if they made sense? Can you give examples?

   ○ At times, did you enjoy the competition, trying to top or overcome your opponent's points of view? Explain your response.

   ○ Do you now see the need for both poles of the polarity you were debating to be acknowledged and honored in our educational system? Explain your response.

   ○ The concept of polarity thinking asserts that unrecognized polarities cost an organization lots of time and energy. How did the debate reinforce that concept for you?

   Debrief Questions

   ● Did you discount your opponent's reasoning, even when it made sense?
   ● Did you find yourself trying to win the competition?
   ● Insights into gaining wisdom from other points of view?
   ● Insights into channeling wasted energy through the mapping process?
   ● Other thoughts?

   Slide 10.5

Polarity Thinking Map

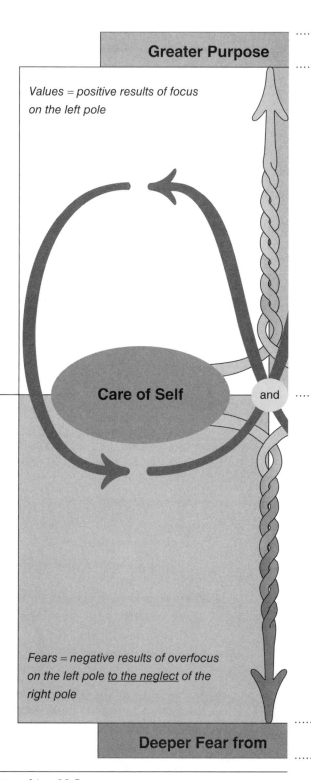

Action Steps

How will we gain or maintain the positive results from focusing on this left pole? What? Who? By when? Measures?

A.

Early Warnings

Measurable indicators (things you can count) that will let you know that you are getting into the downside of this left pole.

A.

Values = positive results of focus on the left pole

Greater Purpose

Care of Self   and

Fears = negative results of overfocus on the left pole <u>to the neglect</u> of the right pole

Deeper Fear from

Source: Map template copyright by Polarity Partnerships, LLC.

Statement (GPS)

Values = positive results of focus on the right pole

Action Steps

How will we gain or maintain the positive results from focusing on this right pole? What? Who? By when? Measures?

A.

and — **Care of Others**

Early Warnings

Measurable indicators (things you can count) that will let you know that you are getting into the downside of this right pole.

A.

Fears = negative results of overfocus on the right pole <u>to the neglect</u> of the left pole

lack of optimization

○ What other ideas or thoughts come to mind after having experienced this activity of turning a debate of two opposing ideas into acknowledging the interdependency of the two poles?

13. As you bring closure to this activity, remind the participants that not all opposing viewpoints are polarities; some require decisions. However, think about decisions such as purchasing one of two reading programs. A decision must be made—either/or thinking. Yet programs may have opposing philosophies that involve a polarity. Identifying that polarity and understanding how each program facilitates leveraging it can be very helpful in improving the outcome.

Chart 10.1 Polarities Reflection Sheet

Consider the polarities mentioned in the chapter. Below is a simple way to rate whether your workplace might benefit from paying attention to these.

Autonomy AND Collaboration

Are we overfocusing on one pole to the neglect of the other? Circle the neglected pole.

Who is experiencing negative results? _____ Students _____ Teachers _____ Building _____?

Color in the number of stars that indicate how crucial this polarity is to reaching school goals, with 5 ☆s being the most crucial: ☆☆☆☆☆

Team Relationships AND Team Tasks

Are we overfocusing on one pole to the neglect of the other? Circle the neglected pole.

Who is experiencing negative results? ___ Students ___ Teachers ___Building _____?

Color in the number of stars that indicate how crucial this polarity is to reaching school goals, with 5 ☆s being the most crucial: ☆☆☆☆☆

Clarity AND Flexibility

Are we overfocusing on one pole to the neglect of the other? Circle the neglected pole.

Who is experiencing negative results? _____ Students _____ Teachers _____ Building?

Color in the number of stars that indicate how crucial this polarity is to reaching school goals, with 5 ☆s being the most crucial: ☆☆☆☆☆

Continuity AND Change

Are we overfocusing on one pole to the neglect of the other? Circle the neglected pole.

Who is experiencing negative results? _____ Students _____ Teachers _____ Building?

Color in the number of stars that indicate how crucial this polarity is to reaching school goals, with 5 ☆s being the most crucial: ☆☆☆☆☆

Conditional Respect AND Unconditional Respect

Are we overfocusing on one pole to the neglect of the other? Circle the neglected pole.

Who is experiencing negative results? _____ Students _____ Teachers _____ Building?

Color in the number of stars that indicate how crucial this polarity is to reaching school goals, with 5 ☆s being the most crucial: ☆☆☆☆☆

Work Priorities AND Home Priorities

Are we overfocusing on one pole to the neglect of the other? Circle the neglected pole.

Who is experiencing negative results? _____ Students _____ Teachers _____ Building?

Color in the number of stars that indicate how crucial this polarity is to reaching school goals, with 5 ☆s being the most crucial: ☆☆☆☆☆

Focusing on the Needs of Students AND Focusing on the Needs of Staff

Are we overfocusing on one pole to the neglect of the other? Circle the neglected pole.

Who is experiencing negative results? _____ Students _____ Teachers _____ Building?

Color in the number of stars that indicate how crucial this polarity is to reaching school goals, with 5 ☆s being the most crucial: ☆☆☆☆☆

Teacher as Lecturer AND Teacher as Facilitator

Are we overfocusing on one pole to the neglect of the other? Circle the neglected pole.

Who is experiencing negative results? _____ Students _____ Teachers _____ Building?

Color in the number of stars that indicate how crucial this polarity is to reaching school goals, with 5 ☆s being the most crucial: ☆☆☆☆☆

11 Students and Polarities

A Tool for Critical Thinking

*C*ritical thinking skills are part of a set of buzzwords, with *twenty-first-century skills, rigor,* and *creativity,* that are bantered about so much that they're more cliché than meaningful concepts. Look at these synonyms for *critical,* however:

Crucial

Essential

Fundamental

Paramount

Key

Pivotal

Polarity tools can scaffold students as they learn to engage in essential, crucial skills such as the following:

- *Analyzing.* Forming a polarity map reveals how well an argument was constructed.
- *Evaluating.* Assessing the current position in an infinity loop of a polarity and learning from past decisions and results can broaden thinking beyond simple problem/solution approaches. Unintended consequences, among other things, often surface.
- *Creating.* The mapping process is an excellent way for students to craft their own positions and support them.

This chapter provides tools for helping students master key Common Core standards, those related to being able to present and support more than one side of an issue, with evidence chosen to influence a specific audience. However, teaching students to think in terms of polarities is useful day in and day out. We'll begin with some common polarities that pertain to goal setting, discipline issues, classroom norms, and more.

Doing so is a high-leverage action step for a crucial polarity in education: *Cognitive Skills AND Noncognitive Skills.* Appendix B, "How Do We Help Students Succeed?" which is part of Activity 9.1, cites expert opinions supporting the value of each pole. Equipping students with polarity tools increases their ability to do the following:

- Understand how and why their viewpoints differ from those of others
- Expand their view of reality
- Use their understanding of another person's viewpoint to invite that person to consider their own
- Better handle situations and choices, both big and little, that involve polarities

These are all crucial abilities that transcend any particular century or set of standards.

MY RIGHTS AND RESPONSIBILITIES

Let's go back to my dad's polarity regarding my brothers and me, which ties closely to other universal polarities such as *My Rights AND My Responsibilities*, as well as *Individual AND Community*.

An eighth-grade teacher at a suburban middle school told me, "My students know all about their rights. If they say, 'You can't make me do that because . . . ' they can quote the school policy or parent threat that applies. But ask them to list their responsibilities as a citizen or a student? They're clueless." To enrich their understanding of citizenship, she had her classes brainstorm both kinds of responsibilities and the negative results of over-focusing on each pole. The exercise not only taught a civics lesson but also was useful for conversations such as, "If you exercise your right to delay working on your part of the team project, what happens to your partner's right to know that everything is under control?" as well as more serious matters.

Another application is in setting classroom norms. Students could collaborate using any of the map-building techniques to complete a map such as this one:

Polarity Thinking Map for Setting Classroom Norms

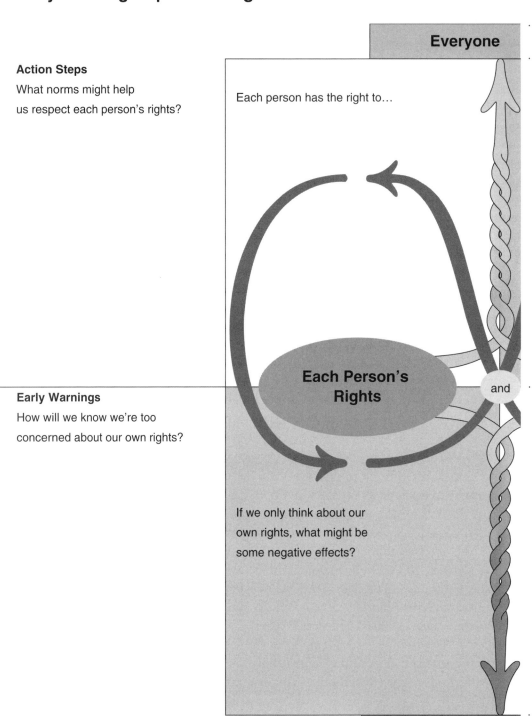

Action Steps
What norms might help
us respect each person's rights?

Each person has the right to...

Everyone

Each Person's Rights

and

Early Warnings
How will we know we're too
concerned about our own rights?

If we only think about our
own rights, what might be
some negative effects?

Winners

Source: Map template copyright by Polarity Partnerships, LLC.

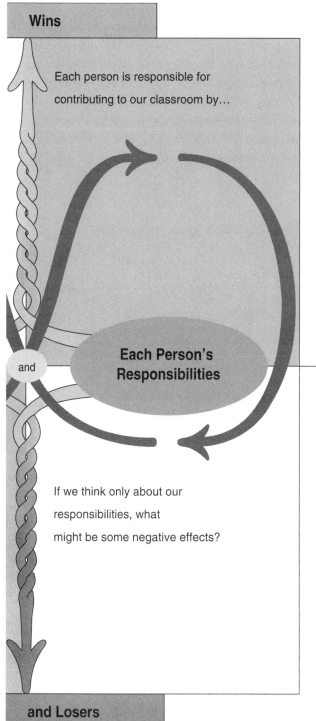

Wins

Each person is responsible for contributing to our classroom by…

Action Steps

What norms might help us be responsible and contribute to making this a great classroom?

and

Each Person's Responsibilities

Early Warnings

How will we know we're overfocusing on our responsibilities in this community?

If we think only about our responsibilities, what might be some negative effects?

and Losers

Then, the norms are actually the action steps that leverage Individual AND Community instead of an abstract list of rules or niceties.

In discipline situations, the mapping process provides a consistent routine that helps students express their view of the situation and listen to others. As an example, I carry a vivid picture in my head from several decades ago of my first-grade teacher, leaning forward on her high heels, yelling at me where all my classmates could hear. "Only a selfish little girl would stand there and refuse to pass the ball to her relay teammates. Go stand in the corner for the rest of recess and think about how they felt when you made them lose."

Yes, I stood in the corner. But not a single glimmer of remorse came to me. Instead, I simmered with the injustice of it all. A complete "discipline" map might have looked like this:

Figure 11.1 My Rights and My Responsibilities

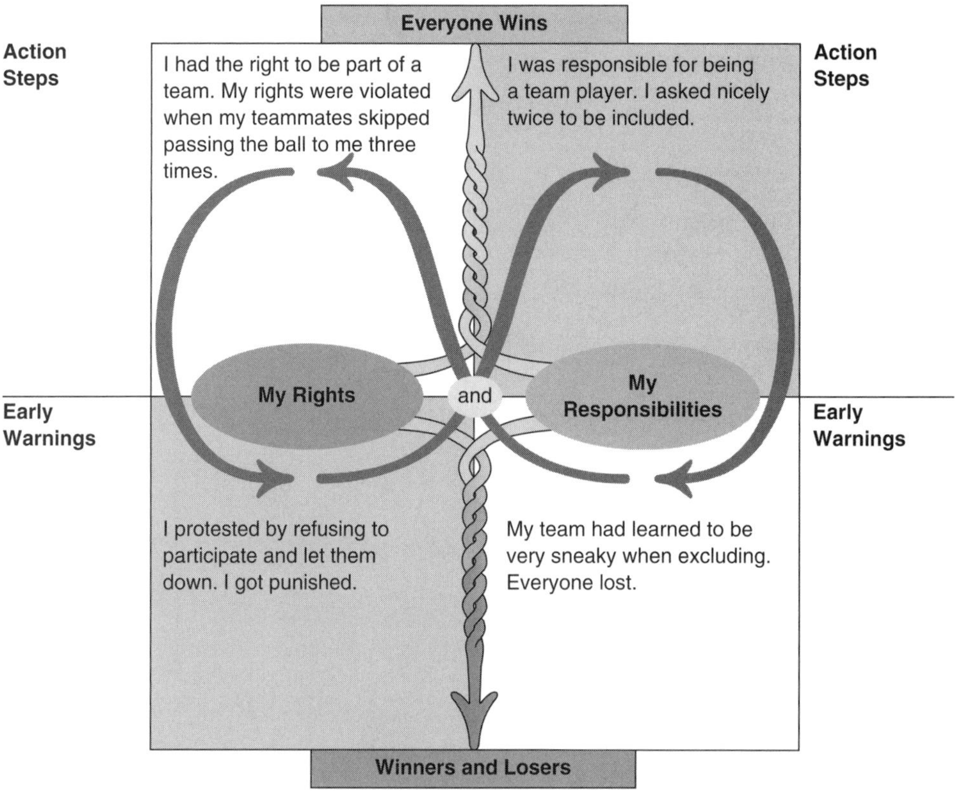

Source: Map template copyright by Polarity Partnerships, LLC.

The teacher, by failing to recognize the polarity and focusing only on responsibilities, got the downside of both poles.

ACTIVITY 11.1: STUDENT DISCIPLINE

When discipline calls for conversations with students, have ready some copies of a blank polarity map. Or make a laminated poster-sized copy of the blank polarity map found on pages 138–139. Also, make several sets of laminated polarity tags, cut to fit the map. Consider stick-on Velcro to make the tags easy to use. Common polarities involved in discipline include the following:

My Rights AND Others' Rights

My Rights AND My Responsibilities

Short-Term AND Long-Term

School Success AND Social Success

1. *Pause.* One of the wisest principals I know directs students sent to the office to a rather comfy chair and says, "Take a seat for just a bit. I need to [jot a note/reschedule a meeting/finish what I was doing]." He says that two-thirds of the time, the student falls asleep. They've lost control because they're tired—they're out of balance on Activity AND Rest. Get them to rest a bit, and the odds of a successful intervention increase significantly.

2. *Suggest, or ask the student to suggest, a polarity.* If students haven't been introduced to polarities, say, "This chart helps me remember to listen to what you have to say *and* explain how it relates to our school rules. Does that seem fair?" Then post the pole name that relates to the student's viewpoint. For my playground incident, "My rights" would have let me voice the injustice only a six-year-old can feel.

3. *Let the student tell his or her side.* Then, help the student write a couple of statements that summarize the values or goals that led to the student's actions—in the upper quadrant for the pole he or she favored.

4. *Ask the student about the downside of those choices.* The first of course is, "Your choice landed you in my office" [or in the hall].

5. *Post the name of the other pole.* Ask, "When you made your choice, what were you ignoring?" Or suggest related school rules or norms.

6. *Use your judgment on consequences.* Sometimes first stating the formal consequences makes sense. Other times, using the map to help the student make an action plan for avoiding repeat offenses will be more productive. Time-consuming, yes, but embedding a model for making better choices provides a sound foundation for helping students learn the very difficult skill of self-regulation.

SHORT TERM AND LONG TERM

Goal setting, cause/effect and if/then logical reasoning, and homework habits are just a few of the areas that benefit from learning how to work with the *Short Term AND Long Term* polarity. Here are a few examples.

Homework. Many students (and adults) are pressure-prompted; the quality of their work improves when a deadline looms. Others start right away, barely stop for milk and cookies before tackling homework (and occasionally develop anxiety problems, a downside of being too conscientious). Conversation prompts for using this polarity with middle school students might map the polarities of *Working Now AND Working Later.* The conversation might sound like this:

> We'll start book commercials Monday, which means you have five whole days to prepare. How many of you think that seems like a long time?
>
> How many of you think you could do all the work on Sunday? What will you do after school today instead of starting your book talk? [Add upside comments to the Working Later pole]
>
> Who plans on starting today? Specifically, what step might you take today? Do you think you'll have time to do anything else? [Add upside comments to the Working Now pole] How does that sound to the rest of you? [Add any negative results from an over-focus on Working Now]
>
> Now think carefully. What else are you going to want to do on Sunday? Saturday? Write it down. Have you ever waited until the last minute and then had to do homework and missed out on other things you wanted to do? What happened and why? [Add any negative results from an overfocus on Working Later]
>
> Let's set a goal here: How far do you want to be by Friday so you can finish by Monday AND do those other things on the weekend?

To help students plan what they will finish by Friday, they need to understand the steps involved in the project—and many can name only two, starting and finishing! Students in Kindergarten to Grade 5 might need to be shown the steps involved.

1. Choose a book you've already read and think your classmates would love.

2. Complete the book commercial organizer your teacher provides.

3. Write an attention-grabbing opener that will create interest in the book among your classmates.

4. Have an adult review your opener and sign off on it (parent, guardian, or teacher). This must be done before Friday.

5. Practice your book commercial at least twice.

Older students need to practice identifying the steps in a project on their own; this is a key skill that struggling students typically lack.

This is a subtle use of polarities to ensure that advice on how to finish on time isn't, "If you start right away, you'll finish in plenty of time." Equally good advice is to plan backward from the deadline to understand how late one can start! These strategies acknowledge the needs of today (short-term) AND the needs of Sunday (long-term for students at this age) and help them plan for making the most of their time.

Goal setting. Being a doctor, playing for the Chicago Bulls, writing a novel, or founding an Internet start-up are some of the most frequent goals I hear from teenagers. All too often, their current actions aren't taking them closer to these lofty, faraway dreams. This polarity helps students think about what they might do *now* in very specific terms to work toward a goal. Instead of *study hard*, they might set a specific short-term goal of "Get a B in algebra" and then find a study partner, ask a teacher about extra resources and sources of help, master a new way of taking notes, and so on.

A teacher and I used a clip from the start of the movie *Space Jam*, where a very young Michael Jordan is practicing free throws on the driveway long past dark. He tells his dad, "I'm going to play for North Carolina. And we're going to nationals. And then I'm going to play for the Chicago Bulls." The students catch on quickly that Michael's long-term *dream* is to play for the NBA, but his short-term *goal* is improving his free throw percentage. It was a quick reality check on whether they were working toward real goals today that might make their future dreams come true.

Logical reasoning. Adolescents are notorious for thinking only of short-term results. Use this polarity to help them think through if/then and cause/effect analyses of the following:

- Their own actions: What were the short-term results? What does it mean for a year from now?
- Character development in stories: How did ___ affect him when it happened? By the end of the book, what did that incident mean to him?

- Historical acts and their short-term and long-term consequences: What were the short-term goals for a law? What happened immediately? What were the long-term results? What can we learn for new situations?

DEVELOPING STUDENT REASONING THROUGH POLARITIES

Some of the most rigorous of the Common Core State Standards are those involving making and supporting arguments. Recall from Chapter 1 that humans in general tend to pay attention only to information that supports what they already believe. Using a polarity map is a robust way to ready students for assignments that fulfill these standards:

- CCSS.ELA-Literacy.W.9–10.1a Introduce precise claim(s), distinguish the claim(s) from alternate or opposing claims, and create an organization that establishes clear relationships among claim(s), counterclaims, reasons, and evidence.
- CCSS.ELA-Literacy.W.9–10.1b Develop claim(s) and counterclaims fairly, supplying evidence for each while pointing out the strengths and limitations of both in a manner that anticipates the audience's knowledge level and concerns. (Common Core State Standards Initiative, 2012a)

Besides tackling these standards, the activity that follows provides opportunities for students with all learning styles to think deeply.[1] The activity emphasizes launching the introverted task of writing with extraverted group discussion. Working with familiar materials helps students bridge into a new writing process and separates teaching content from teaching processes. Those in themselves are a polarity. Too often, we try to do both. For example, we ask students to learn to write a compare/contrast essay focused on a book they're studying. New content and

---

1. See Chapter 12 for a deeper definition of learning styles. An interesting professional learning community discussion is considering how the needs of Extraversion, Introversion, Sensing, Intuition, Thinking, Feeling, Judging, and Perceiving are all met. And if there's a step someone would naturally omit, does it meet the needs of a style different from their own?

new process. An alternative is having them choose their own compare/contrast topic for the first essay. Concentrate instruction on the form of the essay—how does one go about writing a good compare/contrast essay? *Then* have them apply what they learned to an essay with new content.

ACTIVITY 11.2: ON-YOUR-FEET ARGUMENTS

Objectives:

- To help students prepare a reasoned argument that identifies and supports opposing viewpoints on a single issue
- To provide students with a mapping process they can use in many academic situations

Materials:

- Presentation slides for Chapter 11, available at www.corwin.com/positivepower.
- Flipchart paper, markers.
- Masking tape. Use this to make a quadrant grid on the floor so that students will be able to stand in the quadrants as you debrief their flipchart lists.
- Four pieces of flipchart paper to be placed in the four corners of the room, one each labeled as follows:

  - Positive results of focusing on Activity
  - Positive results of focusing on Rest
  - Negative results of overfocus on Activity to the neglect of Rest
  - Negative results of overfocus on Rest to the neglect of Activity

- Copies of any primary source materials students need (see below).
- If you completed Activity 9.1 or 9.2, you might keep the map you created handy to show students how the process can be used to sift through opinions.

Facilitation Instructions for Part 1:

1. Choose an example of a polarity to which your students can relate. Examine possibilities with the four "see it" questions in mind:
   - Is it ongoing? Like breathing?
   - Are the alternatives interdependent? Like inhaling and exhaling?

○ Over time, are both poles or solutions needed?
○ Finally, if we focus on only one upside, will we eventually undermine the greater purpose statement, or GPS?

Look for examples of a common polarity so that you can demonstrate how the same poles can be used to describe many issues. Possibilities include the following:

○ Part AND Whole
○ Individual AND Community
○ Centralization AND Decentralization
○ Tradition AND Change
○ Freedom AND Equality
○ Justice AND Mercy

Sources include these:

○ Fiction. The textbox below contains an excerpt from *Touching Spirit Bear* by Ben Mikaelsen (2001) that illustrates the *Justice AND Mercy* polarity.
○ Historical events that your class has studied. Examples include these:

➢ Prohibition: Individual Freedom AND Community Health

➢ The nuclear arms race: Part (nation) AND Whole (planet)

➢ Current events: Congressional partisanship as a demonstration of Part AND Whole

➢ Government regulations about sales of sugared beverages or vaccinations: Individual Freedom AND Community Health

Many works of fiction grapple with polarities. Use a book or movie that your students are familiar with. For example, *Touching Spirit Bear* can be used to launch mapping Justice AND Mercy, or Punishment AND Restoration, or even Individual AND Society. It tells the story of Cole, an angry middle schooler who has been abused by his father. Cole assaults a classmate so severely that the boy faces possible permanent disabilities. The juvenile court system uses a Restorative Justice Circle, where the victim's parents and attorney, and Cole's parents and attorney, work together under the care of circle facilitator Garvey. At the fourth meeting, Cole is tired of the process. Sure that he's bound for prison anyway, he asks why no one believes that he's sorry.

"All your life you've lied, manipulated people, and tried to avoid consequences," [Peter's lawyer] said. "There is absolutely no reason to believe that you have truly changed inside."

"Great, then get rid of me," Cole said. "Send me someplace where I'm not in your face and can't hurt anyone. But why do I have to go to jail?"

"Cole has a point," said Garvey. "Maybe there is some place other than prison."

"Anyplace he goes, there will be people he could assault," Peter's mother said. "It's not like we can ship Cole to the Arctic Circle."

Garvey's face came alive with thought, and he asked for the feather again. "I'm a native Tlingit," he said. "I was raised in Southeast Alaska. It is possible I could make arrangements to have Cole banished to a remote island on the Inland Passage. This is something First Nations people have done for hundreds of years. Cole could undergo a vision quest of sorts, an extended time alone to face himself and to face the angry spirits inside of him. . . . Banishment isn't a sentence. It's simply a time for Cole to walk his talk. We tell him to give more than lip service to the idea of change, but what chance does he have to prove anything if he's locked up? Sentencing would be delayed until the end of Cole's banishment. Then this same Circle could reevaluate him and decide whether he has walked his talk, and whether a sentence is still necessary." (pp. 55–56; Copyright © 1982 by Vera B. Williams, Greenwillow Books. Used by permission of HarperCollins Publishers.)

Cole *is* sent to a remote island, with primitive conditions, to contemplate what he wishes to make of his life. What are the positive and negative results from justice as punishment and mercy as restoration?

2. Introduce students to polarities. The slides are available at www. corwin.com/positivepower.

[Slide 11.1] Today we're going to look at a set of tools that will help us recognize when we need to solve a problem AND when we're dealing with an ongoing dilemma where each solution only holds part of the truth. [Slide 11.2] Let me give a quick example. Breathe in deeply. Keep breathing in. Now hold your breath. Hold it.

Getting Ready to
Support BOTH
Sides of an Issue

Slide 11.1

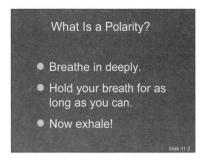

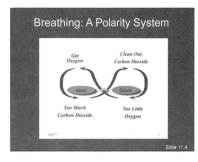

Note: Hold your own breath for at least five seconds.
Now exhale!

[Slide 11.3] Which is better, inhaling or exhaling? Neither, right? Our bodies need both—and they're interdependent. Inhaling and exhaling are an example of a polarity.

[Slide 11.4] Note that inhaling and exhaling are really an infinity loop. When we were holding our breath, our bodies started signaling "Too much carbon dioxide!" so we exhaled. Pretty soon our bodies demand that we inhale to get more oxygen. That's how polarities work. Each pole makes a valuable contribution to the system.

You've worked with polarities your whole lives. When you learned to share, you were working with Mine AND Yours. When you volunteer, you work with Individual AND Community. When families decide how to celebrate birthdays and holidays, they're often working with Tradition AND Change.

[Slide 11.5] So let's clarify just a couple definitions and then dive into trying out a tool. Polarities are interdependent pairs that, over time, need each other. Just like these turtles here. Yes, they can trade off being at the tip of the log, and one can even disappear for a while into the water, but over the long term they need each other. They require "and" instead of "versus" thinking. Note that some issues *do* require "versus" thinking; often, they're problems that can be solved once and for all. We're dealing with messier systems here—polarities that require a different way of thinking.

Why do we care about polarities? Because we can reclaim all the energy that's wasted on arguments, resistance, policy swings, and so on, if we intentionally analyze what we need from both sets of arguments. And that's what we're going to practice: a way to understand what each side values and fears, all in preparation for writing an essay where you fairly argue and effectively support both sides of an issue.

So let's start with a simple polarity system that everyone of us deals with—although some of us leverage it better than others! *Activity AND Rest*. And to start, let's look at athletes who *really* need to handle this one. Just about every athlete benefits from weight training, even if the purpose is balance or endurance. The system looks like this [Slide 11.6]. You start lifting weights heavily, and it's great—

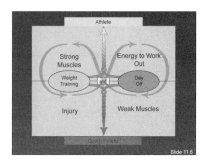

until you pull a muscle or end up too tired to walk. So you take a day off, and pretty soon you're back in the game. But if you don't get back to weight lifting, your strength starts to dwindle, and . . . if you don't get the right balance for you, you'll end up a couch potato instead of an athlete.

So let's try brainstorming the positives and negatives of each pole for the more general polarity of Activity AND Rest, not just lifting weights [Slide 11.7]. Think of being with friends and volunteering and sports and all kinds of things as activity. And sleep and television and relaxing as rest. Head with your group to the flipchart I assign to you. Your group will have two minutes to brainstorm the topic listed on your paper. Choose someone to record who is willing to report to the larger group. Any questions?

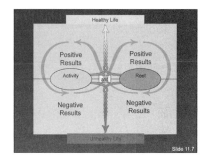

Instructions for the Rest of Part 1:

- After each group has finished brainstorming, ask everyone to gather around the chart for Positive Results of Activity. Ask someone from that group to read the items. Comment that the rich list of positive outcomes draws people toward this pole. However, as wonderful as it all sounds, if we overfocus on any pole, we get its downside.

- Have the group gather around the Negative Effects of Activity quadrant and have someone from the group read the chart. Ask how the group feels after hearing the list. Comment that we often then see the other pole as the solution—here, Rest—because it is the natural self-correction in an interdependent system.

- Move to the Positive Results of Rest. Ask someone to read their group's items. Again, comment that an overfocus will always bring the downside.
- Move the group to the Negative Effects of Rest and have someone read the group's list. Comment that once again the opposite pole can seem like a solution. But all of us continually move through the loop. Circumstances can dictate where we need to be, such as training for a major sports event or studying for a big test or getting injured. However, fighting between the poles as if they are an either/or choice, or choosing one pole as a solution, will lead to a vicious cycle where we're either too busy or too lethargic!
- Ask everyone to form a circle around the quadrants taped out on the floor. Have the four recorders bring the charts with them and stand in the middle, in their proper quadrants, back-to-back and facing the outside of the circle.
  - Ask the two "negative results" recorders to read their items one by one, alternating, and taking a step toward the bottom of the circle each time they read one. Note that you're having them demonstrate the spiraling down of a vicious cycle.
  - Then ask the two "positive results" recorders to do the same, stepping toward the top of the circle. Note that you're having them demonstrate the power of determining the action steps that will capture the best of both poles.
- Ask students to return to their seats. Show on the Activity/Rest polarity slide [Slide 11.7] how a virtuous cycle captures the positives of both sides and the vicious cycle balloons into the negative results area. Display how you would draw your loop. Have them do a quick-write on whether they are moving toward the positive or negative side of one of the poles. Also have them do the following:
  - Write down two action steps they could take to spend more time in the upside of this polarity.
  - Write down one sign that lets them know they're getting too much rest and one that lets them know they're being too active.

Inform them that they'll be using the same process to prepare to write an argumentative essay.

Facilitation Instructions for Part 2:

Use this script or reword it for your classroom to give students a bit more background before you tackle a bigger issue that can serve as the basis for a paper.

Now that we've had an experience with a polarity, let's look a little more deeply at how to work with them. Three steps are key.

[Slide 11.8] Step 1 is *seeing the polarity*. How do we know whether something is a problem to be solved once and for all or a polarity where we need to identify the value of each position? Four key questions can help us decide.

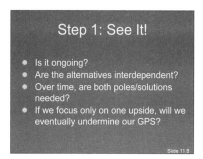

- Is it ongoing? Like activity and rest, our whole lives?
- Are the alternatives interdependent? Just as you need to inhale and exhale to blow out birthday cake candles?
- Over time, are both poles or solutions needed?
- Finally, if we focus on only one upside, will we eventually undermine what is called our greater purpose, like being healthy?

[Slide 11.9] Step 2 is *map it*. That's what we did last time—figuring out what each side contributes to our purpose and the consequences of focusing on only one pole. We add a greater purpose that convinces people at each pole that they want to work together. And we identify a deeper fear—what might happen if we fail to work together.

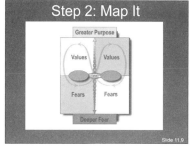

[Slide 11.10] Finally, in Step 3, we *leverage* the polarity to get as much of the positive impact of each pole as we can. To do this, we identify *early warning signs* that we can measure. These will let us know if we're focusing too much on one of the poles. And we develop *action steps,* strategies and practices we can implement to get the best of each side. Our goal? To use those action steps to stay in a virtuous cycle, as shown here with the infinity loop mostly encompassing the upper half of the map. We're trying to avoid a vicious cycle that would spiral us down toward our fears. And here's an important truth: If we overfocus on a pole, we end up with the downside of both.

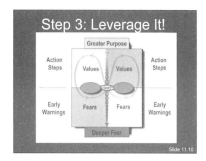

Note: Insert an example familiar to your students from class work. A well-known example of this is Prohibition, which is an example of the pole of Individual Freedom AND Community Health. The

United States saw alcohol as a problem. Solution? Ban alcohol sales. But then the production, sales, and purchase of alcohol went underground. There was still abuse *and* now we had organized crime involved. Alcohol was again legalized, but there are restrictions. The current situation tries to get the upside of people making their own choices, yet protecting members of the community such as children and keeping us safe from hazards such as drinking and driving.

[end of script]

Introduce the specific issue you'll be using to teach polarity mapping, following the process below. Consult Activity 8.1 for other ideas if you would like to adjust the activity. Activity 10.2, Debate, can also be used with students.

- Prepare four pieces of flipchart paper labeled with the positive and negative results of each pole, framed in student-friendly language. For the *Touching Spirit Bear* example given below, use the following labels, one for each chart paper:

    1. Positive results of Cole facing trial in Juvenile Court (Justice)

    2. Negative results of overfocus on jail and punishment to the neglect of helping Cole

    3. Positive results of Cole and Peter's family using Restitution Circle (Mercy)

    4. Negative results of overfocus on helping Cole to the neglect of punishment

  Note: The phrasing above helps students use a specific example to think through the huge issues that surround justice and mercy. Generalizing from this example will be easier than having students try to map justice and mercy abstractly.

  Note: Make two sets of chart paper if more than 24 students are involved.

  Note: A sample map for Touching Spirit Bear *is included at the end of this chapter and as the last slide in the deck, available at* www.corwin.com/ positivepower.

- If you have four groups of students, place one flipchart paper in each corner of the room. The map with the quadrants labeled for

Touching Spirit Bear is shown on Slide 11.11. Assign each group to a starting place. Have the groups spend two minutes brainstorming results for their station. Instruct them that they will move through the stations by their numbers: 1s rotate to 2s and so on, with 4s moving to 1 after the first round.

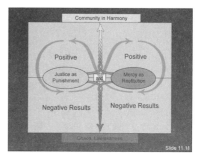

- Have the groups move to the next station, following the infinity loop. Give them about ninety seconds to add to the list the first group started.

- Rotate the groups to the next two stations, following the same instructions.

- After groups have added to their fourth charts, ask them to remain at their last station and prioritize the items listed. Which do they believe are the top five most significant? Have them put stars in front of their selections.

- Ask students, "What did you learn from providing input at all four stations?" Have them choose and move toward the pole that probably best fit their beliefs about the situation being discussed at the start of the exercise. Then ask for volunteers to share what they learned about the opposite point of view from the exercise.

- Display the Common Core Standard, either as published or as your school has reworded it [Slide 11.12].
  - CCSS.ELA-Literacy.W.9–10.1a Introduce precise claim(s), distinguish the claim(s) from alternate or opposing claims, and create an organization that establishes clear relationships among claim(s), counterclaims, reasons, and evidence.
  - CCSS.ELA-Literacy.W.9–10.1b Develop claim(s) and counterclaims fairly, supplying evidence for each while pointing out the strengths and limitations of both in a manner that anticipates the audience's knowledge level and concerns (Common Core State Standards Initiative, 2012a).

- Point out how polarity mapping provides the framework for considering what those at each pole in a debate value and what they fear about the other pole. The structure makes it easy to develop a cohesive argument about how to move forward on an issue.

- If you completed Activity 9.1 or 9.2, show students the original article and then how the pieces fit onto a polarity map as a demonstration of its use.

- Use your preferred technology method to capture the top five most significant results for each quadrant so that all students have access to them and can see them for the next step. A blank map is included in the slide deck [Slide 11.13], with a sample map for *Touching Spirit Bear* included as the last slide [Slide 11.15]. *Or have groups copy their top five to a separate piece of paper, printing in large letters, and tape the charts on the wall, arranged to form the polarity map quadrants. You could then draw the infinity loop on the papers.*

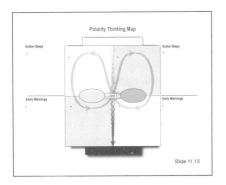

- Have students work in groups of four to organize the maps so that there are three results in each quadrant. Can they see pairs of items, where a negative result of one pole is "solved" by a positive result of the other? Or where a positive result, overdone, will produce a negative result as well? Point out how this helps them organize a cohesive argument. *The sample map is organized this way.*

- Move to action steps. Define action steps again. Have each group brainstorm at least one for each pole and share it with the class.

FROM MAPPING TO WRITING

While students could certainly write essays on the all-class map, the quality of rigorous essays usually improves when students are vested in the arguments they are making. And for teachers, reading a classroom's worth of essays on the same topic can have a few negative results from overfocus on one subject. Here's one solution.

- Introduce the universal polarities listed on page 200 [and Slide 11.14], as well as others, such as Activity AND Rest, that might appeal to your students. Give at least one example of each. Have students work in small groups to think of at least three issues they've seen that might illustrate one of the polarities, writing the polarity *and* topic on sheets of copy paper. *Note: You may wish to collect them, set aside any that are more problems to solve than polarities to leverage, and explain your reasoning to the students.*

What Topics Fit These Polarities?

- Part AND Whole
- Individual AND Community
- Centralization AND Decentralization
- Tradition AND Change
- Freedom AND Equality
- Justice AND Mercy

Slide 11.14

- Post all the suggested topics on a classroom wall. Give each student a self-stick note and ask them to write their names on them. Then, ask them to place their note below the topic that appeals to them most for an essay assignment. Let students know that they'll be able to work in groups of two to four to map their issues, but they will each produce an essay. Allow them to talk with each other and move their sticky notes until they've each chosen a topic.

- Let students work together to form a map with at least five items in each quadrant. Then, they can start working separately to narrow down the items to their top two or three to use in the essay.

In essence, the mapping process provides the mechanics for forming an argument—the bare-bones content of the essay. While writing is mainly an introverted process, gathering ideas is not.

REFLECTION

1. The older the students, the more sophisticated their use of polarity thinking can be. What will work for your students? What might you try? Commit to at least one activity, remembering that it often takes five or six tries for a strategy to be effective for teachers and students.

2. Find another learning standard where polarity thinking might deepen student understanding: A science concept, a literary technique, or a way to think about tackling a mathematics task are a few possibilities.

Polarity Thinking Map for *Touching Spirit Bear*

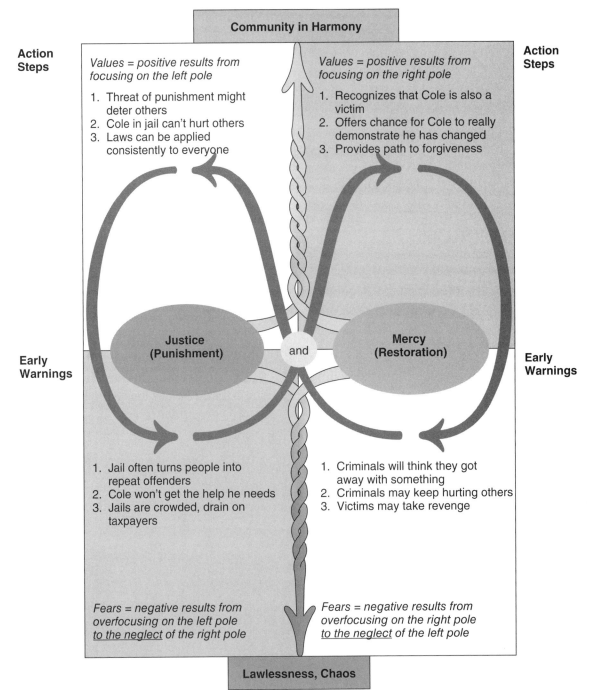

Polarity Thinking Map for Touching Spirit Bear

Community in Harmony

Action Steps

Values = positive results from focusing on the left pole

1. Threat of punishment might deter others
2. Cole in jail can't hurt others
3. Laws can be applied consistently to everyone

Values = positive results from focusing on the right pole

1. Recognizes that Cole is also a victim
2. Offers chance for Cole to really demonstrate he has changed
3. Provides path to forgiveness

Action Steps

Justice (Punishment) and **Mercy (Restoration)**

Early Warnings

1. Jail often turns people into repeat offenders
2. Cole won't get the help he needs
3. Jails are crowded, drain on taxpayers

1. Criminals will think they got away with something
2. Criminals may keep hurting others
3. Victims may take revenge

Early Warnings

Fears = negative results from overfocusing on the left pole to the neglect of the right pole

Fears = negative results from overfocusing on the right pole to the neglect of the left pole

Lawlessness, Chaos

Source: Map template copyright by Polarity Partnerships, LLC.

Part IV

A Closer Look at Why We Believe What We Believe

12 Carl Jung, Neuroscience, and the Truth That We're Wired to Develop Different Viewpoints

One of the biggest benefits of polarity thinking is its usefulness in understanding other people's positions. Values, past experiences, and culture all influence our beliefs, but sometimes the act of mapping polarities helps us gain answers to questions such as the following:

How can they say that their proposal is best practice?

Why aren't they buying in to the reasoning I've presented for making this change?

Why aren't some students responding to this research-based practice?

Who would want to learn this way?

Another tool, though, helps us gain insights into how wise people, even with similar backgrounds and experiences, can hold different beliefs about education. In all my research and writings on education, I've worked with the framework of Jungian personality type. Popularized through the Myers-Briggs Type Indicator (MBTI), it is the most widely used, and perhaps the most widely *mis*-used, theory of human nature in the world.

"Wait," I hear some of you say. "I heard the MBTI has nothing to do with education." When people say this, they've either read reports of research that mistakenly used the MBTI as a diagnostic tool rather than a self-reporting instrument, or they're unaware of significant research that (a) validates Carl Jung's theory and (b) demonstrates its usefulness as a tool in education. Isabel Myers, who worked with her mother Katherine Briggs to develop the MBTI, said that it was her desire that someday all parents, teachers, and students would understand personality type and the impact it has on education.

Actually, there are literally thousands of studies that validate type theory. I'll highlight several in this chapter, especially those with a neuroscience foundation or a direct connection to improving instruction.

Here is the essence of personality type. Jung noted predictable patterns in the following:

- How people are *energized*
- How they *take in information*
- How they *make decisions*
- How they *approach work and life*

Look at the italicized words above. All are essential components in the debates over education. Teachers, students, and administrators all need energy to succeed. Further, the reality that we take in information and make decisions in different ways *drives many of the polarizing debates in education.*

"No wonder I . . . didn't like that curriculum . . . struggle with fidgety students . . . objected to that teaching strategy . . . thought that teacher ran a perfect classroom" are some of the typical responses when people explore their own personality type preferences and reflect on how they influence their education beliefs. Note that I said "influence" and not "determine." Type theory is about a system of preferences, not predestination.

Below, sign your name using the hand you do not usually write with.

_____

How might you describe that task? Most people say it is awkward and unnatural, requiring some thought and effort. Now sign using the other hand.

Most people describe that experience as fluent, natural, and unconscious. The hand with which we write is a physical preference that is part of our innate makeup. We have lots of these—a dominant eye, a favorite foot for kicking balls, a way to cross our arms, and so on. However, which one we use can be influenced by culture (think about prejudices against people who are left-handed of both long ago and, if you think about it, still today in ways such as how most coffee cups are designed). Further, we can develop skills with the nonpreferred side; in fact, success at sports and in many other fields depends on it. What basketball coach would let youngsters dribble, pass, and shoot with only their preferred side? The other team would soon figure out how to block every shot!

Jung postulated that we similarly have mental preferences. These are also innate but are influenced by culture, skills development, our work environment, and more. Countless studies have looked at type, learning styles, and student achievement. Look back, though, at how these mental preferences are defined. Would you expect that teaching to a student's style would improve performance? No, and here's the consensus of type experts on why this is so:

School success requires students to develop skills for learning in every style. Sometimes students need to work alone on set tasks such as mastering math facts or core knowledge about a period in history. Some school tasks require imaginative or innovative independent work, including silent reading and writing. At other times, such as in science labs, students need to engage in hands-on activities, often working in groups. And some of our biggest learning moments happen through high-level group discussions, questioning, and debates. However, some of these activities naturally appeal to some of us more than to others.

While it would not be helpful to allow each child to learn in his or her own style all the time, taking type into consideration in education means the following:

- Ensuring that classrooms "teach around" the learning styles so that no children constantly have to learn in other styles—think of the energy drain of writing with your nonpreferred hand all day long!

- Helping students recognize when tasks require them to learn outside their own style, and providing strategies and skills for them to succeed
- When children struggle with key learning concepts, finding ways to bridge to those concepts via the child's own style

Because of the frequent misunderstandings and misuses of type, let's look at what it *isn't* and then at what it *is*. Then we'll explore its relationship to some of the polarized debates in education and how it might help us leverage our differences.

WHAT TYPE *ISN'T*

As with most things, criticism of type comes from misunderstandings, so let's begin with a clear understanding of what can and can't be done with type theory.

The misconceptions on the left side of Chart 12.1 come from misuse of type. Unfortunately, people frequently take an online survey or paper/pencil tool for finding their preferences and are told, "That's your type." The technical manuals for *all* of these published type instruments (MBTI, Psychological Type Indicator [PTI], Jung Type Indicator [JTI], Golden Personality Type Profiler [GPTP], etc.) indicate that the results need to be interpreted by a qualified practitioner. This can be done in a group session or individually. If being handed results without interpretation was your experience, then validation research on all the instruments shows that there's a 25% to 30% chance that, given the opportunity to work with a qualified individual, you'd conclude that a different set of preferences describes you best.

These instruments have, by statistical standards, *excellent* reliability for self-reporting instruments. But Myers, and developers since her, didn't think people liked to be told who they were. The self-reporting format leads to deep discussions of why people answered one way on a questionnaire, yet think differently about themselves when hearing the theory or participating in an experience. Often people realize they need to be one way at work and another way at home, or that they value one preference but struggle to operate consistently in that manner. These insights are great fuel for self-reflection.

So here's what type is.

WHAT TYPE *IS*

Personality type is a theoretical framework that describes normal differences among normal people. There are four sets of preferences, or eight in

Chart 12.1 Ten Truths About Type

Type is not . . .	Type is . . .
1. A static labeling system	1. A dynamic system that describes common patterns in how people perceive information and make decisions
2. A tool that boxes people in	2. A tool that helps people reflect on who they are and what is important to them
3. A predictor of how an individual will behave	3. A predictor of patterns and tendencies that influence motivations and choices
4. A differentiation system useful for assigning students to their ideal learning practices	4. A differentiation system that helps teachers evaluate whether they favor or place at risk students with certain preferences. They work to "teach around the styles" to ensure all students are motivated and develop flexibility.
5. A predictor of biases	5. A way to add some objectivity to examination of one's strengths and beliefs
6. A label assigned through an assessment or questionnaire	6. A pattern of mental preferences assigned through a combination of theory explanation, experiences, interpretation, and self-assessment. This process may be assisted by wise use of an indicator or sorting tool.
7. An excuse for bad behavior	7. An explanation for how some negative behaviors may become habitual without self-reflection and development
8. Limiting	8. Freeing, while recognizing that although some things can take more effort and energy, they can still be mastered at a high level
9. A framework that predicts school success or failure	9. A framework that helps teachers better meet student needs
10. A cure-all for communication and collaboration	10. A reliable lens that helps people see relationships in a new way, often motivating them to develop new skills for improving relationships

total, which combine to describe 16 types. Each of the four preference sets is a polarity that involves two equally valuable mental processes. Mature people can access either pole, but they still *prefer* one over the other, similar to the handedness exercise earlier in the chapter.

While thousands of studies over the last several decades have validated Jung's theory, perhaps the most fascinating work is the recent research by Dr. Dario Nardi (2011). Working with college students at the University of California, Los Angeles, he used EEG technology to analyze brain patterns as subjects completed a variety of tasks in sessions that lasted from two to three hours. He found that whereas two people selected at random will show similar patterns for about 33% of their neocortex activity, people of the same personality type show more similarities. Half have 70% to 90% in common, and the rest share 50% to 70% of the same brain activity at a statistically significant level.

Here's an example. Most people would agree that physical education majors and English majors tend to have different personalities—and research bears that out. In fact, my husband, a physical education teacher, and I have completely opposite Jungian personality profiles. Over 30 years of marriage confirms that this can be a wonderful combination, but we *are* different.

Take our natural pathways to inspiration. My type usually seeks quiet. We try to let our minds go blank so our unconscious can forge connections among knowledge, theories, experiences, and so on. Suddenly—pop!—we gain new insights. Our brain activity in the main sections of the neocortex, the brain's outer layer, looks like the diagram in Figure 12.1: calm, synchronized, with almost no use of energy.

My husband, in contrast, gets his best ideas while interacting with the environment—examining, moving, rearranging, or observing. Each area of the brain is slightly "switched on," waiting for something to happen, in the same circumstances that produce my best ideas. It looks like the diagram in Figure 12.2.

Nardi calls this the "tennis hop" pattern, the brain being ready to respond to stimulus, just as tennis players assume a ready stance while waiting for an opponent's serve. In Nardi's lab, students with my husband's type preferences showed more brain activity when looking out the window than when completing math calculations that are similar to worksheet activities. Their brain activity increases in response to the outside world, with all the bars in the chart above moving toward maximum activity, in the very same circumstances that shut down my best ideas! Jungian preferences do influence our approaches to learning!

Figure 12.1 Introverted Intuition Brain in Flow State

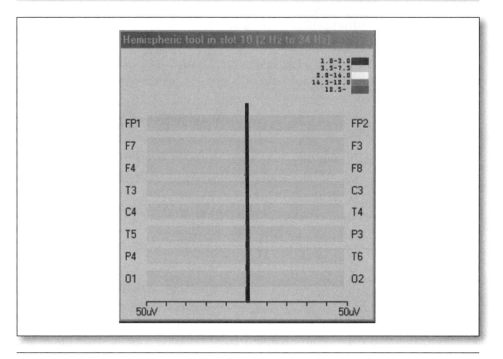

Source: Dario Nardi

Figure 12.2 Extraverted Sensing Brain in "Tennis Hop" Mode

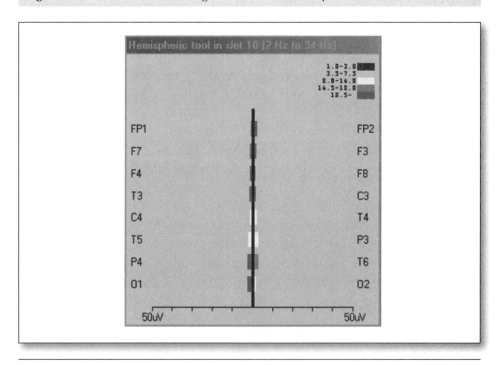

Source: Dario Nardi

Hopefully, these few facts whetted your appetite for more information on how type affects our educational beliefs and practices. Let's look at each of the preference pairs.

HOW WE ARE ENERGIZED

Perhaps the most visible of the type preferences are those for Extraversion and Introversion. In type terms, this polarity doesn't describe who is most outgoing or who has the most friends but, rather, how we are energized:

- People who *prefer* Extraversion get their energy from action and interaction.
- People who *prefer* Introversion get their energy from solitude and reflection.

Everyone needs interaction with other people. All of us need time alone for reflective practice on life in general. The question is how much of each brings energy. You spend some of your time in both worlds, but which do you prefer? Which is more draining?

Let's look at one example of how these preferences might affect education reform. I was working with a school in another country. As we completed a hands-on exercise on Extraversion and Introversion, I asked them to discuss any implications for their classrooms. Here is a summary of what they said:

> One of our schoolwide strategies this year is cooperative learning, with students working in small groups frequently throughout the day. While you were clear that students who prefer Introversion will also benefit from this, we realize that we aren't giving them any time to reflect and prepare for discussions. We need more protocols, such as the ones you've introduced, to make sure all students have energy for cooperative learning.

Note that they weren't talking about whether student collaboration was "right" or "wrong" but about how to make it work for all students. That's the power of a neutral framework for describing how we teach and how students learn.

Below is set of continuums you can use to consider whether Extraversion or Introversion best describes you.

Chart 12.2 Extraversion (E) or Introversion (I): How Are You Energized?

Mark where you would place yourself on each continuum. It is perfectly normal to mark some on each side. Remember that you have skills with each preference; your task is to reflect on which is naturally more energizing and which is more draining, even though you do both.

E | | | | | | I

I get my best ideas
during discussions.

I prefer to discuss ideas after I've
had a chance to reflect on my
perspective.

E | | | | | | I

I like to talk through possible
solutions to a difficulty I'm having.

I like to think through possible
solutions to a difficulty I'm having.

E | | | | | | I

When there is a lull in
conversation, I frequently jump in.

When there is a lull in conversation,
I get lost in thought.

E | | | | | | I

I often share new ideas quickly
so I can get input from others.

I often work to perfect ideas on
my own before I'm comfortable
sharing them.

E | | | | | | I

I like to try new ideas before
discussing or reflecting on them.

I like to read/reflect on new ideas
before trying them.

E | | | | | | I

People usually know what I am
thinking; I say it.

People often ask to find out what I
am thinking.

E | | | | | | I

My ideal learning environment is
full of variety and activity.

My ideal learning environment is
full of concentration and reflection.

E | | | | | | I

I enjoy learning through trial and
error.

I like to think through possible
solutions and try the best one first.

E | | | | | | I

I tend to focus on the outer world
of people and things.

I tend to focus on the inner world
of thoughts, books, and ideas.

E | | | | | | I

I get my best ideas when
interacting with the world.

I get my best ideas when I'm alone.

Research Supporting Consideration of Extraversion and Introversion in Education

In a meta-analysis of research on type in education, Lawrence (2009) found that students who prefer Extraversion did their best work when they had opportunities to think out loud through discussions, group work, and active projects. They also benefited from being able to observe how classmates worked on problems and hearing what they considered as important. Students who preferred Introversion did their best work when they could reflect first, processing their thoughts and experiences at their own pace and being able to think before presenting or answering questions.

Felder, Felder, and Dietz (2002) redesigned introductory engineering courses at North Carolina State University to include more hands-on, collaborative work, in response to past studies of engineering students, which showed that those who preferred Extraversion earned lower grades and were less likely to stay enrolled in the major. They looked at students with high and low college acceptance indices (a combination of high school GPA and SAT scores) and found that while the course design made no difference for students with a higher index, for the lower students in the new courses, the Extraverted students outperformed their Introverted peers by a full letter grade in those courses and dropped out of the program at a much lower rate. Their study perhaps shows an *over*correction in course design to meet the needs of Extraverted students, but it lends weight to the need for both interactive and reflective learning activities to meet the needs of all students.

Reflection Questions: Extraversion, Introversion, and Education Strategies/Policies

- As a child, how easy was it for you to sit still and read? Usually, those who prefer Extraversion struggle to sit still more than those who prefer Introversion.
- Is Extraversion or Introversion honored more through the education policies in your workplace? How is time allocated between action and reflection? Between collaboration and individual work, for both adults and students?
- Think about your response to intervention strategies. Might they be biased toward Extraversion or Introversion? For example, computer-based interventions often require sitting still with little interaction with other students or adults; this may be more difficult for Extraverted students. Small-group, discussion-based interactions may be more difficult for Introverted students.
- In my research and work with instructional coaching, I constantly find that teachers who prefer Introversion seek more support as they launch literature circles and other small-group activities than do Extraverted teachers. How might Introverted teachers need to adjust these activities to ensure that they maintain their own energy levels?

- Billings and Roberts (2012) found that teachers expressed surprise that allowing students to talk about a complex text before engaging in a writing task increased the length and quality of their writing. Given that writing is an Introverted activity, through the lens of type, allowing Extraverted students to talk first is a natural way to improve their writing process. How else might our views on the "right" way to provide assignments or tasks hamper learning for either Extraverted or Introverted students?

WHAT INFORMATION CATCHES YOUR ATTENTION: SENSING AND INTUITION

Jung identified two starting places in the process of perceiving the world around us:

- People who prefer Sensing *first* notice the real world of information collected through their five senses and through past experience
- People who prefer Intuition *first* notice the unseen world of hunches, connections, and analogies.

All of us can do both. The question is where we start. For example, where does your mind go first when examining the drawing in Figure 12.3?

Figure 12.3 The Hearing Forest and Seeing Field by Hieronymus Bosch

Source: Wikimedia Commons

This exercise isn't a definitive test for Sensing or Intuition; your past experiences with writing about art or your notions of why I included the picture may influence how you respond. When I use the picture in workshops, I circulate to find the three clearest examples of each preference to illustrate the different starting places of perception.

The clearest Sensing responses follow this pattern: "Tree with owl and dog, two ears in the forest, eyes in the ground, trees, birds . . . What could this be? Maybe a fairy tale illustration?" They first note the details and then move to interpretation and finding meaning.

The clearest Intuitive responses follow this pattern: "Once upon a time the Wise woman of the forest . . ." or "This seems to be an interpretation of the wisdom of nature, if we would only look and listen and . . ." They go straight to interpretation or finding meaning and then circle back to use supporting details.

We can all of course do both, and our background and mind-set (as well as our general like or dislike of the picture) will influence how long we spend with each process, but our innate mental preference for Sensing or Intuition influences how we process information, whether that information is in pictures, words, actions, the physical world, books, movies—in the myriad ways we encounter information every day.

Work through the continuums in Chart 12.3 to reflect on which preference best describes your natural approach.

Research Supporting Consideration of Sensing and Intuition in Education

Lawrence (2009), in an overview of major research on Sensing, Intuition, and education, found that students who preferred Sensing thrived when teachers took a sequential approach to new material, provided firsthand experiences and opportunities to practices showed them exactly what was expected, and demonstrated the usefulness of what they were learning. Students who preferred Intuition thrived when they pursued new material in their own way, often hopping from concept to concept; had choices in the content they studied and the ways they could solve problems; when challenged to discover ideas for themselves; and when allowed to explore new skills rather than practice existing ones.

Myers, McCaulley, Quenk, and Hammer (1998) found that Intuitives outperform Sensing types on nearly every standardized test of learning. Myers (1993) identified that although 70% to 75% of the population prefers Sensing, 82% of the National Merit Scholarships go to Intuitive students. Wilkes (2004), in an item-by-item analysis of student responses, concluded that the performance difference on the PSAT, the determinant of National Merit Scholarships, is due to the Intuitive style of guessing rather than a difference in intelligence.

Much of the realm of education favors the Intuitive world of symbols and abstraction; reading itself is an Intuitive exercise, for example. Recall that two of the types showed more brain activity looking out the window at the real world than while doing worksheets (Nardi, 2011). Those were Sensing students who also preferred Extraversion!

Many educator biases can be traced back to these preferences. For example, teachers who prefer both Introversion and Sensing naturally prefer a basal reading program approach to instruction, whereas those who prefer Extraversion and Intuition are attracted to a more whole language approach (Lehto, 1990). While instruction has moved to a more balanced approach since this study took place, one can assume that part of the reason the "reading wars" were so contentious was that our beliefs in part derive from this basic personality difference.

Chart 12.3 Sensing (S) or Intuition (N): What Information Grabs Your Attention?

Mark where you would place yourself on each continuum. It is perfectly normal to mark some on each side. Remember that you have skills with each preference; your task is to reflect on which is naturally more energizing and which is more draining, even though you do both.

S | | | | | N

I tend to use facts and what's worked in the past as my guides.
I tend to use ideas, connections, and the new insights they bring as my guides.

S | | | | | N

I think of myself as practical, down-to-earth.
I think of myself as original, thriving on doing things differently.

S | | | | | N

I like step-by-step instructions—why start if you aren't sure you have accurate directions?
I tend to jump into things without reading directions, following my hunches.

S | | | | | N

Curriculum provides structure for teaching and learning.
Curriculum provides ideas that can be modified and improved.

S | | | | | N

I notice the "trees" of practical and factual details.
I notice the "forest" of patterns and meanings.

S | | | | | N

I tend to focus on the here and now, what is happening in the present.
I often find myself pondering possibilities for the future.

S | | | | | N

For me, long-term planning is six to twelve months.
For me, long-term planning is three to five years.

S | | | | | N

I prefer receiving clear instructions and getting answers to all my questions.
I prefer receiving clear goals and charting my own way to meet them.

S | | | | | N

I prefer student assignments that require accuracy to ensure fairness in grading.
I prefer student assignments that allow them to be unique.

S | | | | | N

I like to try a strategy multiple times, working to improve it.
I like to try a variety of strategies and may not use them more than once.

Reflection Questions: Sensing, Intuition, and Education Strategies/Policies

- Sensing teachers and students tend to seek more practice before moving on to new learning (as discussed on page 86). How much practice is embedded in your response to intervention programs? Do some (possibly Intuitive) students complain?
- One emphasis in the Common Core State Standards for both mathematics and language arts is on questions and problems that can be approached in multiple ways and that could have more than one answer. How might teachers' (and students') preferences for Sensing and Intuition affect their comfort with these more open-ended tasks?

HOW DO YOU MAKE DECISIONS: THINKING OR FEELING?

If *Star Trek* made one contribution to society (and I'd argue for more, given how store doors and flip phones work . . .), it was personifying two very different sets of criteria people use in making decisions:

Spock: "Logic would dictate . . ."

McCoy: "But there are people involved! You can't . . ."

In Jungian terms, Spock begins with a Thinking preference in decision making and McCoy with a Feeling preference, defined as follows:

- When making decisions, people who prefer Thinking *first* consider logic, if-then and pro-con reasoning, and the precedents being set. Objectivity is the goal.
- When making decisions, people who prefer Feeling *first* consider the values involved and the impact on people by stepping into their shoes. Subjectivity is the goal.

Both are rational ways of making decisions; the quickest way to see a logical decision turn into a disaster is to neglect the values and feelings of those who are expected to implement that decision. Or a leader can lose the respect of his or her team by being continually inconsistent in an effort to please everyone until chaos seems to reign. (Note that Captain James T. Kirk listened to both Spock and McCoy, a great model for leadership.)

Recent research shows that our brains use different neural pathways to process empathetic lines of reasoning and analytical lines of reasoning

Chart 12.4 Thinking (T) or Feeling (F): Which Decision Criteria Might You Emphasize?

Mark where you would place yourself on each continuum. It is perfectly normal to mark some on each side. Remember that you have skills with each preference; your task is to reflect on which is naturally more energizing and which is more draining, even though you do both.

T | | | | | | F

My decisions are based on logic, awareness of precedents, and cause/effect reasoning.

My decisions are based on community values and awareness of the impact on people.

T | | | | | | F

I tend to first see flaws in ideas and practices.

I tend to first see the positives in other people's ideas and practices.

T | | | | | | F

Fairness comes through consistent implementation of rules and policies.

Fairness comes through consideration of individual needs and circumstances.

T | | | | | | F

I am more skeptical than trusting

I am more trusting than skeptical.

T | | | | | | F

I prize bringing a logical order to processes and learning.

I prize relationship building in processes and learning.

T | | | | | | F

I look first for competency in team members.

I look first for good relationships with team members.

T | | | | | | F

If someone shares a problem with me, I tend to analyze and solve it.

If someone shares a problem with me, I tend to sympathize before checking if they are seeking advice.

T | | | | | | F

I tend to favor math and science topics.

I tend to favor the humanities and cultural studies.

T | | | | | | F

Debate and competition motivate me.

Consensus and cooperation motivate me.

T | | | | | | F

Using objective data to inform instruction comes naturally for me.

Using subjective data to inform instruction, such as information on student engagement, comes naturally for me.

and that the other pathway shuts down when one is being used (Case Western University, 2012). It is thus possible for intelligent education leaders to get so wrapped up in an analytical analysis of data and research while choosing or implementing reform efforts that they lose track of the human side of the equation and neglect to build support or answer critique.

Knowing your natural preference for Thinking or Feeling provides avenues for avoiding being too objective or too subjective for specific situations—and for understanding how reasonable people can reach different conclusions with similar sets of facts.

Research Supporting Consideration of Thinking and Feeling in Education

Lawrence (2009), in a review of research on type in education, concluded that Thinking students thrive when they are instructed by teachers who are logically organized, they receive feedback that tracks their progress on objective learning goals, and they are allowed to analyze and critique ideas and materials, avoiding emotional issues to keep thinking clear. Feeling students learn best when teachers value having a personal rapport with students, they can help others and respond to their needs, they receive feedback that shows warm appreciation for their efforts and abilities, and they care deeply about the topics they are studying.

Mathematics teachers tend to prefer Thinking—not surprising, given its logical, orderly content base. A majority of elementary teachers prefer Feeling (approximately 70%); the percentage of Thinking teachers increases with each grade level. In contrast, about 75% of school principals prefer Thinking. This difference in decision-making style often leads to misunderstandings.

Nardi (2011) found that two of the types that prefer Introversion and Thinking show active use of the logic centers of their brains but very little use of the main auditory processing centers. One way to interpret this is that they rely on internal, logical models instead of on input from others. In contrast, two of the types that prefer Introversion and Feeling show the *most* activity of all the types in the main auditory processing centers. They show a keen interest in the input of others; they are innately good at listening. These findings have major implications for the skills and practices these types need to work together effectively.

Reflection Questions: Thinking, Feeling, and Education Strategies/Policies

- Much of the support for zero-tolerance policies comes from overfocus on the Thinking (especially Sensing/Thinking) view of fairness as consistent implementation of a rule as well as cause/effect reasoning. Feeling-based decision makers are often aware of reasons for exceptions or ways in which such rules might unfairly impact certain students. Are there voices for each side in your community?

- With the growing body of brain research demonstrating how objective and subjective reasoning shut each other down, what does this mean for data-driven decision making? What action steps might add needed subjective criteria to such decision processes?

- Think back to Chapter 3 on *Academic Success AND Whole Child Success.* How might people who prefer Thinking and Feeling view this issue? Use the upper quadrants of the map on pages 50–51 and the continuums on page 226 to assist your analysis.

HOW DO YOU APPROACH LIFE: JUDGING OR PERCEIVING?

The framework of type concludes with an overall look at how we orient our lives: toward planning and closure or toward spontaneity and openness?

- Those who prefer a Judging orientation tend to prefer planning and then working that plan. Deciding, or coming to closure, is motivating.

- Those who prefer a Perceiving orientation tend to prefer staying open to new information, incorporating it into a more spontaneous approach to life. Remaining flexible is motivating to them.

Both are valuable and responsible ways of approaching life. In education, the Judging side drives calendars, learning benchmarks, curriculum mapping, graduation standards, and other areas that allow us to organize the world of learning. The Perceiving side allows for flexibility for students with different needs, for emerging events, for new practices and research discoveries, and for dealing with the unexpected. Which best describes your natural approach?

Chart 12.5 Judging (J) or Perceiving (P): How Do You Approach Life?

Mark where you would place yourself on each continuum. It is perfectly normal to mark some on each side. Remember that you have skills with each preference; your task is to reflect on which is naturally more energizing and which is more draining, even though you do both.

J | | | | | | P

I thrive when I can plan my work and work my plan.

I thrive when I can stay open to the moment.

J | | | | | | P

I tend to plan my free time as well as my work life.

Although I organize my work life, I lead a spontaneous personal life.

J | | | | | | P

Work before play is my preferred style.

I tend to mix work and play.

J | | | | | | P

I feel comfortable implementing a plan.

I feel comfortable responding to surprises.

J | | | | | | P

I like to decide quickly and get to work.

I like to seek more options to ensure we've made the best decision.

J | | | | | | P

Finishing early is naturally appealing, although I know more time could bring new insights.

I enjoy the process of searching and seeking options and sometimes struggle to bring closure.

J | | | | | | p

I may call for a decision even if more data might be found.

I might delay a decision even if we seem to have a lot of data.

J | | | | | | P

I'd describe myself as goal oriented.

I'd describe myself as process oriented.

J | | | | | | P

I have a built-in clock; I know how long projects or classroom activities will take.

I may underestimate how long projects or classroom activities will take.

J | | | | | | P

I know human limits and avoid overcommitment for myself and others.

I often make new commitments and then struggle to meet all of them.

> ## Research Supporting Consideration of Judging and Perceiving in Education
>
> Lawrence (2009) concluded from a review of research on type in education that Judging students thrive when learning experiences have clear structure with milestones and accountability, as well as established completion points. Perceiving students prefer open exploration, assignments that feel like play, and novelty in tasks to spark their interests.
>
> Many studies show that students who prefer Perceiving, especially if they also prefer Sensing, are overrepresented in alternative high schools in the United States. I once conducted a workshop for over one hundred members of a curriculum and instruction department for a large urban school district. Only one of the participants preferred Sensing and Perceiving and exclaimed, "This explains so much of my own school experiences!" The head of the department commented, "It also means that perhaps you're the only person in the room who might have insights into the needs of students who are struggling the most?" Sensing and Perceiving teachers are underrepresented in general, making up only 13% of all teachers (and are usually found in physical education, business education, and other noncore subjects), whereas they represent over 27% of the general population.
>
> About 85% of school principals prefer Judging, compared with about 50% of the general population. The culture of U.S. schools shows a definite bias toward the Judging approach to life.

Reflection Questions: Judging, Perceiving, and Education Strategies/Policies

- Think about your school's or district's use of pacing guides; curriculum maps; grouping students by age level; school daily, weekly, and yearly schedules; and homework policies. If one thinks of Judging and Perceiving as a polarity where the best outcome involves accessing the values of each pole, what action steps might incorporate more of a Perceiving approach to learning?
- Loose-tight leadership (Sagie, 1997) incorporates both Judging (setting clear goals) and Perceiving (granting autonomy in reaching those goals). How well are you managing the tension between clear expectations and multiple pathways for meeting them?

WHY TYPE AS A FRAMEWORK FOR MOVING BEYOND POLARIZATION?

In summary, type adds to our ability to move beyond polarization because it is a tool for the following:

- Rethinking where our own positions come from and how the needs of others might differ from our own
- Considering which teachers might favor/struggle with implementing a new strategy or practice
- Evaluating the effectiveness of teaching, learning, and intervention strategies for students with different learning preferences

Further, type provides a framework for understanding what cultures as a whole value, including our own culture. Type is universal; people around the world use the same mental preferences. My professional organization, the Association for Psychological Type International, has members in over forty countries, from England to South Africa to Saudi Arabia to Chile to Indonesia. However, cultures differ in how they value the preferences. Some of the current agendas in education reform in the United States closely align with what type professionals call the cultural *archetype.*

Archetypes are different from stereotypes or labeling. For example, people from other countries often *stereotype* Americans as loud, overbearing, and quick to voice decisions, all characteristics of Extraversion. The best data we have on type distribution show that about 50% of Americans prefer Extraversion. However, think about the behaviors that are valued in corporations and rewarded in schools, such as voicing ideas quickly, being at ease in social situations, and participating in class. In other words, we value Extraversion more than Introversion in the United States. It is our cultural *archetype.* In contrast, type experts within cultures such as Korea and Japan have looked at their values and determined an archetype for Introversion.

Analysis by type experts of the preference pairs has again and again pointed to Extraversion, Sensing, Thinking, and Judging as the overall U.S. archetype, although the modal, or most common, type is ISFJ, at 14%, with ESTJ at 9% (Myers et al., 1998).

Let's look at how type preferences influence educator beliefs about the four main issues discussed in Part II of this book.

TYPE AND *ACADEMIC SUCCESS* AND *WHOLE CHILD SUCCESS*

When policies reinforce ESTJ values, the U.S. archetype, one might do well to consider whether "majority rules" means that important considerations are being devalued or overlooked.

From a personality type perspective, the Achievement pole reflects the U.S. cultural archetype of ESTJ preferences, and the Whole Child pole reflects the very different values of INFP preferences. One of my colleagues, the late Gordon Lawrence, surveyed over twelve hundred people to develop common values statements for each type. He then asked one hundred people of each type to critique the statements that applied to them to ensure that they reflected values, not behaviors. Chart 12.6 lists a few for these two types.

Chart 12.6 Comparison of ESTJ and INFP Values

ESTJ	INFP
• Common-sense practicality	• Creativity, curiosity, and exploring
• Consistency and standard procedures	• Helping people find their potential
• Concrete, present-day usefulness	• Seeing the big picture possibilities
• Having things settled and closed	• Adaptability and openness
• Rules, objective standards, and fairness according to the rules	• Compassion and caring; attention to feelings
• Systematic structure and efficiency	• An inner compass; being unique
• Scheduling and monitoring	• Perfecting what is important

Source: Lawrence (1998).

While it is *not* true that everyone who prefers ESTJ tends toward the Academic Success pole or that every INFP tends toward the Whole Child Success pole, it is safe to say that accountability, flexibility, and choice are more consistent with the values in the left column than those in the right column. Further, because of our cultural norms and the fact that about two-thirds of our country prefers Sensing (and about two-thirds of leaders in businesses, education, and government prefer TJ), the values on the right can be easily overlooked.

TYPE AND *TEACHER EVALUATION FOR ACCOUNTABILITY AND FOR PROFESSIONAL GROWTH*

Most type experts concur that the preferences for how we take in information and make decisions, the two middle letters of the type code, drive our core communication style. As you read the chart that follows, think about how these differences might affect one's notion of ideal teacher observation and evaluation practices.

Chart 12.7   Type Preferences and Communication Styles

Sensing and Thinking	Sensing and Feeling	Intuition and Feeling	Intuition and Thinking
Prefer efficient, factual communication that stays on topic	Prefer warm, harmonious communication that meets each person's needs	Prefer big-picture communication that taps into ideas and future potential	Prefer big-picture communication that focuses on concepts and competencies

Pajak (2003) identified four distinct models of clinical supervision and noted how they tie to Jungian type preferences. He believed that our type preferences thus influence how we undertake teacher observation and how we might view others' practices. Following, these are listed in the order in which they were originally developed:

- Original clinical models. These models concentrate on competence, theoretical concepts, and developing personal teaching styles. Pajak noted that these describe the values of the Jungian preferences for Intuition and Thinking.
- Artistic/humanistic clinical models. These models emphasize interpersonal relationships, harmony, providing support, and meeting the needs of each teacher. They match the concerns of those who prefer Sensing and Feeling.
- Technical/didactic clinical models. These models measure performance against set processes and procedures for teaching that are based in research, striving for efficiencies. These might appeal most to those who prefer Sensing and Thinking.
- Developmental/reflective clinical models. These models encourage reflection and emphasize fostering personal growth, guided by ideals and values, and might appeal most to those who prefer Intuition and Feeling.

A review of the polarity map on pages 76–77 shows that the "Measurement Model for Teacher Evaluation" pole is closer to the Thinking models described by Pajak and the "Growth Model for Teacher Evaluation" pole is closer to the Feeling models.

Chart 12.11 at the end of this chapter describes common traps or struggles teachers with different type preferences may experience as they begin teaching. Reflection Question 2 for this chapter provides a discussion exercise to help you understand any type biases that might affect how we rate other teachers. What do you want to see when you walk into a classroom? What might strike you unfavorably about teachers with type preferences different from yours?

On the macro level, though, the question is, "Are there any type biases in how the new evaluation systems being rolled out nationwide were constructed?"

- The emphasis on checklists, where items such as "Students are making eye contact with teacher" are used as a measure of engagement, comes from an overfocus on quantifying, a Sensing/Thinking bias.
- The emphasis in some systems toward efficient use of class time can undervalue the needs of many Feeling students for caring relationships with teachers.
- An emphasis on group work can overemphasize the needs of Extraverted teachers and students to the neglect of the needs of Introverted teachers and students.

These are just a few examples of the ways in which using the framework of type can help us get beyond personal biases, the dangers of confirmation bias, and other dilemmas discussed in Chapter 2.

TYPE AND *MATHEMATICS EDUCATION FOR KNOWLEDGE AND PROBLEM SOLVING*

Remember that the *Sensing AND Intuition* preference polarity describes profound differences in the information that first draws one's attention. Look at Chart 12.12 on page 242 at the end of this chapter. The two learning styles on the left-hand side both include Sensing. There is a relationship between this side and the Mastering Math Knowledge pole, summarized in the "Math Wars" Polarity Thinking Map on pages 102–103 at the end of Chapter 5. Carly and Tim, in the opening story of Chapter 5 (page 78), both preferred Introversion and Sensing. Wes preferred Introversion and Intuition, while Roslyn, the principal, preferred Extraversion and Intuition. You can see how their reactions to the new curriculum fit their own learning styles. These fictional educators were composites built from research interviews and coaching work in many districts.

Here's an example of how the Sensing AND Intuition polarity can help teachers develop new or improve existing practices. In one district, as I prepared for a weeklong workshop on differentiating instruction when engaging students in solving math problems that involve higher-level thinking, I ran across the research of Stein, Smith, Henningsen, and Silver

(2009) on the factors that cause teachers to proceduralize such tasks. The factors struck me as type related; Sensing teachers would struggle with some of the factors while Intuitive teachers would struggle with others.

I wrote up my hypotheses and, as a first step in testing them out, showed them to a teacher who disliked using such problems and avoided using much of the district's chosen curriculum because of its problem-based emphasis. She read my hypotheses and said, "No wonder . . . this is *exactly* why I hate using those problems with students—I know I might make these mistakes. But if teachers of my type tend to have these struggles and it isn't just *my* problem, that means you can coach me to implement them well, right?" And that next fall she asked to work with me to do so.

Later in the workshop as we discussed these common traps, such as failing to activate prior knowledge, turning rich problems into procedures, failing to get students to justify answers, or failing to summarize key learning points, Sensing teachers told me the following:

- I do struggle with "overprocedurizing" a task. Many students don't grasp a concept even after following the six-step process that I had them do on the lab sheet. Some can do the six steps; others don't have to and can go straight to the big idea.
- I would be likely to specify specific steps or procedures in an effort to help students succeed—I often think I've discovered the "best" method for tackling a problem.

Intuitive teachers mentioned very different struggles:

- I get frustrated when asked to break tasks down into smaller steps, especially when I already understand the task.
- Sometimes it is hard to explain/justify an answer because it just is, and I don't always know how to break it down (Kise, 2007).

Helping teachers understand *why* they struggled with these problems that are at the heart of leveraging the *Math for Knowledge AND Math for Problem Solving* increased their ability to overcome these difficulties. Again, type doesn't limit us to our own learning styles but points out what we prefer and what might be more uncomfortable or difficult. That can turn "This is wrong and won't help students" into "I can see the benefits if I can learn to do this well."

The same differences in approach to mathematics are evident in students. I filmed over one hundred students completing the same mathematics tasks. Only Intuitive students used numbers to find common denominators and solve problems, no matter their math achievement scores. Written numbers are abstractions; Sensing students worked with concrete tools such as pictures, diagrams, and color tiles to find the answers (Kise, 2012).

Another huge difference was in the information they sought, both when and how. Students who preferred Sensing asked far more questions before tackling problems in the filming project. No student who preferred both Introversion and Intuition asked a single question, even though an equal percentage of these students struggled to complete the problems. And most of the Extraverted students talked with the facilitator constantly as they worked the problems. Again, think about the implications for "ideal" mathematics instruction, especially in "personalized learning" interventions that involve technology solutions.

TYPE AND THE CCSS, *STANDARDIZATION AND CUSTOMIZATION*

Key to the entire impetus behind the Common Core was the drive for students to be "college and career ready," especially for STEM careers (science, technology, engineering, and mathematics). People with different preferences even have different purposes in mind for pursuing education. Intuitives are far less concerned about whether course work will be practical and are overrepresented in majors such as philosophy, art history, and history. Some shudder at the thought of a "college and career ready" diploma, especially if they also prefer Feeling!

With regard to producing more STEM graduates, though, possibly the most researched area connected with personality type has to do with the very clear patterns in the careers people with different type preferences chose. People of every type can—and do—succeed in any career, but we self-select into different occupations in predictable ways. This results in some types being overrepresented in certain careers—in other words, that the percentage of that type is higher in a given career than in the general population. For example, it shouldn't be surprising that ESTPs, whose "tennis hop" brain patterns (shown in Figure 12.2), show a distinct readiness to respond to the environment, are overrepresented in fields such as emergency medicine, marketing, and law enforcement. INFPs, whose brain patterns show an ability to listen longer and more intensely to others than the other fifteen types, are overrepresented in psychology and other counseling fields. Technical fields appeal more to Thinking types, while people-oriented fields appeal more to Feeling types. These patterns never predict individual behavior but are strong enough that education policies need to take them into consideration.

Look again at Chart 12.6 and the very different values sets it lists: The Standardization pole reflects the U.S. cultural archetype of ESTJ preferences and the Customization pole the very different values of INFP preferences.

Chart 12.6 Comparison of ESTJ and INFP Values

ESTJ	INFP
• Commonsense practicality	• Creativity, curiosity, and exploring
• Consistency and standard procedures	• Helping people find their potential
• Concrete, present-day usefulness	• Seeing the big picture possibilities
• Having things settled and closed	• Adaptability and openness
• Rules, objective standards, and fairness according to the rules	• Compassion and caring; attention to feelings
• Systematic structure and efficiency	• An inner compass; being unique
• Scheduling and monitoring	• Perfecting what is important

Source: Lawrence (1998).

While it is *not* true that everyone who prefers ESTJ is an advocate for the Common Core State Standards or that every INFP yearns for customized education, it is safe to say that many of the decisions and processes that produced the Common Core are more consistent with the values in the left column than those in the right column. But refer again to the learning styles outlined in Chart 12.12. An overemphasis on standardization makes it more difficult to provide the Intuitive learning styles on the right side of that chart with the optimal experiences that are driven by their own interests and ideas. They are often motivated by learning what no one else is learning! It is very possible that many famous "school failures" such as Einstein, John Dewey, and Steve Jobs shared one of these learning styles. Again, the fact that two-thirds of the population of the United States prefers Sensing may mean that the needs of the other third are undervalued.

REFLECTION

1. Reconsider the values of ESTJ and INFP, listed in Chart 12.6 above. While there are fourteen other types, many people find that they relate more to one list than the other. Also, reflect on which of the

learning styles described in Chart 12.12 might have fit you best during your school years. Consider the following:

- Were you content to follow the education prescribed for you? Or did you thrive when given choices and chances for independent study?
- While students who prefer Introversion and Intuition make up only about 12% of the population, their strong values around authentic learning and pursuing their own interests deeply can place them at risk in "standardized" environments. What might be early warning signs that these students are not benefiting from such an environment?
- When did you personally benefit from a standardized curriculum? From independent study or choices in what/how you learned?

2. Studies around the world indicate that a majority of leaders (60%–80%) prefer the Thinking and Judging style. Consider both confirmation bias and our drive to conform to the opinions of those around us (page 19). Thinking/Judging leaders have plenty of opportunity to reinforce with each other that their views on leadership are the only acceptable style. Consider how the strengths and associated weaknesses of Thinking and Judging (Myers et al., 1998, p. 353) correlate with the positive and negative results of focusing on the pole of Measurement Model for Teacher Evaluation on the Polarity Thinking Map for Teacher Effectiveness on pages 76–77 at the end of Chapter 4:

Chart 12.8 Thinking/Judging Strengths and Weaknesses

Thinking/Judging Strengths	Thinking/Judging Weaknesses
• Focus on creating logical order and structures in the organization and its processes	• Creating logical structures that unintentionally limit others' flexibility, creativity, and perspectives
• Using logical reasoning to quickly analyze problems	• Moving so quickly to decisions that those who are judging don't allow the amount of process time others need
• Emphasizing efficiency	• Emphasizing efficiency over inclusion and consultation—failing to involve others in analysis and decision making
• Those who are judging value competence, set high standards for themselves and others	• Placing such value on their own high standards that those who are judging fail to recognize alternative standards and positive contributions from others that are different from theirs

Now consider how the Feeling style (Kirby, 1997, pp. 28–29) compares with the positive and negative results of focusing on the Growth Model for Teacher Evaluation pole of that same polarity map. Remember that this is a far more rare leadership style.

Chart 12.9 Feeling Strengths and Weaknesses

Feeling Leadership Strengths	Feeling Leadership Weaknesses
• Focusing on meeting and supporting the needs of people	• Focusing on the needs of people to the detriment of long-range, strategic plans, and decisions
• Including others in the processes of information gathering and decision making	• Feeling overwhelmed by the emotions of people impacted by decisions or external events
• Evaluating alternatives by the values of an organization, a culture, and . . . the impacts they will have on those involved	• Overpersonalizing decisions
• Working for consensus and win-win decisions	• Needing consensus before making decisions—even when that is not possible

ACTIVITY 12.1: REFLECTING ON BIASES

3. Join with two to four others. To consider how type might affect your own practices and the successes and struggles of those with whom you work, try the following protocol.

a. Look through Chart 12.11: Common Type-Related Classroom Management Traps.

 i. Mark with one highlighter color the traps you know you've struggled with at some point.

 ii. Mark with another color the traps you think might be hindering teachers with that preference from accepting or implementing a strategy that you advocate or that is part of your school's overall strategy (literature circles or silent reading time or a scripted curriculum are a few examples).

b. Begin with the person whose first name comes last in the alphabet. Use the following process, until each person has had a chance to choose an item to discuss.

 i. The first person chooses a trap and reads it aloud *without making any further comment.*

ii. Round robin, each person then comments on the statement by

1. Sharing his or her reaction

2. Giving an example

3. Agreeing or disagreeing with it

4. Making a connection to type preferences or other topics

iii. The first person then shares why he or she chose it.

This protocol honors Extraversion and Introversion by giving everyone a chance to reflect on the chart before discussion begins. Sensing is honored by working from a given chart and allowing discussion of past experiences while Intuitive types can make connections and add information. Thinking types have a chance to critique and agree or disagree, while Feeling types can discuss things from a values standpoint. Judging types appreciate the structure, while Perceiving types enjoy the spontaneity of not knowing exactly which items will be discussed.

4. Consider a recent change that involved you or your staff. How were the needs of Judging types met? What about Perceiving types? Common needs are shown in Chart 12.10.

Chart 12.10   Judging and Perceiving Preference Needs During Change

During change, Judging types report needing . . .	During change, Perceiving types report needing . . .
• Clear goals and time frames for changing.	• A plan that is clearly open to changing goals and time frames as circumstances unfold.
• Clear priorities: What needs to be done? What will be left undone?	• A process for incorporating late-breaking information and situational changes.
• Assurances that surprises will be minimized.	• Flexibility around how each person will implement the changes while reaching the same goals.

Source: Adapted from Kise and Russell (2008, p. 41).

Chart 12.11 Common Type-Related Classroom Management Traps

Chances are that you've learned how to avoid some of these traps. What strategies do you use? What made you aware of the needs of students who aren't like you?

Extraverted teachers might . . .	**Introverted teachers might . . .**
• Look for outward enthusiasm as a sign of student engagement. • Not give enough wait time for Introverted students to process their thoughts. Some at-risk students I've worked with describe it this way: "By the time I'm ready to say something, all the good stuff has been said." • Give second and third prompts when a student delays in responding, thinking the student needs more information. This actually interrupts the Introverted process and causes a longer delay. • Overwhelm and tire out Introverted students, for whom just being in school all day is difficult, trying to get them to show more enthusiasm.	• Mistake the Extraverted need to share thoughts as rude blurting out. Extraverted students often solidify their thoughts by speaking them, so when they're asked to wait, they can honestly say, "I forgot" when finally called upon. • Require too much quiet, causing Extraverts to lose focus. All students need quiet for difficult tasks such as test taking, but Extraverts often need more breaks in that quiet. • Overestimate how long Extraverted students can read or write quietly without sharing their thoughts. • Delay hands-on learning too long while providing background information or explanations.
Sensing teachers might . . .	**Intuitive teachers might . . .**
• Think that Intuitive students are sloppy or heedless of directions. • Overstructure assignments, relying on procedures rather than letting students discover underlying concepts. • Emphasize factual learning or basic skills, believing that students can't do "higher level thinking" without that foundation. • Grow almost too comfortable with what they've learned to do well in the classroom.	• See a student's need for clarity as a lack of creativity. • Understructure, not wanting to stifle the imagination or individuality of students. • Emphasize themes and projects or drama, and miss teaching or reinforcing fundamental skills. • Embrace almost any change, jettisoning techniques or curriculum that should be kept.
Thinking teachers might . . .	**Feeling teachers might . . .**
• Be unaware that Feeling students struggle to learn in classrooms where put-downs or sarcasm are common. • View the Feeling need for positive reinforcement as ploys for attention. • Need to smile at students more. • Fail to bend rules when exceptions would help motivate students.	• Get drawn into unproductive arguments, trying to reason with a Thinking student who just wants to argue for argument's sake. • Offer too much nonspecific praise. • Not hold fast enough on rules. • Strive for building relationships over providing rigor.
Judging teachers might . . .	**Perceiving teachers might . . .**
• "Rush" Perceiving students toward completion. • Stick to schedules, cutting short exploratory time. • Lock into a lesson idea too soon, not seeking other possibilities. • See Perceiving students as unmotivated or one step from being irresponsible.	• Change deadlines and plans, frustrating Judging students. • Fail to provide enough classroom routine. • Underestimate or overestimate how long activities might take. • Not give enough parameters; students don't know when they're done.

Chart 12.12   Student Learning Styles, Activities, and Motivating Words

Introversion and Sensing "Let Me Master It"	*Introversion and Intuition* "Let Me Think"
Motivating activities Labs Demonstrations Read and think Time lines Hands-on manipulatives Programmed learning Computer-assisted learning Direct instruction Clear writing assignments	**Motivating activities** Reading Research Imaginative or open-ended writing assignments Self-paced tutorials Brain twisters Independent study Independent projects
Motivating words: Read, identify, list, label, name, notice, observe, apply, analyze, graph, examine, work, prepare, do, organize, complete, answer, listen	**Motivating words:** Read, think, consider, design, evaluate, clarify, speculate, dream, envision, paraphrase, brainstorm, create, elaborate, illustrate, write, reflect, chew on, make connections, compare, contrast, compose
Extraversion and Sensing "Let Me Do Something"	*Extraversion and Intuition* "Let Me Brainstorm"
Motivating activities Videos Group projects Contests Games Skits Songs Physical activities Class reports Hands-on manipulatives	**Motivating activities** Problem solving Improvisations, drama, role-play Discussions and debates Experimenting Group projects Work with ideas Field trips Self-instruction Developing models
Motivating words: Build, show, assemble, tell, discover, make, demonstrate, figure out, touch, design, suggest, solve, choose, construct, examine, explore, discuss	**Motivating words:** Create, discover, pretend, design, develop, discuss, synthesize, collaborate, find a new . . . , generate, visualize, evaluate, problem solve, experiment, invent, hypothesize

Conclusion

Moving Beyond Polarization in Education

Let's go back to where we started. Take a deep breath and hold it as you read this paragraph. Can you feel your anxiety increase? Or your energy drain away as you pursue this crazy notion of inhaling without exhaling? Perhaps a touch of panic, even?

Now exhale and feel your spirits lift as you acknowledge the value of both poles in this simple yet crucial system. Our brains excel at picking up early warning signs that we're out of balance on the breathing cycle. For example, if you turn up the resistance on a stationary bike and pedal as hard as you can, your brain, ever so protective of its own oxygen safety margin, will interpret the increasing fatigue in your legs as a sign that your oxygen supply is compromised and scream, "Stop!" well before your legs actually tire out.

In education, though, we aren't heeding early warning signs because we aren't recognizing polarities that are as essential as breathing in and out. We're too intent on action steps—or too afraid of the "problems" those action steps are supposedly solving—to note the downsides of our "solutions."

One might even say we're seeing late warning signs for many polarities in education—warnings as obvious as the alarm that sounds when a patient's oxygen level sinks to dangerous levels. At least, we *should* be alarmed by repeated patterns in reforms and policy reversals that aren't moving us forward.

So how can move beyond polarization? By helping people see the difference between problems and polarities. As one of the early reviewers of this book wrote, *"It's one of those 'Why didn't I think of that?' kind of ideas that, once you have it, you really can't see another way to do it."*

To start helping others "see," pick an issue within your own team or building or education community where you now recognize that a polarity is at work. Think about who might be open to exploring it through this new lens. The slides in Chapter 7 are ready to go at www.corwin.com/positivepower to help you walk others through the concepts. Then show them a map on a relevant issue. You could use any map in this book. Or you might create a simpler map using the simple blank polarity thinking map available at www.corwin.com/positivepower. Pick out just a couple of the positive and negative results for each pole to begin a conversation. Or use the common polarity we used with Pete's team back in Chapter 1. Have they seen pendulum swings in how we support students?

Students as Lifelong Learners

Positive Results From Student Responsibility for Learning

1. Students learn from natural consequences.

2. Students develop skills for independence.

3. Students develop high expectations.

Positive Results From Teacher Responsibility for Student Learning

1. Students learn from success.

2. Students given organization tools and taught skills.

3. Students with less home support are better off.

Student Responsibility for Learning — and — **Teacher Responsibility for Student Learning**

Negative Results

1. Higher student failure rates.

2. Students victims of learned helplessness.

3. Immature students don't learn from natural consequences.

Negative Results

1. Teachers create too many safety nets.

2. Teachers, not students, own work completion.

3. Students settle for easy assignments.

Student Failure

Source: Map template copyright by Polarity Partnerships, LLC.

You can share some of the action steps on page 22 that turn this into a virtuous cycle, emphasizing how the system needs adjustment over time. The polarity is there; the question is whether it is being leveraged well.

Remember, though, that not all issues are polarities. For example, one problem absolutely needs to be solved in education:

We're wasting the energy of educators by channeling it into "solutions"

that are destined to create more problems

because in fact the problems are polarities that cannot *be solved!*

We can continue to see cycles of reform.

Reforms will continue to create new problems.

Problems will continue to drain our energy.

And the vicious cycles will continue . . .

OR we can start creating virtuous cycles by

Seeing polarities

Mapping them

Assessing how well we're working with them

Learning from where we are as we

Leverage the positive power of our differences.

The latter sounds like a better plan, doesn't it? If our greater common purpose is a meaningful education for each child, then certainly we can find the motivation to pursue it together!

Appendix A

A PACT Process Case Study

While Chapters 7 through 11 of *Unleashing the Positive Power of Differences* are designed to help you begin using the tools of polarity thinking immediately, more in-depth processes that allow for collection and analysis of data, as well as analysis of multiple polarities, can be even more powerful. Let's look at how Central Middle School[1] benefited from using a formal process for PACT Steps 3 and 4, assessing and learning.

Administrators and teachers at Central Middle School had implemented new homework and grading policies. Acting on the belief that all students can learn if given time and support, they were experimenting with accepting late homework without penalties and allowing test retakes.

Halfway through the year, I introduced the staff to polarity thinking, and we mapped the two poles of *Teacher Responsibility AND Student Responsibility* as they applied to these specific policies. At the end of the session, the teachers in general reported that talking about their successes and concerns with the new policies had been of great value. However, they weren't sure where to focus going forward.

The school's leadership team decided that it needed a survey for PACT process Step 3, *assessing*, before developing that focus. Drawing on the polarity map generated by the entire staff, we developed a survey to assess how frequently staff members were experiencing key positive and negative results for each pole.

Figure A.1, on pages 250–251, shows the resulting summary report with the survey statements and scores. Note that all of the statements use the stem, "*Based on what I've observed or experienced in the last six months, I'd say . . .*

---

1. Names and details have been changed for confidentiality.

THE RESULTS

The results are consistent with other polarity thinking maps: The positive and negative results of each pole are in the four quadrants, with the *greater purpose statement* at the top and *deeper fear* at the bottom. The score contained within the black oval (65 in Figure A.1) is an overall indicator of how well the participants believe the polarity is currently being leveraged. Note that this score falls within the "good" range. Although this school chose not to, one can also compare answers from different demographic groups, such as teachers, administrators, and specialists.

The graphs given for the quadrants show the mean scores for each question; the mean scores for the quadrants are shown within the arrows that point to the survey questions. Note that every statement is phrased so that a high score contributes to better results on the overall score for the polarity.

STEP 4: LEARNING

Key themes of this step of the process are "How do these results inform our understanding of how we are leveraging this polarity?" "How did we get here?" "What is key to achieving/continuing a virtuous cycle?" The goal is to articulate a solid rationale for the next step of the process: designing the *action steps* and *early warnings* that will result in leveraging the polarity well in the future.

Rather than acting as a diagnostic, the results foster informed conversations about where to best concentrate future efforts. If the questions are well-designed, the discussion draws on collective experience within the organization rather than hearsay or the experience of just a few team members.

As the Central Middle School leadership team met, we discussed several key questions, such as these:

- What do these results confirm? What is a surprise?
- Which policies or actions might be tied to these results?
- Are our current actions, and any changes we have made, having the desired impact?
- On what might we concentrate more? Less?
- Where might we be most at risk as we try to sustain success?

While my goal as a facilitator is to allow conclusions to form via the collective wisdom of the group, I made the following notes as I reviewed the results and prepared for the team meeting.

- The overall score of 65 indicates that, while they see room for improvement, survey participants believe that the school is experiencing a virtuous cycle for this polarity. Our goal is to note where these results suggest that we create/refine/revisit action steps and early warnings.
- The higher mean scores on the Student Responsibility pole indicate that participants believe they are seeing positive results from the current focus on this pole—students have been encouraged to take more responsibility with the new policies and, according to the teachers, are doing so. What practices might be having this effect?
- Note that Item C in the lower quadrant of the Student Responsibility pole received a score of 55. "Sometimes" isn't a particularly low rating, but we might probe deeper into grading data for such items as the number of students chronically turning in late work or who fail to improve grades on test retakes.
- In the upper quadrant for the Teacher Responsibility pole, the "Sometimes" score for Question B may call for more discussion of action steps to provide in-school homework support. And with the "Sometimes" score for Question C, we may wish to investigate whether the policy of allowing retake tests is improving student learning outcomes.
- The lowest-scoring quadrant was the negative results of an overfocus on teacher responsibility to the neglect of student responsibility. If teachers feel the policies are burdensome, that may affect future leveraging of this polarity.
  - Respondents could enter comments on each item. For Question A in this quadrant, three respondents indicated that many students do not seem to be studying for tests but instead are taking them "cold" to find out what they need to study. Developing potential action steps to ensure that students give their best effort each time might be a priority, especially since this is the lowest-scoring item on the survey.
  - For Question B, comments about the workload focused on finding time for makeup quizzes or creating alternate-form tests. Is there an interest in looking at ways the school schedule might support makeup opportunities? Or ideas for lessening the workload of administering a test multiple times?
- During our original mapping exercise, we heard many comments about late homework interfering with curriculum pacing. However, notice that the answer to Question C in the lower Teacher Responsibility quadrant indicates that this seldom happens. We can probably concentrate action step planning elsewhere, although determining an early warning for this item may be important.

Note how the discussion has the power to focus the planning of action steps; all too often, action plans tackle too many different goals and strategies. The full PACT process, with the addition of a formal survey, provides a sound basis for selecting the most important areas for action.

PACT ASSESSMENTS AND YOUR ORGANIZATION

The Polarity Maps Public Library contains several generic tools for schools. Mini-PACTs exist for the following polarities.

- Academic Success AND Whole Child Success
- Teacher Responsibility for Learning AND Student Responsibility for Learning
- Teaching Reading Skills and Strategies AND Student Choices in Reading Materials

Readers willing to engage in a free debriefing (via phone) of one of these tools may contact jane@janekise.com to schedule a survey opportunity.

Existing surveys for all of the topics discussed in this book can also be customized for a team, school, or district. As can be seen in the preceding case study, the data often focus the action plans on the areas respondents view as most troublesome and may help you avoid the problem of the "squeaky wheel getting all the grease."

Organizations about to embark on major initiatives or those in the midst of processes that seem to be not fully leveraging polarities may wish to engage in a fully customized process. In these cases, the surveys may contain questions for several polarities, including ones that deal with change efforts, leadership distribution, and other universal organizational polarities. Contact jane@janekise.com, or visit www.polaritypartnerships .com to learn more.

Figure A.1 Sample PACT Survey Result

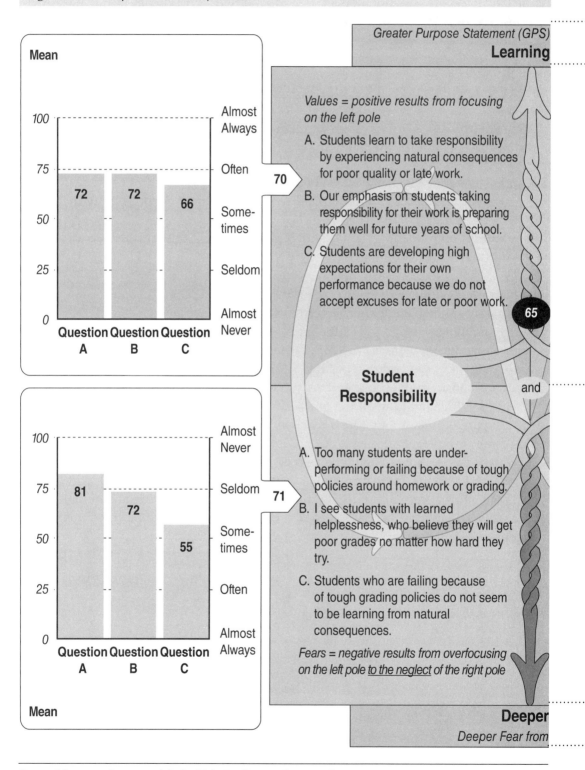

Source: Map template copyright by Polarity Partnerships, LLC.

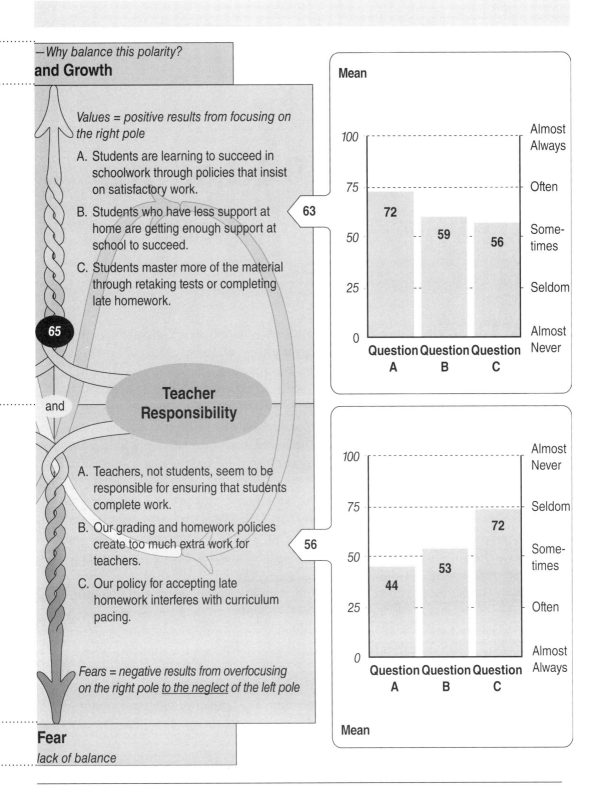

—Why balance this polarity?
and Growth

Values = positive results from focusing on the right pole

A. Students are learning to succeed in schoolwork through policies that insist on satisfactory work.

B. Students who have less support at home are getting enough support at school to succeed.

C. Students master more of the material through retaking tests or completing late homework.

63

65

Teacher Responsibility

and

A. Teachers, not students, seem to be responsible for ensuring that students complete work.

B. Our grading and homework policies create too much extra work for teachers.

56

C. Our policy for accepting late homework interferes with curriculum pacing.

Fears = negative results from overfocusing on the right pole to the neglect of the left pole

Fear
lack of balance

Mean

100		Almost Always
75		Often
72	59	56 Some-times
50		
25		Seldom
0		Almost Never
Question A	Question B	Question C

Mean

100		Almost Never
75		Seldom
		72
50	53	Some-times
44		
25		Often
0		Almost Always
Question A	Question B	Question C

Appendix B

Chapter 9 Reading

How Do We Help Students Succeed?

Most teachers live for those moments when every student eagerly digs in to complete an assignment—not for a grade or a reward but because he or she is intrinsically motivated. We know that trying to motivate adults or students via extrinsic rewards doesn't work in the long run, unless the work is boring and repetitive (Deci, Koestner, & Ryan, 1999; Pink, 2009). Since we aren't working to create classrooms where boring, repetitive work is the norm, we want students to develop a desire to learn and to work hard—and that internal motivation involves self-discipline, right?

In the past, people thought that intelligence, not perseverance or self-discipline, predicted school success. Until the 1960s, dropping out of high school was an option since plenty of good jobs existed for people who lacked a diploma; the graduation rate was only about 60%. However, as manufacturing occupations diminished, earning that diploma became more and more crucial for earning a living wage—and schools found themselves tasked with educating all students.

Researchers quickly realized that students from poverty struggled in school. In the 1970s, Hart and Risley (1995) identified the huge vocabulary gap between students from families with different levels of income. In response, preschool programs provided richer language experiences. While short-term effects were promising, the learning gap grew again as students journeyed through school.

Researchers then found differences in the nature of parent-child interactions.

> Extrapolated to the first four years of life, the average child in a professional family would have accumulated 560,000 more instances of encouraging feedback than discouraging feedback, and an average child in a working-class family would have accumulated 100,000 more encouragements than discouragements. But an average child in a welfare family would have accumulated 125,000 more instances of prohibitions than encouragements. (Hart & Risley, 1995, p. 5)

This "encouragement" gap is even harder to overcome, since discouragement affects curiosity, self-confidence, and willingness to take intellectual risks. Attention turned to whether interventions in early childhood education could teach these traits.

In *How Children Succeed: Grit, Curiosity and the Hidden Power of Character,* Paul Tough (2012) terms the vocabulary and other knowledge-based programs "the cognitive hypothesis": If we fill young children with the right input, eventually they'll acquire the knowledge and skills needed for success in school. Many researchers and practitioners in psychology, economics, and education are challenging that hypothesis.

> What matters most in a child's development, they say, is not how much information we can stuff into her brain in the first few years. What matters, instead is whether we are able to help her develop a very different set of qualities, a list that includes persistence, self-control, curiosity, conscientiousness, grit, and self-confidence. (p. xv)

Advocates for this position believe that K–12 character education can help students develop these crucial noncognitive skills.

The work of Carol Dweck of Stanford (2006) also supports the importance of noncognitive factors. Students with a "fixed intelligence" mindset, believing that you either are or aren't smart, are less likely to persevere on difficult problems. Further, the quality of their problem-solving strategies deteriorates as problems increase in difficulty. Students with a "growth" mind-set, believing hard work makes you smarter, not only persevere but also improve their strategies. Whereas "fixed" mind-set students made comments such as "This problem is stupid," the "growth" mind-set group said, "This problem is hard, but it's more interesting."

Related research found that teachers trained in a "fixed" mind-set complimented underachieving students to improve their self-esteem. Those trained in a "growth" mind-set actively worked with the students to understand why they weren't learning and brainstormed new ways to assist them (Feinberg, 2004). Thus, both teachers and students needed to internalize that working hard would make them more successful.

But is it possible to nurture self-discipline? Many educators remembered the "marshmallow experiment." Walter Mischel (Mischel, Ebbesen, & Raskoff Zeiss, 1972) of Stanford offered preschoolers a marshmallow to eat but told them that if they waited to eat it until the researcher returned to the lab room, they could have two. When Mischel followed up on his subjects years later, those who had waited the longest had better social skills and higher SAT scores. His early conclusion was that the ability to delay gratification is key to success.

However, Mischel (Mischel et al., 1972) himself pointed out that those able to wait knew how to distract themselves. They sang songs, played with a toy, or made up stories while waiting for the researcher to return. Mischel concluded that using willpower to "bear up" is the wrong approach, especially for difficult or boring tasks. The essential skills involved distracting oneself or changing circumstances so that temptations are less tempting! These strategies involve skills that can be taught. Organizations such as the KIPP schools have created measures and progress reports for attributes such as politeness, self-control, and the ability to focus.

Then, subsequent researchers found that a predictable, trustworthy environment had a major impact on how long students would wait for those marshmallows (Kidd, Palmeri, & Aslin, 2013). They recommended that schools focus on creating trustworthy learning environments to support students from more turbulent homes.

Critics, though, think the pendulum is swinging too far toward noncognitive skills as the key to success. E. D. Hirsch (2013), founder of the Core Knowledge Foundation, faults *How We Succeed* for downplaying the importance of knowledge. He contends that in the era of No Child Left Behind, schools have emphasized tests, not knowledge. "On the contrary," Hirsch writes, "'mere information' has been disparaged in favor of how-to strategies and test-taking skills. What Tough calls 'the cognitive hypothesis' with regard to academics might better be called the 'how-to hypothesis.'"

Hirsch (2013) points to research from the National Longitudinal Survey of Youth; it shows that the biggest single predictor of student success is a general vocabulary measure that serves as a proxy for general knowledge. The second biggest factor is fine motor skills, which also ties to cognitive skills. Noncognitive skills come in third. Self-discipline can't overcome a lack of knowledge.

In his article "Why Self-Discipline Is Overrated," Alfie Kohn (2008) provides more reasons to be concerned about the emphasis on self-discipline, which he defines as using willpower to accomplish desirable things. In contrast, self-control helps us avoid temptation or delay gratification. People with too much self-control have problems, too, lacking the spontaneity, flexibility, and creative expression that lead to a balanced life. Further, there are limits to the value of perseverance. We need to be able to ask for help, focus energy toward our interests and talents, and learn from failure. He summarizes that success comes from knowing when to persevere or follow the rules and when these actions will not be helpful.

Most troubling to Kohn, though, is that if schools focus on buckling down and trying harder, then it becomes easy to ignore unjust societal, economic, or educational structures. We may fail to question whether schoolwork is meaningful, requiring self-discipline, or not worth doing, requiring self-control. He concludes that

> *to identify a lack of self-discipline as the problem is to focus our efforts on making children conform to a status quo that is left unexamined and is unlikely to change.* . . . Aside from its philosophical underpinnings and political impact, there are reasons to be skeptical about anything that might produce overcontrol. Some children who look like every adult's dream of a dedicated student may in reality be anxious, driven, and motivated by a perpetual need to feel better about themselves, rather than by anything resembling curiosity. In a word, they are workaholics in training.

At KIPP Schools, which emphasize both cognitive and noncognitive skills, the college graduation rate for low-income students is four times the national average. However, their graduates receive a level of support that society doesn't offer to every high school graduate—and it still isn't enough. KIPP's own website states that they have a long way to go toward their goal of graduating their students at the same rate as high-income students. Do we understand how to help every student yet lack the national will to support them? Or have we yet to find what really helps all students succeed?

References

Akinbami, L. J., & Liu, X. (2011, January 12). Asthma prevalence, health care use, and mortality: United States, 2005–2009. *National Health Statistics Reports,* No. 32. Retrieved from http://www.cdc.gov/nchs/data/nhsr/nhsr032.pdf

Alberti, S. (2012). Making the shift. *Educational Leadership, 70*(4), 24–27.

American Federation of Teachers. (n.d.). Teacher development and evaluation. Retrieved from http://www.aft.org/issues/teaching/evaluation.cfm

Anderson, L. H. (2002). *Catalyst.* New York, NY: Penguin Group.

Association for Supervision and Curriculum Development. (2012a). *Making the case for educating the whole child.* Retrieved from http://www.wholechild education.org/assets/content/mx-resources/WholeChild-MakingTheCase .pdf

Association for Supervision and Curriculum Development. (2012b). The whole child. Retrieved from http://www.wholechildeducation.org/

Barnes, G., Crowe, E., & Schaefer, B. (2007). *The cost of teacher turnover in five school districts: A pilot study.* Washington, DC: National Commission on Teaching and America's Future. Retrieved from http://nctaf.org/wp-content/uploads/ 2012/01/NCTAF-Cost-of-Teacher-Turnover-2007-full-report.pdf

Barth, R. S. (2005). Turning book burners into lifelong learners. In R. DuFour, R. Eaker, & R. DuFour (Eds.), *On common ground: The power of professional learning communities* (pp. 114–133). Bloomington, IN: National Educational Service.

Bill & Melinda Gates Foundation. (2010). *Working with teachers to develop fair and reliable measures of effective teaching.* Seattle, WA: Author.

Bill & Melinda Gates Foundation. (2013). *Ensuring fair and reliable measures of effective teaching: Culminating findings from the MET Project's three-year study.* Seattle, WA: Author.

Billings, L., & Roberts, T. (2012). Think like a seminar. *Educational Leadership, 70*(4), 68–72.

Boaler, J. (2008). *What's math got to do with it? How parents and teachers can help children learn to love their least favorite subject.* New York, NY: Penguin Books.

Boaler, J. (2012, October). Jo Boaler reveals attacks by Milgram and Bishop: When academic disagreement becomes harassment and persecution. Retrieved from http://stanford.edu/~joboaler/

Bransford, J. D., Brown, A. L., & Cocking, R. R. (Eds.). (1999). *How people learn: Brain, mind, experience and school.* Washington, DC: National Academy Press.

Brooks, J. G., & Dietz, M. E. (2012). The dangers and opportunities of the Common Core. *Educational Leadership, 70*(4), 64–67.

Brown Center on Education Policy at Brookings. (2012). *The 2012 Brown Center report on American education: How well are American students learning?* Washington, DC: Author.

Bruchac, J. (2003). *Our stories remember: American Indian history, culture, and values through storytelling.* Golden, CO: Fulcrum.

Bust, B. (2013, January 7). The school cliff: Student engagement drops with each school year. Retrieved from http://thegallupblog.gallup.com/2013/01/the-school-cliff-student-engagement.html

Campbell, D. T. (1975). Assessing the impact of planned social change. In G. M. Lyons (Ed.), *Social research and public policies: The Dartmouth/OECD conference* (pp. 3–45). Hanover, NH: Dartmouth College, Public Affairs Center.

Case Western Reserve University. (2012). Empathy represses analytic thought, and vice versa: Brain physiology limits simultaneous use of both networks. *ScienceDaily.* Retrieved from http://www.sciencedaily.com/releases/2012/10/121030161416.htm

Clarke, J. (2012). Invested in inquiry. *Educational Leadership, 69*(5), 60–64.

Collins, J. (2001). *Good to great: Why some companies make the leap and others don't.* New York, NY: HarperCollins.

Columbia world of quotations. (2013). Retrieved from http://quotes.dictionary.com/The_test_of_a_firstrate_intelligence_is_the

Common Core State Standards Initiative. (2012a). Common Core State Standards for English language arts & literacy in history/social studies, science, and technical subjects. Retrieved from http://www.corestandards.org/assets/CCSSI_ELA%20Standards.pdf

Common Core State Standards Initiative. (2012b). Common Core State Standards for mathematics. Retrieved from http://www.corestandards.org/assets/CCSSI_Math%20Standards.pdf

Cronin, J., Dahlin, M., Adkins, D., & Kingsbury, G. G. (2007). *The proficiency illusion.* Washington, DC: Thomas B. Fordham Institute.

Damasio, A. (1994). *Descartes' error: Emotion, reason, and the human brain.* New York, NY: Penguin Books.

Danielson, C. (2007). *Enhancing professional practice: A framework for teaching.* Reston, VA: ASCD.

Darling-Hammond, L. (2010). *The flat world and education: How America's commitment to equity will determine our future.* New York, NY: Teachers College Press.

Darling-Hammond, L. (2012, March 5). Value-added evaluation hurts teaching. *Education Week.* Retrieved from http://www.edweek.org/ew/articles/2012/03/05/24darlinghammond_ep.h31.html?r=453642

Dawkins, R. (1996, November 12). Science, delusion and the appetite for wonder [Speech on BBC1 Television]. Retrieved from http://www.edge.org/3rd_culture/dawkins/lecture_p1.html

Deci, E. L., Koestner, R., & Ryan, R. M. (1999). A meta-analytic review of experiments examining the effects of extrinsic rewards on intrinsic motivation. *Psychological Bulletin, 125*, 627–668.

Delpit, L. (1995). *Other people's children: Cultural conflict in the classroom.* New York: New Press.

Dewey, J. (1990). *The school and society & The child and the curriculum.* Chicago, IL: University of Chicago Press. (Original works published 1902)

Dillon, S. (2011, May 4). Failing grades on civics exam called a "crisis." *New York Times.* Retrieved from http://www.nytimes.com/2011/05/05/education/05civics.html?_r=0

Downey, M. (2012). Bill Gates in Atlanta: Don't rush teacher evaluations. Do it right [Web log message]. Retrieved from http://blogs.ajc.com/get-schooled-blog/2012/07/12/bill-gates-in-atlanta-dont-rush-teacher-evaluations-do-it-right/

Durlak, J. A., Weissberg, R. P., Dymnicki, A. B., Taylor, R. D., & Schellinger, K. B. (2011). The impact of enhancing students' social and emotional learning: A meta-analysis of school-based universal interventions. *Child Development, 82,* 405–432.

Dweck, C. (2006). *Mindset: The new psychology of success.* New York, NY: Random House.

Dweck, C. S., & Leggett, E. L. (1988). A social-cognitive approach to motivation and personality. *Psychological Review, 95*(2), 256–273.

Erdrich, L. (1999). *The birchbark house.* New York, NY: Hyperion.

Ericsson, K., Prietula, M. J., & Cokely, E. T. (2007). The making of an expert. *Harvard Business Review, 85*(7/8), 118.

Felder, R. M., Felder, G. N., & Dietz, E. J. (2002). The effects of personality type on engineering student performance and attitudes. *Journal of Engineering Education, 19*(1), 3–17.

Feinberg, C. (2004, July 1). A possible dream: A nation of proficient schoolchildren. *Ed.magazine* (the news source of the Harvard Graduate School of Education). Retrieved from http://www.efficacy.org/Resources/TheEfficacyLibrary/tabid/227/Default.aspx

Fisch, K., McLeod, S., & Xplane. (2007). *Did you know?* Retrieved from http://shifthappens.wikispaces.com/file/view/Text%20of%20Did%20You%20Know%2020.pdf

Fishbane, M. (2007, August 30). Teachers: Be subversive. Jonathan Kozol, author of *Letters to a Young Teacher,* talks with Salon about why No Child Left Behind squelches learning and about reading Rilke's sonnets to first graders. *Salon.* Retrieved from www.salon.com/2007/08/kozol/

Fosnot, C. T., & Dolk, M. (2002). *Young mathematicians at work: Constructing fractions, decimals, and percents.* Portsmouth, NH: Heinemann.

Freedman, M. (1992). Initiative fatigue. *Strategic change, 1*(2), 89–92.

Freedman, S. G. (2005, November 9). "Innovative" math, but can you count? *New York Times.* Retrieved from http://www.nytimes.com/2005/11/09/education/08education.html?pagewanted=all

Gates, B. (2013, April 3). A fairer way to evaluate teachers. *Washington Post.* Retrieved from http://articles.washingtonpost.com/2013-04-03/opinions/38246518_1_teacher-evaluation-systems-classroom-observations-student-test

Gewertz, C. (2012, November 29). Testing group scales back performance items. *Education Week.* Retrieved from http://www.edweek.org/ew/articles/2012/11/30/13tests.h32.html?tkn=UPLFfYzJ%2BlzJu%2FQzgzku%2BR

Gilovich, T. (1991). *How we know what isn't so.* New York, NY: Free Press.

Gladwell, M. (2000). *The tipping point: How little things can make a big difference.* New York, NY: Little, Brown.

Haidt, J. (2012). *The righteous mind: Why good people are divided by politics and religion.* New York, NY: Pantheon Books.

Hart, B., & Risley, T. R. (1995). The early catastrophe: The 30 million word gap by age 3. *American Educator, 27*(1), 4–9.

Hiebert, J. (1999). Relationships between research and the NCTM standards. *Journal for Research in Mathematics Education, 30*(1), 3–19.

Hill, H., Blunk, M., Charalambous, C. Y., Lewis, J. M., Phelps, G. C., Sleep, L., & Ball, D. L. (2008). Mathematical knowledge for teaching and the mathematical quality of instruction: An exploratory study. *Cognition and Instruction, 26*(4), 430–511.

Hill, H., & Ball, D. L. (2009). The curious—and crucial—case of mathematical knowledge for teaching. *Phi Delta Kappan, 91*(2), 68–71.

Hilton, P. (1998, May). Review: *The Pleasures of Counting* by T. W. Körner. *American Mathematics Monthly, 105*(5), 481–485.

Hirsch, E. D. Jr. (2001a). Breadth versus depth: A premature polarity. *Common Knowledge, 14*(4). Retrieved from http://www.coreknowledge.org/mimik/mimik_uploads/documents/22/BreadthVSDepth.pdf

Hirsch, E. D., Jr. (2001b). The roots of the education wars. In T. Loveless (Ed.), *The great curriculum debate: How should we teach reading and math?* (pp. 13–24). Washington, DC: Brookings Institution Press.

Hirsch, E. D., Jr. (2013). Primer on success: Character and knowledge make the difference. *EducationNext, 13*(1). Retrieved from http://educationnext.org/primer-on-success/

History literacy failing among American students: Study faults colleges' lack of core subject requirements. (2012, October 10). *Huffington Post Education.* Retrieved from http://www.huffingtonpost.com/2012/10/10/study-rates-colleges-base_n_1954987.html

Jackson, R. R. (2009). *Never work harder than your students and other principles of great teaching.* Reston, VA: ASCD.

Jehlen, A. (2012). Boot camp for education CEOs: The Broad Foundation Academy. *Rethinking Schools, 27*(1), 25–34.

Johnson, B. (1992). *Polarity management: Identifying and managing unsolvable problems.* Amherst, MA: HRD Press.

Johnson, B. (2012). *The polarity approach to continuity and transformation.* Sacramento, CA: Polarity Partnerships, LLC.

Kerr, S. (1995). On the folly of rewarding A, while hoping for B. *Academy of Management Executive, 9*(1), 7–14.

Keiser, J. (2010). Shifting our computational focus. *Mathematics Teaching in the Middle School, 16*(4), 217–223.

Kidd, C., Palmeri, H., & Aslin, R. N. (2013). Rational snacking: Young children's decision-making on the marshmallow task is moderated by beliefs about environmental reliability. *Cognition, 126,* 109–114. Retrieved from http://dx.doi.org/10.1016/j.cognition.2012.08.004

Killion, J. (2012). Taking the long view on Common Core [Blog post]. Retrieved from http://blogs.edweek.org/edweek/learning_forwards_pd_watch/2012/11/taking_the_long_view_on_common_core.html

Killion, J., & Kennedy, J. (2012). The sweet spot in professional learning: When student learning goals and educator performance standards align, everything is possible. *Journal of Staff Development, 33*(5), 10–17.

Kim, K. H. (2011). The creativity crisis: The decrease in creative thinking scores on the Torrance tests of creative thinking. *Creativity Research Journal, 23*(4), 285–295.

Kirby, L. (1997). Psychological type and the Myers Briggs Type Indicator. In C. Fitzgerald & L. K. Kirby (Eds.), *Developing leaders: Research and applications in psychological type and leadership development* (pp. 3–31). Palo Alto, CA: Davies-Black.

Kise, J. A. G. (2007). *Differentiation through personality types: A framework for instruction, assessment, and classroom management.* Thousand Oaks, CA: Corwin.

Kise, J. A. G. (2012). *The impact of student Jungian psychological types on student approaches to mathematical tasks.* Unpublished manuscript.

Kise, J. A. G., & Russell, B. (2008). *Differentiated school leadership: Effective collaboration, communication, and change through personality type.* Thousand Oaks, CA: Corwin

Kohn, A. (1998). Only for my kid: How privileged parents undermine school reform. *Phi Delta Kappan, 79*(8), 568–577.

Kohn, A. (2008). Why self-discipline is overrated: The (troubling) theory and practice of control from within. *Phi Delta Kappan, 90*(3), 168–196. Retrieved from http://www.alfiekohn.org/teaching/selfdiscipline.htm

Lavon, R. (2009). *Real justice in the age of Obama.* Princeton, NJ: Princeton University Press.

Lawrence, G. (1998). *Descriptions of the 16 types.* Gainesville, FL: Center for Application of Psychological Type.

Lawrence, G. (2009). *People types and tiger stripes: Using psychological type to help students discover their unique potential.* Gainesville, FL: Center for Applications of Psychological Type.

Lehto, B. A. (1990). A comparison of personalities and background of teachers using a whole language approach and a basal approach in teaching elementary reading. *Dissertation Abstracts International, 51*/03-A, 740.

Leithwood, K., Louis, K. S., Anderson, S., & Wahlstrom, K. (2004). *How leadership influences student learning.* New York, NY: Wallace Foundation.

Lengel, J. G. (2012). The kindergarten education gap. Retrieved from http://www.powertolearn.com/articles/teaching_with_technology/article.shtml?ID=171

Lester, W. (2005, August 17). Poll shows America's love-hate relationship with math. *Lawrence Journal-World.* Retrieved from http://www2.ljworld.com/news/2005/aug/17/poll_shows_americas_lovehate_relationship_math/

Littky, D. (2011). Whoever wanted a standardized child anyway? In R. F. Elmore (Ed.), *I used to think . . . but now I think* (pp. 101–111). Cambridge, MA: Harvard University Press.

Lockhart, P. (2009). *A mathematician's lament: How school cheats us out of our most fascinating and imaginative art form.* New York, NY: Bellevue Literary Press.

London Mathematical Society, Institute of Mathematics and Its Applications, and Royal Statistical Society. (1995). *Tackling the mathematics problem.* London, England: Author.

Lopez, S. J. (2011). The highs and lows of student engagement. *Phi Delta Kappan, 93*(2), 72–75.

Loveless, T. (2012). The Common Core initiative: What are the chances of success? *Educational Leadership, 70*(4), 60–63.

Ma, L. (1999). *Knowing and teaching elementary mathematics.* Mahwah, NJ: Lawrence Erlbaum.

Madison, B. L., & Hart, T. A. (1990). *A challenge of numbers: People in the mathematical sciences.* Washington, DC: National Academy Press.

Margolis, J. (2010, June 22). Why teacher quality is a local issue (and why Race to the Top is a misguided flop) (No. 16023). *Teachers College Record.* Available at http://tcrecord.org

Marklow, D., & Pieters, A. (2012). *The Metlife survey of the American teacher: Teachers, parents and the economy.* New York, NY: Metropolitan Life Insurance Company. Retrieved from https://www.metlife.com/assets/cao/contributions/foun dation/american-teacher/MetLife-Teacher-Survey-2011.pdf

Mathematics. (2005). *Online encyclopedia and dictionary.* Retrieved from http://www.fact-archive.com/quotes/Mathematics

Marzano, R. J. (2003). *What works in schools: Translating research into action.* Reston, VA: ASCD.

Marzano, R. J. (2011). *The Marzano teacher evaluation model.* Englewood, CO: Marzano Research Laboratory.

Marzano, R. J. (2012). The two purposes of teacher evaluation. *Educational Leadership, 70*(3), 14–19.

Matthews, J. (2005, May 31). 10 myths (maybe) about learning math. *Washington Post.* Retrieved from http://www.washingtonpost.com/wp-dyn/con tent/article/2005/05/31/AR2005053100656_4.html

McMurrer, J. (2008). *Instructional time in elementary schools: A closer look at changes for specific subjects.* Washington DC: Center on Education Policy. Retrieved from http://www.cep-dc.org/displayDocument.cfm?DocumentID=309

Milteer, R. M., Ginsburg, K. R., & Council on Communications and Media, Committee on Psychosocial Aspects of Child and Family Health. (2012). The importance of play in promoting healthy child development and maintaining strong parent-child bond: Focus on children in poverty. *Pediatrics, 129*(1), 204–213. Retrieved from www.pediatrics.org/cgi/content/full/129/1/e204

Mielke, P., & Frontier, T. (2012). Keeping improvement in mind. *Educational Leadership, 70*(3), 10–13.

Mikaelsen, B. (2001). *Touching spirit bear.* New York, NY: Scholastic.

Miller, D. (2009). *The book whisperer: Awakening the inner reader in every child.* San Francisco, CA: Jossey-Bass.

Ministry of Education. (2006). *Nurturing every child.* Singapore: Author.

Mintz, A. I. (2012). The happy and suffering student: Rousseau's *Emile* and the path not taken in progressive educational thought. *Educational Theory, 62*(3), 249–265.

Mischel, W., Ebbesen, E. B., & Raskoff Zeiss, A. (1972). Cognitive and attentional mechanisms in delay of gratification. *Journal of Personality and Social Psychology, 21*(2), 204–218.

Mooney, M. E. (1988). *Developing life-long readers.* Katonah, NY: Richard C. Owen.

Moore, E. (2000, April 3). My turn: Why teachers are not those who can't. *Newsweek, 135*(14), 13.

Myers, I. B., McCaulley, M., Quenk, N., & Hammer, A. (1998). *MBTI manual: A guide to the development and use of the Myers-Briggs Type Indicator* (3rd ed.). Palo Alto, CA: Consulting Psychologists Press.

Myers, I. B., with Myers, P. B. (1993). *Gifts differing: Understanding personality type.* Palo Alto, CA: Consulting Psychologists Press.

Nakamura, T., Takahashi, A., & Kurosawa, S. (1989). *Jugyookenkyuu no susumekata, fukamekata, norikirikata* [The lesson study] (Vol. 10). Tokyo, Japan: Tooyookan Suppansha.

Nardi, D. (2011). *The neuroscience of personality.* Los Angeles, CA: Radiance House.

National Council of Teachers of Mathematics. (1980). *An agenda for action.* Reston, VA: Author. Retrieved from http://www.nctm.org/standards/content.aspx?id=17278

National Council of Teachers of Mathematics. (2000). *Principles and standards for school mathematics.* Reston, VA: Author.

National Mathematics Advisory Panel. (2008). *Foundations for success.* Washington, DC: U.S. Department of Education.

Newton, X., Darling-Hammond, L., Haertel, E., & Thomas, E. (2010). Value-added modeling of teacher effectiveness: An exploration of stability across models and contexts. *Educational Policy Analysis Archives, 18*(23). Retrieved from http://epaa.asu.edu/ojs/article/view/810/858

No Child Left Behind (NCLB) Act of 2001, Pub. L. No. 107–110, § 115, Stat. 1425 (2002).

Omar, S. (2012). Question at heart of Chicago strike: How do you measure teacher performance? *U.S. News on NBC News.com.* Retrieved from http://usnews.nbcnews.com/_news/2012/09/11/13808109-question-at-heart-of-chicago-strike-how-do-you-measure-teacher-performance?lite

Paige, M. (2012). Using VAM in high-stakes employment decisions. *Phi Delta Kappan, 94*(3), 29–32.

Paine, L., & Ma, L. (1993). Teachers working together: A dialogue on organizational and cultural perspectives of Chinese teachers. *International Journal of Educational Research, 19*(8), 675–718.

Pajak, E. (2003). *Honoring diverse teaching styles: A guide for supervisors.* Alexandria, VA: ASCD.

Pallas, A. (2012, May 15). The worst eighth-grade math teacher in New York City [Blog post]. Retrieved from http://eyeoned.org/content/the-worst-eighth-grade-math-teacher-in-new-york-city_326

Partnership for Assessment of Readiness for College and Careers. (2012). About PARCC. Retrieved from http://www.parcconline.org/about-parcc

Partanen, A. (2011, December 29). What Americans keep ignoring about Finland's school success. *The Atlantic.* Retrieved from http://www.theatlantic.com/national/archive/2011/12/what-americans-keep-ignoring-about-finlands-school-success/250564/

Perkins, D. N., Farady, M., & Bushey, B. (1991). Everyday reasoning and the roots of intelligence. In J. F. Voss, D. N. Perkins, & J. Segal (Eds.), *Informal reasoning and Education* (pp. 83–106). New York, NY: Routledge.

Peter Hilton quotes. (2013). *Inspirational quotes, words, sayings.* Retrieved from http://www.inspirationalstories.com/quotes/peter-hilton-computation-involves-going-from-a-question-to/

Pink, D. (2009). *Drive: The surprising truth about what motivates us.* New York, NY: Riverhead.

Project RED. (2012). Project RED: The research. Retrieved from http://www.projectred.org/about/research-overview.html

Put Kids First Minneapolis. (2011). Contract for student achievement. Retrieved from http://www.putkidsfirstminneapolis.org/index.php?option=com_content&view=article&id=60&Itemid=40

Ramstetter, C. L., Murray, R., & Garner, A. S. (2010). The crucial role of recess in schools. *Journal of School Health, 80*(11), 517–526.

Ravitch, D. (2012, March 13). Why are teachers so upset? [Blog post]. Retrieved from http://blogs.edweek.org/edweek/Bridging-Differences/2012/03/why_are_teachers_so_upset.html

Reeves, D. B. (2005). Putting it all together. In R. DuFour, R. Eaker, & R. DuFour (Eds.), *On common ground: The power of professional learning communities* (pp. 45–64). Bloomington, IN: National Educational Service.

Regents of the University of California. (2003). How much information? 2003. Retrieved from http://www2.sims.berkeley.edu/research/projects/how-much-info-2003/execsum.htm

Resnick, L. B. (1999). Making America smarter. *Education Week Century Series, 18*(40), 38–40. Available at http://www.edweek.org/ew/articles/1999/06/16/40resnick.h18.html?qs=Making+America+smarter

Riley, J. L. (2011, July 29). Was the $5 billion worth it? *Wall Street Journal.* Retrieved from http://online.wsj.com/article/SB10001424053111903554904576461571362279948.html

Root-Bernstein, R., & Root-Bernstein, M. (2013). The art and craft of science. *Educational Leadership, 70,* 16–21.

Rosales, J. (2012, February 7). How bad education policies demoralize teachers. *NEA Today.* Retrieved from http://neatoday.org/2012/02/07/how-bad-education-policies-demoralize-teachers/

Sagie, A. (1997). Leader direction and employee participation in decision making: Contradictory or compatible practices? *Applied Psychology: An International Review, 46,* 387–415.

Schmidt, W. H., & Burroughs, N. H. (2012). How the Common Core boosts quality and equality. *Educational Leadership, 70*(4), 54–58.

Schmoker, M. (2012). The madness of teacher evaluation. *Phi Delta Kappan, 93*(8), 70–71.

Schochet, P. Z., & Chiang, H. S. (2010). *Error rates in measuring teacher and school performance based on student test score gains.* Washington, DC: National Center for Education Evaluation and Regional Assistance. Retrieved from http://www.eric.ed.gov/PDFS/ED511026.pdf

Schoenfeld, A. J. (2004). The math wars. *Educational Policy, 18*(1), 253–286.

Stein, M. K., Smith, M. S., Henningsen, M. A., & Silver, E. A. (2009). *Implementing standards-based mathematics instruction: A casebook for professional development* (2nd ed.). New York, NY: Teachers College Press.

Stigler, J. W., & Hiebert, J. (1997). Understanding and improving classroom mathematics instruction: An overview of the TIMSS video study. *Phi Delta Kappan, 79*(1), 467–483.

Tapping America's Potential. (2005, July). *The education for innovation initiative.* Retrieved from http://www.uschamber.com/sites/default/files/reports/050727_tapstatement.pdf

Tough, P. (2012). *How children succeed: Grit, curiosity, and the hidden power of character.* New York, NY: Macmillan.

U.S. Department of Education. (2012). What we do. Retrieved from http://www2.ed.gov/about/what-we-do.html

Wagner, T. (2006). Rigor on trial. *Education Week, 25*(18), 28–29.

Wason, P. (1960). On the failure to eliminate hypotheses in a conceptual task. *Quarterly Journal of Experimental Psychology, 12,* 129–140.

Weisberg, D., Sexton, S., Mulhern, J., Keeling, D. Schunck, J., Palcisco, A., & Morgan, K. (2009). *The widget effect: Our national failure to acknowledge and act on differences in teacher effectiveness* (2nd ed.). New York, NY: New Teacher Project.

Westen, D., Blagov, P. S., Karenski, K., Hamann, S., & Kilts, C. (2006). Neural bases of motivational reasoning: An fMRI study of emotional constraints on partisan political judgment in the 2004 U.S. presidential election. *Journal of Cognitive Neuroscience, 18,* 1947–1958.

Wilkes, J. W. (2004, July). *Why do intuitives have an advantage on both aptitude and achievement tests?* Paper presented at the International Conference of the Association for Psychological Type, Toronto, Canada.

William, D. (2011). *Embedded formative assessment.* Bloomington, IN: Solution Tree.

Yazzie-Mintz, E. (2010). *Charting the path from engagement to achievement: A report on the 2009 High School Survey of Student Engagement.* Bloomington, IN: Center for Evaluation & Education Policy.

Zhao, Y. (2009). *Catching up or leading the way: American education in the age of globalization.* Alexandria, VA: ASCD.

Zhao, Y. (2012). Common sense vs. Common Core: How to minimize the damages of the Common Core [Blog post]. Retrieved from http://zhaolearning.com/2012/06/17/common-sense-vs-common-core-how-to-minimize-the-damages-of-the-common-core/

Suggestions for Further Reading

Haidt, J. (2012). *The righteous mind: Why good people are divided by politics and religion.* New York, NY: Pantheon.

Kise, J. A. G. (2006). *Differentiated coaching: A framework for helping teachers change.* Thousand Oaks, CA: Corwin.

Kise, J. A. G. (2013). *Intentional leadership: 12 lenses for focusing your strengths, managing your weaknesses, and achieving your purpose.* St. Paul, MN: ShareOn.

Johnson, B. (2002). *Polarity management: Identifying and managing unsolvable problems.* Amherst, MA: HRD Press.

Oswald, R., & Johnson, B. (2010). *Managing polarities in congregations.* Herndon, VA: The Alban Institute.

Index

Note: Figures are indicated by an *f* following the page number.

Ability grouping, 140–152
Academic achievement
 cross-school comparisons of, 119
 gap in, 36, 252–253
 means to, 252–255
Academic standards, 37, 45
Academic Success AND Whole Child
  Success, 32–52
 assessing polarity of, 46
 focusing on academic achievement,
  36–41
 focusing on whole child achievement,
  41–46
 leveraging polarity of, 47–49
 mapping it, 35–36
 personality types and, 231–232
 seeing it, 33–35
 thinking map for, 50–51
Accountability
 school, 38
 teacher, 54
Achievement gap, 36, 252–253
Action steps, 18
 Academic Success AND Whole Child
  Success, 47–49
 principles for developing, 152
 Standardization AND Customization,
  123–125, 128
 Teacher Evaluation as a Measure of
  Effectiveness AND as Guide for
  Professional Growth, 69–74
Activity AND Rest, 12–14, 12*f*, 13*f*
ACT tests. *See* College admissions tests
Adequate yearly progress, 39, 45
Alberti, S., 125
Alternative schools, 118
American Academy of Pediatricians, 35

American Association of Pediatrics, 42
American Federation of Teachers, 55, 58
Anderson, Laurie Halse, *Catalyst*, 119–120
Apprenticeship, teacher, 63–64
Archetypes, 231
Argument and reasoning, 198–208
Assessment of polarity, 14
 Academic Success AND Whole Child
  Success, 46
 case study, 246–247
 guided activity on, 147–149
Assessments
 authentic, 123
 performance-based, 114, 120
 standardization and, 108–109
Assigned texts, 25–26
Association for Supervision and
  Curriculum Development (ASCD),
  34–35
Authentic assessments, 123
Autonomy AND Collaboration, 173–174

Ball, D. L., 95
Barth, Roland, 35–36
Biases, 19, 24
Big ideas, 97–98
Bill and Melinda Gates Foundation,
  58, 113
Billings, L., 222
Boaler, Jo, 80, 87
Bonuses, 64–65
Book study, with polarity tools, 162–170
Bosch, Hieronymus, The Hearing Forest
  and Seeing Field, 222f
Brain
 decision making, 225, 227
 personality type, 217, 218*f*

"Brainstorming" learning style, 80, 86, 242
Breathing cycle, 2, 3f, 11–12, 11f
Briggs, Katherine, 213
Broad Foundation, 38
Brooks, J. G., 107, 112
Brown Center, 113
Bruchac, Joseph, 112
Burroughs, N. H., 109, 124
Business Roundtable, 34
Business values, in education, 71, 111–112

Calculators, 90–91
Cambridge Education, 58
Campbell, Donald, 61
Career preparation. *See* Employment preparation
Care of Self AND Care of Others, 135–136, 138–139
CCSS. *See* Common Core State Standards
Centers for Disease Control, 43
Centralization AND Decentralization, 178
Character education, 253
Charter schools, 38–39
Chicago Teachers Union, 53
China, 96, 97
Churchill, Winston, 121
Clarity AND Flexibility, 175
Clarke, John, 118
Classic education, 33–34
Classroom management traps, 241
Classroom norms, polarity thinking map for, 192–193
Classrooms
    Autonomy AND Collaboration, 173
    Team Relationships and Team Tasks, 174
Class time, 37
Cognitive hypothesis, 253, 254
Cognitive Skills AND Noncognitive Skills, 191, 253–255
Collaboration, teacher, 64–65, 96–97. *See also* Autonomy AND Collaboration
College admissions tests, 92, 119–120
College preparation, 108
Collins, J., 60
Common Core State Standards (CCSS), 98, 106, 107–115, 122–125, 198, 207, 225, 236–237
Communication styles, 232–233
Competition AND Cooperation, 173

Conditional Respect AND Unconditional Respect, 62, 176–177, 179–181
Confirmation bias, 19
Constructivist learning, 90, 92
Content AND Process, 78–104, 109, 119
Continuity AND Change, 175–176
Core curricula, 106. *See also* Common Core State Standards (CCSS)
Core Knowledge, 110–111
Costs. *See* Financial issues
Critical Analysis AND Encouragement, 178
Critical thinking, 190–210
Culture, personality type preferences by, 231
Curriculum
    Academic Success AND Whole Child Success, 39–40, 45
    core, 106
    Mastery of Knowledge AND Mastery of Problem Solving, 96
    scope of, 114–116, 125

Damasio, A., 24
Darling-Hammond, L., 26, 62–63, 65
Data, for instructional purposes, 49
Dawkins, Richard, 87
Debate activity, 182–188
Decision making
    personality type and, 225–228
    role of emotions in, 24
Deeper fears, 14, 18
    Academic Success AND Whole Child Success, 36
    Mastery of Knowledge AND Mastery of Problem Solving, 82
    Standardization AND Customization, 107
    Teacher Evaluation as a Measure of Effectiveness AND as Guide for Professional Growth, 56
Dehn, Max, 88
Delpit, Lisa, 116–117, 156
Dewey, John, 32, 237
Dickens, Charles, 105
Dietz, E. J., 221
Dietz, M. E., 107, 112
Dignity in Schools, 39
Discipline, 195
Districts. *See* School districts
Diversity, 112, 116
Dropouts, 39, 40
Dweck, Carol, 253

Early warning signs, 18
  Academic Success AND Whole Child
    Success, 46
  Mastery of Knowledge AND Mastery of
    Problem Solving, 94
  Standardization AND Customization,
    121–122
  Teacher Evaluation as a Measure of
    Effectiveness AND as Guide for
    Professional Growth, 68–69
Educational Leadership (magazine), 71, 156
Educational Testing Service, 58
Education for Innovation Initiative, The
    (Tapping America's Potential), 34
EEG (electroencephalography), 217
Effective teachers, 53–77
Efficiency, 83–84, 92–93, 107
Einstein, Albert, 237
Electroencephalography (EEG), 217
Employment preparation, 34, 56, 82, 87,
    108, 111–117, 119. *See also* Twenty-first
    century skills
Energy, personal sources of, 219–222
Engagement, of students, 40, 45, 47–48,
    49, 86–90, 118
Equity, in education. *See also* Inequalities
  core knowledge and, 110–111
  mathematics education, 89–90
  providing equal opportunities, 42, 47
Erdrich, Louise, 116
Evaluation models, 233–234
Expectations, for student achievement,
    37, 44
Extraversion, 219–222

Fears, associated with poles, 14
Feedback, for teachers, 64
Feeling personality type, 225–228, 239
Felder, G. N., 221
Felder, R. M., 221
Fidelity to the Intervention AND
    Innovation With the Intervention, 178
Financial issues
  customization costs, 120
  standardization and economies of scale,
    108–109
  teacher evaluation costs, 61, 71, 73
Finland, 32–33, 42, 47, 69–70, 117
Fitzgerald, F. Scott, 4, 136–137
Flexible thinking, 87
Focusing on the Needs of Students
    AND Focusing on the Needs
    of Staff, 177

Fordham Institute, 119
Frontier, T., 56, 64

Gates, Bill, 61, 73, 106–107
Gedanken experiments, 125
Geography, 99
Goal setting, 197
Gradual release of responsibility, 84
Greater purpose statement (GPS),
    14, 18, 107
  Academic Success AND Whole Child
    Success, 33
  Mastery of Knowledge AND Mastery of
    Problem Solving, 82
  Teacher Evaluation as a Measure of
    Effectiveness AND as Guide for
    Professional Growth, 56
Grouping. *See* Ability grouping

Haidt, Jonathan, 19, 26
Hammer, A., 223
Harlem Children's Zone, 43, 48
Hart, B., 252
Harvard University, 58
Hiebert, J., 85
Higher-level thinking, 114
High-leverage action steps, 69–71, 123–124
High-stakes teacher evaluations, 56
High-stakes testing, 40–41
Hill, H., 95
Hilton, Peter, 88, 89
Hiring of teachers, 60
Hirsch, E. D., Jr., 33, 110–111, 254
History, 99
Homework, 196–197
Homogeneous Grouping AND
    Heterogeneous Grouping,
    140–152, 154–155
Hong Kong, 78

Individual AND Community, 3–4, 25,
    44, 191–194
Individual AND Team, 173
Inequalities. *See also* Equity, in education
  academic disregard as contributor to, 44
  academic focus as contributor to, 39
  school choice as contributor to, 38–39
Information explosion, 35–36
Information intake, personality types and,
    222–225
Initiative fatigue, 7–8
Inquiry-based learning, 90, 92
Instructional methods, 83–86, 90, 123–124

Introversion, 219–222
Intuition, 222–225, 234–235

Jackson, R. R., 85–86
Jackson, Shirley, "The Lottery," 24–25
Jobs, Steve, 237
Johnson, Barry, 8
Jordan, Michael, 197
Judging personality type, 228–230,
    238, 240
Jung, Carl, 6, 213–214, 217
Justice AND Mercy, 178

Kennedy, J., 73–74
Kerr, Steven, 114
Killion, J., 73–74, 122
KIPP charter schools, 37, 254, 255
Kohn, Alfie, 89, 255
Korea, 78

Language arts, 99, 110, 223
Lawrence, Gordon, 221, 223,
    227, 230, 232
Leadership, 37, 238–239
Learning about the polarity, 15
    case study, 247–248
    guided activity on, 149
Learning AND Doing, 131f
Learning styles
    "let me brainstorm," 80, 86, 242
    "let me do something," 86, 242
    "let me master it," 79, 84, 86, 242
    "let me think," 79, 86, 242
    personality types and, 214–215, 217,
        221, 235–236, 242
"Let me do something" learning style,
    86, 242
"Let me think" learning style, 79, 86, 242
Leveraging polarities
    Academic Success AND Whole Child
        Success, 47–49
    guided activity on, 149–151
    Mastery of Knowledge AND Mastery
        of Problem Solving, 94
    need for, 4–5
    PACT model, 15
    presentation on, 131–137
    process of, 10, 15, 18
    Standardization AND Customization,
        122–123
    Teacher Evaluation as a Measure of
        Effectiveness AND as Guide for
        Professional Growth, 69–71

Lifelong learning, 35–36
Life orientation, 228–230
Literacy, 110
Littky, D., 123
Lockhart, Paul, 87–88, 91
Logical learning style, 80
Logical reasoning, 197–198
London Mathematical Society, 84

Making the Case for Educating the Whole
    Child (ASCD), 34
Manipulatives, 93
Mapping the polarity
    Academic Success AND Whole Child
        Success, 35–36
    guided activity on, 144–147
    Mastery of Knowledge AND Mastery of
        Problem Solving, 82
    PACT model, 14
    reading with the tool of, 162–170
    Standardization AND
        Customization, 107
    Teacher Evaluation as a Measure of
        Effectiveness AND as Guide for
        Professional Growth, 55–57
    Teacher Responsibility AND Student
        Responsibility, 20–23f
Marathon training, 12–14
Margolis, J., 65
Marzano, R. J., 90
Mastery learning style, 79, 84, 86, 242
Mastery of Knowledge AND Mastery of
    Problem Solving, 78–104
    focusing on knowledge, 83–88
    focusing on problem solving, 88–94
    greater purpose statement, 82
    leveraging polarity of, 94
    mapping it, 82
    "math wars" thinking map, 102–103
    personality types and, 234–236
    seeing it, 81–82
    thinking map for, 100–101
    transforming polarity of, 94–98
Math anxiety, 78, 85
Mathematically Correct, 81–82
Mathematics, 110
Mathematics Education for Knowledge
    and Problem Solving. See Mastery of
    Knowledge AND Mastery of Problem
    Solving
Math wars, 78–104
MBTI. See Myers-Briggs Type Indicator
    (MBTI)

McCaulley, M., 223
Measures of Effective Teaching (MET), 58
Merit pay, 59
Mielke, P., 56, 64
Mikaelsen, Ben, *Touching Spirit Bear*,
   200–210, 206–208, 210
Miller, Donalyn, *The Book Whisperer*,
   164–170
Mind-set, fixed vs. growth, 253
Minnesota, 120
Mintz, A. I., 45
Mirel, Jeff, 65–66
Mischel, Walter, 254
Montgomery County, Maryland,
   Professional Growth System, 64, 74
Mooney, Margaret, 84
Moore, Emily, 69–70
Motivation
   intrinsic, 43, 48, 252
   of students, 43, 48, 84, 91, 252–254
   of teachers, 70
Myers, Isabel, 213, 223
Myers-Briggs Type Indicator (MBTI),
   213–242
My Rights AND My Responsibilities,
   191–194, 194*f*

Nardi, Dario, 217, 227
Narrative writing, 111–112
National Assessment of Educational
   Progress, 109, 122
National Council of Teachers of
   Mathematics (NCTM), 81, 82, 89, 92
National Longitudinal Survey of
   Youth, 254
Native Americans, 112, 116
NCLB. *See* No Child Left Behind
   (NCLB) Act
NCTM. *See* National Council of Teachers
   of Mathematics
New Teacher Project, 67
No Child Left Behind (NCLB) Act,
   34, 37, 40, 45, 58, 106

Obama, Barack, 54
Objectivity, 60, 107
Open-school initiatives, 121
Overfocusing, 16*f*, 18. *See also* Unintended
   consequences of solutions
   Academic Success AND Whole Child
     Success, 38–41, 44–46
   Mastery of Knowledge AND Mastery of
     Problem Solving, 85–88, 91–94

Standardization AND Customization,
   111–115, 119–121
Teacher Evaluation as a Measure of
   Effectiveness AND as Guide for
   Professional Growth, 60–63, 66–68

PACT. *See* Polarity Approach to
   Continuity and Transformation
   (PACT)
Paige, M., 63
Pajak, E., 233
Parent-child interactions, 253
Partnership for Assessment of
   Readiness for College and Careers
   (PARCC), 108
Partnerships, non-school, 43, 48
Pedagogy. *See* Instructional methods
Pendulum-swinging in educational
   policy and practice, 2, 4, 8, 10, 26,
   176, 245, 254
Perceiving personality type, 228–230, 240
Performance assessments, 114, 120
Personality types, 213–242
   Academic Success AND Whole Child
     Success, 231–232
   brain activity and, 217, 218*f*
   classroom management traps by, 241
   educational applications of, 221, 223,
     227, 230
   extraversion/introversion, 219–222
   factors in formation of, 214
   facts and misconceptions
     about, 215–218
   judging/perceiving, 228–230
   learning styles and, 214–215, 217, 221,
     235–236, 242
   manifestations of, 213
   Mastery of Knowledge AND Mastery of
     Problem Solving, 234–236
   MBTI and, 213
   of teachers, 227, 230, 233–235
   polarity thinking and, 230–231
   sensing/intuition, 222–225
   Standardization AND Customization,
     236–237
   Teacher Evaluation as a Measure of
     Effectiveness AND as Guide for
     Professional Growth, 232–234
   thinking/feeling, 225–228
Phi Delta Kappan (magazine), 71, 156
Phonics instruction, 18
Pink, Daniel, 48, 70
Play, benefits of, 42–43

Polarities. *See also* Assessment of polarity;
    Learning about the polarity;
    Leveraging polarities; Mapping the
    polarity; Seeing the polarity
    characteristics of, 29
    common, 172–189
    debate activity on, 182–188
    defined, 8
    examples of, 3–4, 8
    interdependence of, 8
    misdiagnosis of, as problems to solve,
        4, 8, 10, 55, 245
    students and, 190–210
    unsuccessful dealings with, 13–14
Polarity Approach to Continuity and
    Transformation (PACT), 14–15,
    142, 246–251
Polarity thinking
    benefits of, 191, 212
    critical thinking and, 190–210
    debate activity on, 182–188
    defining, 2–3
    factors contributing to, 19, 24
    goal of, 35
    guided activity on, 142–152
    guiding team through, 140–155
    introducing team to, 130–139
    presentation on, 131–137
    reflection sheet, 189
    using tools of, 156–171
Power standards, 98, 124
Preparation time, for teachers, 96–97
Preparing to Do the Work AND Doing the
    Work, 97, 130, 174
Principals, personality types
    of, 227, 230
Problems
    caused by "solutions," 4, 9
    seeing polarities as, 4, 8, 10, 55, 245
Problem solving, vs. content knowledge,
    78–104
Process knowledge. *See* Content AND
    Process
Professional development
    effective, 67, 124
    evaluation systems for, 64
    polarity tools for, 156–171
    standards for, 73–74
Progressive education, 33–34, 45
Project-based learning, 118
Project RED (Redesigning
    Education), 37
Put Kids First Minneapolis, 59

Quenk, N., 223
Quick-write process, 136

Race to the Top, 54, 74, 108
Ranking of schools, 38–39
Ranking of teachers, 54, 64–65, 73
Reading articles/books, with polarity
    tools, 158f
Reading First, 123
Reading instruction, 164–170, 223
Reardon, Sean, 36
Reason
    biases defended with use of, 19
    group exercise of, 26
    in decision making, 24
Reasoning and argument, 198–208
Reeves, D. B., 98
Reform, shortcomings of, 4
Resistance, 15, 55
Respect. *See* Conditional Respect AND
    Unconditional Respect
Responsibility. *See* Teacher Responsibility
    AND Student Responsibility
Rethinking Schools, 35, 39
Risely, T. R., 252
Roberts, T., 222
Rousseau, Jean-Jacques, 45
Russell, Bertrand, 89

Sahlberg, Pasi, 42
Salaries, teacher, 59, 64–65
Santoro, Doris, 62
SAT tests. *See* College admissions tests
Schmidt, W. H., 109, 124
Schmoker, M., 72
Schoenfeld, A. J., 81, 83
School choice, 38–39
School districts
    Autonomy AND Collaboration, 173
    Team Relationships and Team Tasks,
        174–175
School Responsibility AND Societal
    Responsibility, 178
Schools
    Autonomy AND Collaboration, 173
    Team Relationships and Team Tasks, 174
Science, 99
Science, technology, engineering, and
    mathematics (STEM) careers, 37, 236
Seeing the polarity, 10
    Academic Success AND Whole Child
        Success, 33–35
    guided activity on, 144

Mastery of Knowledge AND Mastery of
Problem Solving, 81–82
PACT model, 14
Standardization AND Customization,
106–107
Teacher Evaluation as a Measure of
Effectiveness AND as Guide for
Professional Growth, 54–55
Segregation, 38–39
Self-discipline, 253–255
Self-esteem, 44
Sensing, 222–225, 234–235
Short Term AND Long Term, 196–198
Singapore, 43, 65
SMALL steps, 14–15, 142
Smarter Balanced Assessment
Consortium, 108, 114
Social justice, 89–90, 112
Solutions
role of, in polarities, 5, 7–8
unintended consequences of, 4, 9, 16
unsustainability of, 4, 8, 18, 55, 245
Staff, needs of, 177
Standardization AND Customization,
105–128
focusing on customization, 115–121
focusing on standardization, 107–115
greater purpose statement, 107
leveraging polarity of, 122–125, 128
personality types and, 236–237
seeing it, 106–107
thinking map for, 126–127
transforming polarity of, 121–122
Standardized tests. See also College
admissions tests
personality types and, 223
teacher evaluation based on, 53, 54
Standards. See also Standardization AND
Customization
academic, 45
effectiveness of, 122
power, 98, 124
teacher, 66–67
Stanford University, 58
Star Trek (television show), 225–228
STEM careers, 37, 236
Stigler, J. W., 85
Strict Disciplinarian AND Lenient
Disciplinarian, 178
Students. See also Teacher Responsibility
AND Student Responsibility
attitudes of, 49
discipline, 195

engagement of, 40, 45, 47–48, 49,
86–90, 118
needs of, 177
polarities and critical thinking for,
190–210
polarity thinking activity for, 199–208
Student-teacher relationship, 176

Tapping America's Potential Coalition, 34
Teacher as Lecturer AND Teacher as
Facilitator, 178
Teacher-centered Instruction AND
Student-centered Instruction, 86
Teacher education programs, 32, 57, 70.
See also Teacher knowledge and
training
Teacher Evaluation as a Measure of
Effectiveness AND as Guide for
Professional Growth, 53–77
focusing on evaluation as a measure of
effectiveness, 58–63
focusing on evaluation as guide for
professional growth, 63–68
greater purpose statement, 56
mapping it, 55–57
personality types and, 232–234
seeing it, 54–55
thinking map for, 76–77
transforming polarity of, 68–69
Teacher evaluation systems
apprenticeship as component
of, 63–64
effective use of, 64
fairness of, 72–73
objectivity of, 60
professional basis of, 65, 71–72
resources required by, 61, 71, 73
response-to-intervention model for, 74
value-added measures, 58–59
Teacher knowledge and training,
95, 97, 124. See also Teacher
education programs
Teacher Responsibility AND Student
Responsibility, 9–10, 14–17,
20–23f, 244, 246–251
Teachers
accountability of, 54
apprenticeship of, 63–64
collaboration of, 64–65, 96–97
compensation of, 59, 64–65
dismissal and turnover of, 56–57,
59, 62–63
effective, 53–77

experience and knowledge of,
41, 63–64, 116
mathematics, 95
morale of, 62
personality types of, 227, 230, 233–235
preparation time of, 96–97
ranking of, 54, 64–65, 73
Teacher-student relationship, 176
Teach for America, 58
Teaching methods. *See* Instructional
methods
Teaching Process and Teaching Skills, 158*f*
Teaching profession, 69–70
Teaching to the test, 39–41
Team Relationships and Team Tasks,
174–175
Tenure, 65–66, 67
Test preparation, 39–41, 113
Thinking personality type, 225–228, 238
Tools, for addressing polarity thinking,
14–17, 19, 24, 156–171
Tough, Paul, 42, 253
Tracking, 141
Training for Work AND Doing the Work.
See Preparing to Do the Work AND
Doing the Work
Trust, 63
Twenty-first century skills, 109, 113–114,
117–118. *See also* Employment
preparation

Unintended consequences of solutions,
4, 9, 16. *See also* Overfocusing
Unions, 54

United States
cultural archetype of, 231
math anxiety in, 78
standardized testing in, 47
state oversight of education in, 106
teacher education in, 57
teacher preparation time in, 96–97
U.S. Chamber of Commerce, 34
U.S. Department of Education, 43

Value-added measures (VAM), 58–59, 63
Values, associated with poles, 14
Vicious cycles, 12–13, 13*f*, 16, 17*f*,
53, 55, 245
Virtuous cycles, 12, 12*f*, 245
Vocabulary, 252, 254

Wagner, Tony, 117
Washburn Center for Children, 48
Weisberg, D., 67, 68
Whole child approach. *See* Academic
Success AND Whole Child Success
Whole Child Initiative, 34
Whole language instruction, 18, 223
Wilkes, J. W., 223
Workforce preparation. *See* Employment
preparation
Working Now AND Working Later, 196
*Working With Teachers to Develop Fair and
Reliable Measures of Effective Teaching*
(Bill & Melinda Gates Foundation), 58
Work Priorities AND Home Priorities, 177

Zhao, Yong, 47, 115

CORWIN
A SAGE Company

The Corwin logo—a raven striding across an open book—represents the union of courage and learning. Corwin is committed to improving education for all learners by publishing books and other professional development resources for those serving the field of PreK–12 education. By providing practical, hands-on materials, Corwin continues to carry out the promise of its motto: **"Helping Educators Do Their Work Better."**

learningforward
Advancing professional learning for student success

Learning Forward (formerly National Staff Development Council) is an international association of learning educators committed to one purpose in K–12 education: Every educator engages in effective professional learning every day so every student achieves.